SEA·KAYAKER
MAGAZINE'S
HANDBOOK OF

SAFETY AND RESCUE

Doug Alderson
Michael Pardy

Ragged Mountain Press / McGraw-Hill

Camden, Maine • New York • Chicago • San Francisco • Lisbon • London • Madrid •
Mexico City • Milan • New Delhi • San Juan • Seoul • Singapore • Sydney • Toronto

The McGraw·Hill Companies

1 2 3 4 5 6 7 8 9 0 DOC DOC 0 9 8 7 6 5 4 3

Library of Congress Cataloging-in-Publication Data
Alderson, Doug.
    Sea kayaker magazine's handbook of safety and rescue / Doug Alderson and Michael Pardy.
        p.   cm.
    Includes bibliographical references and index.
    ISBN 0-07-138890-7
    1. Sea kayaking—Safety measures—Handbooks, manuals, etc. 2. Rescue work—Handbooks, manuals, etc. I. Title: Handbook of safety and rescue. II. Pardy, Michael. III. Sea kayaker. IV. Title.
    GV784.55.A43 2003
    796.1´224´0289—dc21   2003000633

Questions regarding the content of this book should be addressed to
Ragged Mountain Press
P.O. Box 220
Camden, ME 04843
www.raggedmountainpress.com

Questions regarding the ordering of this book should be addressed to
The McGraw-Hill Companies
Customer Service Department
P.O. Box 547
Blacklick, OH 43004
Retail customers: 1-800-262-4729
Bookstores: 1-800-722-4726

Photographs by Doug Alderson and Michael Pardy unless noted otherwise.
Illustrations by Chris Hoyt unless noted otherwise.

Warning: This is an instructional book for a potentially dangerous activity. Sea kayak rescue takes paddlers into harm's way, exposing them to risks in excess of those normally encountered in sea kayaking. The information in this book is not intended to replace instruction by qualified teachers, and the authors recommend that readers seek instruction before attempting a rescue. Even after such instruction, this book cannot substitute for good personal judgment on the water. By using this book the reader releases the authors, publisher, and distributor from any liability for any injury, including death, that may result from attempting the techniques covered within. It is understood that you paddle and attempt rescues at your own risk.

"But why had we come, if not to depend upon our own resources and in so doing, discover more about them? There are circuits and juices in every person that are the heritage of millions of years of evolution and survival in wild country. They need exercising—add a twinge of fear and wonder, and they can bring the world into focus with astonishing clarity."

James Baldwin

"A ship in the harbour is safe, but that is not what ships are built for."

William Shedd

Contents

1 Judgment and Safety   3

Judgment • Decision Making • Safety and Risk • Leadership

2 Health and Fitness   18

Fueling a Human-Powered Craft • Power and Endurance •
Medical Conditions

3 Environment   28

Weather Systems • Personalized Weather Forecast • Local
Weather Effects • Waves • Tides and Currents • Local Wave
Effects • Forecasting Sea State • Campsites

4 Safety and Rescue Gear   54

How to Choose Gear • Kayak Safety Features • Paddling Gear •
Paddling Clothing • Rescue Gear • Communication Gear •
Additional Safety and Rescue Aids

5 Paddling Technique   76

Adequate Reserves • Skills • Forward Stroke • Brace Strokes •
Paddling in Wind and Waves • Paddling in Tidal Current •
Paddling in Rough Seas

Preface

We believe that participating in the natural world is an essential component of a full life, and sea kayaking is an ideal way to do that. Sea kayaking provides the opportunity to get out and explore the planet, to experience the risky immediacy of nature. We have traveled by sea kayak long enough and far enough to be thrown a few curves. So far, thorough preparation and due diligence have provided us with many eventful trips and just as many safe returns.

Advising others on how to plan a trip and judge the risks is a path fraught with peril. In deciding what to include in this handbook, we have chosen the advice, preparations, and techniques on which our own comfort, and at times our lives, have depended. Not everything that works for us will be right for all paddlers in all situations. With every stroke of the paddle, each kayaker must independently decide how best to move forward, explore, and meet a personal challenge.

Inherent in these decisions is the acceptance of physical effort and consequence. The decisions you make on the water are important not just to you but to the people who care about you. Your safe passage also is important to the sport, to the agencies that govern our access to the water, and to those who stand by to risk their safety when we find ourselves in harm's way.

It is our hope that the information and advice offered in these pages stimulates personal growth, encourages outdoor adventure, and supports many safe passages.

Acknowledgments

In paddle sports, we have always had encouragement and support. The community of paddlers is a remarkable network. Stand on the shore with a paddle in your hand and they will come. Do you need a hand? Do you want to paddle with us? Where are you going? Is there anything you need? Did you hear the weather forecast? Cool boat! On those days when nothing went right and we truly did not feel strong enough to paddle, we were encouraged to rest. When lazy, we were challenged to get out and get wet. One cannot become an expert in isolation; we extend our sincere thanks to the innumerable paddlers who have drawn us out from the shelter of home to the wonders of the coastline.

In the preparation of this book, the members of the Victoria Canoe & Kayak Club, Victoria, British Columbia, have endured personal injury, damaged kayaks, lost gear, cold days, wet camps, considerable water up the nose—and not once, to my face, did they complain. My heartfelt thanks go out to the entire sea kayak group.

—Doug Alderson

The path to this book has been a long one, and along the way, I have had a lot of support and encouragement. I would like specifically to thank my partner Kari and my son Rowan for their patience and encouragement while I struggled and rejoiced through the writing of the book. In addition, thanks to all the staff at Ocean River Sports, who put up with my distraction over the past year—their enthusiasm for the out-of-doors and sea kayaking continues to be an inspiration.

—Michael Pardy

Introduction

Sea kayaking is more than just a recreational activity. We also use the remarkable little craft known as a sea kayak to meet personal challenges and explore the boundary between land and water. The transition from beach to open water is a significant one, and it is not surprising that so many people see it as a voyage of personal discovery as well as physical challenge.

Risk is inherent to sea kayaking, and each time you leave the beach you must accept the potential for harm. But your accepted level of risk should be consistent with your desires. Too little risk can lead to boredom; too much can push the experience beyond excitement and into anxiety. The boundary between excitement and anxiety is not well defined; its exploration is a natural part of sea kayaking that will occasionally lead to the need for a rescue.

The nature and extent of the risks you are willing to accept will vary with your experience, your surroundings, and your choice of paddling partners. Along with the acceptance of risk comes the responsibility to understand the consequences of your actions. We work to maintain our safety by carefully planning each trip, acting on our plans while on the trip, and reflecting on the effectiveness of our plans after the trip is over. Most of the time our plans are sufficient to maintain an adequate level of safety; when these plans fail, we must perform a rescue.

In the language of sea kayaking, the term *rescue* has many interpretations. It often refers to the techniques used to get a paddler back into a kayak after a capsize. For us, *rescue* takes on a larger meaning, encompassing all the decisions and actions necessary to return a kayaker to full function after any event that compromises his or her safety. This broader concept of a rescue includes the decisions and actions of the entire paddling group. When one member of a group encounters difficulties that necessitate a rescue, other members in the group are also likely to be vulnerable. Keeping the entire group safe and secure is part of the rescue.

Rescue techniques are divided into two general categories: self rescues and assisted rescues. Any rescue technique must accomplish three goals: get the water out of the kayak; get the paddler back in; and stabilize the affected kayak. Moreover, as rescuer, you must manage your own safety and that of the group, shaping your actions to lower overall risk and move the group as a whole to a condition of greater safety. This larger project requires techniques and skills beyond a kayak roll or an assisted reentry.

While the precise method for a reentry can be described, the unfolding of a rescue is seldom straightforward. Thoughtful training and practice in moderately rough sea conditions reduce the chance of an otherwise simple reentry turning into an extended rescue. Like climbing a ladder where one foot keeps up with the other, rescue skills need to keep pace with paddling skills. Skills develop only as they are practiced. Most of our time paddling is in calm conditions, and it is easy to develop bad habits because the demands on our skills are low. Consistent practice of good technique and good judgment on many fine days near home will help prepare you for the unexpected rough day on a distant trip. Your actions will be consistent with your most common practice, so strive to use good techniques and good judgment at all times.

Both safety and rescue rely on effective decision making. Take the time to clearly identify a problem and gather as much information as you can before making a choice and carrying out your plan. A structured approach to decision making helps ensure safety on the water; furthermore, it allows us to develop good judgment. In the aftermath of the problem, allow time to reflect on the outcome. Recognize sound decisions and review poor ones.

The book is broadly divided into two sections—one on safety, the other on rescue. Chapter 1 describes the framework and the relationship of the two sections. Chapters 2 through 7 deal with safety. Chapters 8 through 10 are concerned with rescue. Throughout the book we emphasize the fundamental principles of the skills, leaving the particular choices to your judgment. Nuances of style or subtle advantages between two techniques or alternatives in gear are left to personal choice. Although we focus on single-seat decked kayaks, the principles of safety and rescue remain the same for all varieties of kayaks, including doubles, folding kayaks, sit-on-tops, and homebuilts. We describe techniques that work reliably for a wide variety of kayaks and paddlers. These techniques need to be tested and practiced and then modified to suit your personal needs.

There is no one right way to be safe or to conduct a rescue. The admonition to always travel in groups of three at sea is good advice, but reliance on others to come to your rescue in all conditions is fundamentally un-safe. Traveling with partners increases safety and decreases risk, but each paddler is independently responsible for his or her own safety. Partners do not replace the need for personal skill and judgment. Sea kayakers venture out to escape order and predictability. Consequently the content of this book must be interpreted and adapted to each specific context of paddler and environment. We have tried to provide descriptive guidelines rather than prescriptive rules. Guidelines rely on the use of judgment; rules seek to replace judgment. It is our belief that the realm of the sea kayaker is too infinitely variable to be governed by rules. In the end, you as a paddler will have to make the decisions regarding your own safety.

When using a marine chart the kayaker will be working in nautical miles (6,080.2 feet). Nautical charts explicitly give both true and magnetic bearings on the compass rose and the kayaker can work with a marine deck compass and magnetic compass bearings without the need to convert bearings to degrees true. On topographical maps, on the other hand, distances are given in land miles (5,280 feet) or kilometers (3,280.8 feet, 0.62 land mile). A hand compass is typically used with topo maps, and common practice for map work is to work in True directions and compensate for the local magnetic deviation either by calculation or by making a declination adjustment on the body of the compass. When sea kayakers use a combination of marine compasses, land compasses, charts, and maps, they encounter a variety of techniques and methods of measurement. The trip plan should include a clarification of how the navigation will be done.

Throughout this book, we will use nautical miles and magnetic compass bearings.

Judgment and Safety

1

Good judgment is at the heart of safe paddling. This point of view informs all the advice in this book. It is certain that if you paddle along an open coast, you will have an adventure; it is not certain what that adventure will be. At all points along the way, look back to see where you have been, look around to see where you are, and look forward to see what lies ahead. The past and present are certain; the future is yet to unfold.

Judgment

Judgment is the filter through which knowledge, skills, and experience are translated into actions, and as such it is enhanced by reflection. *Knowledge* can be acquired through study, reading, research, and paddling with knowledgeable partners. If you are planning a trip to a new area, take time to research its natural history, weather, and marine hazards. This research will reveal new avenues of investigation. Perhaps the area is known for gap winds. Armed with this fact, you can research gap winds, expand your knowledge of the subject, and develop appropriate skills. You can improve your chances of success by preparing yourself intelligently.

Skills include physical abilities such as capsize-recovery and mental abilities such as planning and navigation. Skills need to be practiced on a regular basis or they will not work well when you need them. Many of us learn capsize-recovery skills in courses and neglect to practice them afterward. When you need to get back into your boat, your technique should be quick and reliable. The mental skills of planning and navigation need regular practice to remain sharp for the foggy or stormy day when plans have to change. In rescue scenarios, judgment and leadership need to be fast and effective.

Experience requires more than repetition. To gain experience, you have to paddle in new places and with new partners and face new challenges. If you are planning a multiday trip through an area of strong tidal currents and you don't have much experience in currents, you could take a course that includes paddling in currents or take a couple of shorter trips in mild currents. If you don't have the time to prepare in this way, consider planning the trip during a quarter moon, when currents are at their weakest. With this experience and some reflection under your belt, you should be more skilled, more confident, and safer, because your judgment will have expanded to include new knowledge, skills, and experience. Exploring

3

The Changing Sea

"One of the challenges of sea kayaking is that every time the paddler snaps the spray deck in place and pushes off from shore, he or she is instantly in an environment that is potentially dangerous. Wind, tidal currents, reflecting waves, and water that are cold enough to lower the core temperature and kill by hypothermia are factors of the sea. On a calm day with flat water and sunshine, the smooth glide of the boat can lull a paddler into complacency and the warning signs of the surrounding environment can go unnoticed. A line of clouds on the horizon, a shift of wind from one quarter to the next, or whitecaps a mile offshore where an hour earlier there had been none, all paint a picture of the constant interplay of sea and sky. The freedom and ease of paddling on calm days can quickly become a battle of nerves and stamina when these signs are ignored or misinterpreted. It isn't the sea that takes lives and brings grief to shore bound families; it is the careless drift of the mind that accepts the moment of calm without looking beyond for what surely will be a change. The kayak allows the freedom of travel, but it also demands that the paddler be observant and have both skill and judgment to deal with the realities of the sea."

—*Chris Duff*, On Celtic Tides

the boundaries of your experience is a necessary and risky part of advancing your skills.

Reflection allows you to refine your judgment and better assess the risks and consequences for future outings. The easiest way to reflect on your experience is to maintain a paddler's logbook and other written records of each trip. In the logbook, keep track of your experiences, paying particular attention to your happy successes and your near misses. Without a written record, memories are incomplete, and the logbook serves as a memory aide. For a half-day outing in familiar territory, the only other written record might be a note given to someone at home, stating where you are going and when you can be expected back. A three-week trip along an open coast, however, can generate additional documents, including a float plan, a budget, a menu, a dead-reckoning log, daily navigation calculations, photography notes, and nature notes. In the evening, snug around the camp stove making tea, you and your paddling partners can compare the weather forecast with

Some paddling destinations require calm weather and good judgment.   (GREG SHEA)

your logbook notes on weather systems evolving over the past several days. Routes, campsites, tidal information, times, and distances can be confirmed or modified with reference to logbook documents.

There are always new challenges in paddling, and we cannot predict the consequences of our actions with absolute accuracy. Making mistakes and suffering the consequences are part of learning. Difficulties are important signposts to the boundary between good judgment and bad. Your successes and your difficulties are valuable experiences for acquiring judgment and improving decision making.

At its best, good judgment leads to good seamanship. The expert sea kayaker has heightened awareness and superior judgment, and frequently appears to make the best decision with ease. What might appear to be a spontaneous decision is the product of thorough but subtle observation and partly unconscious but refined judgment. The path from proficiency to expertise is well known and simple: expertise is achieved by deliberate training and diligent practice.

Decision Making

Decision making turns information into action, and is the inseparable complement of judgment. Good judgment without decision making is useless; decisions uninformed by good judgment are usually disastrous. A decision-making model can help you identify key problems, available resources, and potential solutions. A clearly defined approach helps you cope with changing circumstances and stress. Many factors can cause you to adjust and adapt. Lack of time, limited information, severity of consequences, or changes in leadership might require a new approach. Rescue scenarios impose high-speed, high-risk, high-stress decisions on paddlers. Pre-planned and well-practiced decision making is necessary to make difficult rescues successful.

A practical model for decision making follows five steps:

- Identify the problem.
- Gather information.
- Make a choice.
- Take action.
- Reflect on the outcome.

Decision making, however, is seldom as straightforward as an orderly series of steps makes it sound. Typically, we take a step or two forward and then pause to check and refine our judgments. Each situation will involve external factors that change the time available, stress levels, and consequences of taking action. There can be a good deal of rethinking where decision making occurs in a changing setting.

Trip planning usually leaves lots of time to make decisions. During a trip, deciding to launch from a surf beach may not impose time restrictions, but the consequences of the action may be significant. Rescues are typically defined by the need for quick decision making, under high levels of stress, with potentially desperate consequences. In all cases,

Decision making is a complex mental skill that improves with coaching and practice. The five steps are more circular than linear, interacting more or less continuously.

the foundations of decision making are the same.

Mental skills can be practiced and developed in the same way as physical skills. Deliberate practice with decision making during many regular routines will help develop the skills for those circumstances when, under stress, there is very little time to make the right decision and take effective action to forestall dire consequences. We can practice deliberate decision making when planning a day trip or before landing on a rocky shore with breaking waves. Participating in simulated rescue scenarios helps us learn to work quickly and efficiently under stressful conditions.

Barriers to Good Judgment

Negative attitudes and excessive stress are barriers to good judgment. Decisions come from judgments based on information about personnel, equipment, and the natural environment. High levels of stress or complacent attitudes decrease our ability to gather good information. Without good information and a concerned attitude, there is an increased likelihood of making a poor decision. It is important to continually reflect on the quality of judgment and information used to make decisions. An awareness of the impact of stress and attitude will help bolster our judgment when it is most necessary.

Five negative attitudes interfere with judgment:

- Macho: "I can do it without any instruction or help."
- Invulnerability: "It won't happen to me."
- Resignation: "What's the use in doing anything?"
- Impulsiveness: "Do something quickly."
- Antiauthoritarian: "The rules don't apply to me."

Recognizing these negative attitudes in yourself and others is the first step in com-bating the effects. When things begin to go wrong, chances are that one or more or these attitudes will be present. If negative attitudes stand in the way of good judgment, work on changing them.

Too much or too little stress is a barrier to good judgment. Under excessive stress, we are anxious and can even panic; we become unable to make good decisions. With inadequate stress, we become bored and complacent. A lack of awareness leads to insufficient information and errors in judgment. Each of us has an optimal level of stress that fluctuates with our experience, knowledge, skills, and the complexity of the tasks we are working on. An important point to keep in mind when working with others is that some people have lower thresholds of optimal stress than others. The group will function best when everyone is comfortable and alert.

Stress is the body's response to any demand made upon it. The stressors can be physical, physiological, or psychological, and many are a normal daily part of life. Stress keeps us on our toes, helping to prevent accidents by keeping us aware of what goes on around us. Many individuals seek out additional stress as a way of maintaining excitement in their lives. When we experience excessive stress over a long time, however, we react by turning inward, becoming less observant, limiting our awareness, and crippling our decision-making abilities.

Sources of stress include the following:

- *Physical stressors* are found in the environment. They include water and air temperature, noise, sea state, and wind speed.
- *Physiological stressors* include dehydration, hypothermia, fatigue, lack of physical fitness, sleep loss, disease, and poor nutrition.
- *Psychological stressors* are related to social and emotional factors in our lives. They include heavy mental workloads, difficult problems to solve, anticipated conse-

quences, conflict between group members, and personal problems.

Using the decision-making model introduced earlier helps cope with the psychological stressors. In times of stress, using this model can help keep you calm and focused. Rough seas and vital rescues require you to control your emotions and keep a level head. Stress levels quickly become excessive when conditions are difficult and the consequences of a quick decision are important. During planned practice sessions, role-playing and rescue scenarios are a great way for individuals and groups to experience handling stressful situations.

During a trip, stress can build. Be aware of accumulating stress, and actively deal with stressors. Individuals who are operating beyond their optimal levels of stress exhibit changes in behavior. Watch for changes in yourself and others, because these changes may indicate excessive stress.

There are some simple things you can do to help reduce the buildup of stress during a trip.

- Keep rested.
- Drink lots of water.
- Stay nourished.
- Keep warm.
- Solve problems early.
- Speak up if you are feeling anxious.
- Use checklists to aid your memory.

Safety and Risk

Decision making for safety is all about reducing risk, which is the potential for injury or loss. Always when kayaking, we work to minimize the chance of harm, knowing that not all risk can be eliminated. The classic model of risk assessment defines two categories of danger: human and environmental.

A good choice of paddling partner can brighten an otherwise dreary day. (GREG SHEA)

Human dangers are those within our control, including the gear we take along, the routes we choose, and the people we paddle with—their skills, equipment, and interactions. The capability of a group is a measure of their collective judgment, experience, and leadership, factors that change as the members interact and mature as paddlers and leaders.

Environmental dangers are those beyond our control, caused by weather, sea, or shoreline terrain. Wind, sun, fog, and cold temperatures are examples. Winds over 8–10 knots, currents over 1–2 knots, and surf over 1.5 feet (0.5 m) are dangerous to novices, though not necessarily to paddlers with more skill.

Where's Amanda?

We were paddling off the west coast of Ireland, and as we headed toward Aran Mhor we could tell that conditions outside the island were not going to be easy. As we made our way round the north tip of the island, we came upon a gap between the main island and a large rock stack that challenged us to try to get through. The gap was plenty wide, 50 yards, but the rough conditions meant that passage through the opening would require steady nerves.

One of the paddlers, Amanda, decided to go around the outside of the rock stack, while the others started taking turns making their way carefully through the gap. Paddlers who made it through kept a watchful eye on those behind them.

It took twenty minutes to get everyone through the gap. Once all the paddlers were safely on the other side, someone thought to ask: "Where's Amanda?"

Suddenly the realization dawned on us that she had never come around the corner. Everyone had been so focused on the excitement of the passage that we had totally forgotten about her.

Just then Adrian spotted a paddle waving from a few hundred yards away, and he paddled toward it. As he got closer, he realized that Amanda was waving her paddle not from the boat but from the water. She had been capsized by a large wave. She had been in the water for twenty minutes and was quite cold. Once back in her boat she said she was fine and ready to continue, but she definitely wanted to remain with the group.

We decided to head down the west side of Aran Mhor and around the southern tip, and into Aran Sound for shelter. This took a slow and difficult two hours because of the size of the swells. By the time we got to the campsite, Amanda was completely exhausted.

On reflection, this incident showed how easy it is to focus on the more demanding paddling and not give due attention to the easier sections. It's when we let our guard down that the sea will have us!

—Mike McClure

Actual versus Perceived Risk

It is useful to think of risks in terms of the frequency and severity of their associated harmful outcomes. Fortunately, the *actual* consequences of risks gone awry are seldom as severe as they could be. Exiting a kayak and swimming in the surf zone has the *potential* to inflict traumatic injury, but if you're properly prepared, some water up your nose and mild hypothermia are the most common outcomes. Not warming up your muscles and joints before paddling increases both the frequency and severity of injury, but minor sore backs are a far more common outcome than major trauma.

Perceived risk can be a psychological barrier to reasonable adventures. We rely on our past and present experiences to interpret the world around us. Unfortunately, we often misinterpret the world, perceiving risk where none exists. Some individuals shy away from sea kayaking because of the perception that it is a dangerous sport. In particular, they express concern about getting trapped upside down in a kayak. If they overcome this initial anxiety and learn the wet exit, they will quickly discover that it is actually harder to stay in an overturned kayak than it is to come out. Intermediate paddlers can perceive risk in currents, surf, or strong winds that may limit their experiences and hamper their growth as sea kayakers. Knowledge, experience, and skill help us separate fact from fiction.

The boundaries between perceived and actual risk shift as we develop knowledge, skills, and experience. One of the qualities that defines an expert kayaker is his or her ability to separate perception from reality, and it goes two ways. The expert will be able to identify a risk, avoid it, and travel safely where others fall blindly into the hole. Alternatively, the expert may see a safe route where others perceive only an impassable hazard. Resolving the boundary between perceived and actual risk is an important part of safety and enjoyment. Paddlers must approach and investigate this boundary and

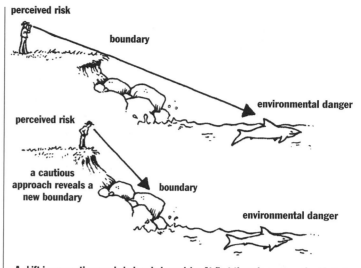

A shift in perception can help break down risks. At first there is a perception that stepping over the edge brings the risk of injury from shark attack. However, after a closer examination of the situation, a new boundary emerges. Shark attack is not a certainty. Stepping into the water only increases the risk potential for shark attack. Knowledge of shark behavior will decrease the risk potential. The human danger of reckless behavior, jumping into the water and thrashing about, increases the risk potential.

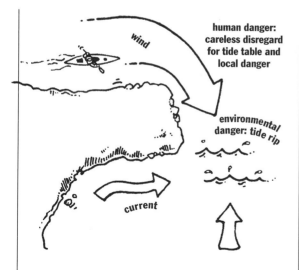

In sea kayaking, both human and environmental dangers play a role in creating actual risks. At a tide rip, the combination of the human danger of overconfidence and the environmental danger creates an actual risk of capsize. The careless paddler has a low perceived risk of rounding the headland. The actual risk is high. This is an unsafe situation—the classic accident waiting to happen.

Likewise, perceived risks arise from human assessments, often incorrect. There is little danger in paddling in large swell and light winds. The cautious group, unaccustomed to paddling in swell, has a high perceived risk where there is a low actual risk. If they decide that it is too dangerous to leave camp to move to the south beach, they will be safe but will limit their opportunities. An experienced leader could sensibly gather information and then make a plan to safely explore the coastline.

cross over it to explore the other side. Exploration is at the heart of developing good judgment, and we must submit to the fact that judgment is imperfect and accidents will happen. Effective risk management enables us to explore the boundaries of perceived risk while ensuring that the accidents we suffer are ones we can survive.

Safety Management

When you make decisions that reduce actual risk while exploring the boundary of perceived risk, you are practicing safety management. The decision-making model introduced earlier will give some structure to the process. You start by assessing risk, then managing it. Risk assessment consists of identifying the human and environmental dangers and gathering all the pertinent information. Deciding to do something about those risks is risk management. Finally, when you take the time to reflect on the outcome of your experiences, you will learn how to better judge similar circumstances in the future.

Safety management is decision making focused on reducing risk. This involves continuous risk assessment and risk management.

Risk Assessment

Risk assessment begins with identifying the human and environmental dangers.

To assess risk associated with human dangers, you need to gather information about:

- The emotional condition of group members.
- The physical condition of group members.
- The condition of equipment.
- The goals of the trip.
- Skills of the group members.
- Knowledge of the group members.
- Experience of the group members.
- The nature of the leadership.

Environmental dangers fall into the three categories of weather, sea state, and shoreline. Information needed for risk assessment of weather dangers includes:

- Strength and direction of wind.
- Location and direction of travel of high-pressure and low-pressure systems.
- Type and amount of precipitation.
- Visibility.
- Whether the weather is improving, stable, or deteriorating.

Information needed for risk assessment of sea-state dangers includes:

- Height, direction, and shape of wind waves and swell.
- Strength, direction, and timing of the current.
- Height and timing of the tides.
- Whether the sea state is improving, stable, or deteriorating.

Information needed for risk assessment of shoreline dangers includes:

- Nature of the shoreline.
- Frequency and quality of landing sites.

ENVIRONMENTAL AND HUMAN DANGERS ASSOCIATED WITH SEA KAYAKING

This is a partial list of environmental and human dangers. Accidents and incidents are the result of some overlap between these two sets of dangers. You can use the list as a starting point for examining risk and managing your safety. The list can be used during planning, during a trip, and during reflection to identify potential problems, to devise strategies for coping with these problems, and to reflect on the sources of problems encountered on the trip.

Environmental Dangers

Animals
Cold water
Currents
Tides
Surf
Illness
Lightning
Loose rocks
Loose logs
Stoves and fires
Uneven terrain
Vehicles
Weather
Wet and slippery terrain
Equipment failure

Human Dangers

Errors in planning
Exceeding ability
Failure to follow instructions
Horseplay
Rushing to meet a schedule
Inadequate supervision
Poor choice of equipment
Ineffective instruction
Poor hygiene
Poor body position
Poor technique
Attitudes toward risk
Stress
Fatigue
Lack of knowledge or skill
Lack of experience
Poor communication
Poor leadership
Preconceived goals and expectations
Peer pressure
Overconfidence
Misinformation

- Sources of fresh water.
- Alternative access and egress points such as roads.
- Location of communication centers.
- Location of medical and emergency services.

As the sum of human dangers and environmental dangers rises, so does the level of risk. A greater sum implies increased overall risk. It is important to note that greater risk does not necessarily mean that harm will occur, only that there is a greater potential for harm. The safe paddler works to identify the dangers and then works to lessen the risk. For example, touring in a new area, a paddler may not have sufficient local knowledge to identify a dangerous body of water. In order to decrease the risk, paddlers must reduce the number of human dangers.

Part of the information you need to gather is on the severity of potential outcomes. Some experiences have no harmful outcomes, others produce minimal harm, while yet others can lead to severe injury and loss. Experiences affecting the safety of the group can be categorized in three ways:

- *Events* do not, strictly speaking, have harmful outcomes. They occur commonly dur-

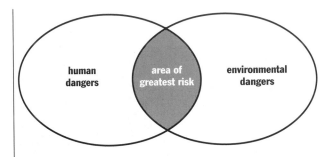

human
dangers

area of
greatest risk

environmental
dangers

A greater number of dangers lead to increased risk. However, risk is greatest when human dangers overlap with environmental dangers. An example would be a lack of warm waterproof clothing (human danger) coupled with cold wind and rain (environmental danger).

ing the normal daily routine of paddling—for example, an unexpected capsize in calm water as you turn around to talk to your buddy and get your paddle caught. You roll up and keep on paddling—wet, but none the worse for wear. This was an *event*.

- *Incidents* result in minimal harm. These are the "near misses" that we all love to regale our paddling partners with at the pub between trips. Bad timing while landing through the surf, being capsized three revolutions in a wave, rolling up, and making it to shore unharmed would qualify as an *incident*.

- *Accidents* have harmful outcomes. The harm can be minor tendinitis or a broken rudder cable. It can also be severe, ending the trip or requiring major boat repair. In any case, it can be categorized as an accident.

Taking Action

Safety management includes choosing a strategy to mitigate potential harm. For paddlers, the primary strategies are to avoid, reduce, or accept the different risks we face.

- *Risks can be avoided* by consciously choosing not to accept a specific danger. For example, by staying at a site for an extra day

and therefore not paddling in 25-knot winds and 4-foot chop, we avoid the dangers of the wind and waves.

- *Risks can be reduced* by employing safety equipment and safety procedures to decrease the frequency and severity of accidents. For example, limiting the length of open crossings and wearing a personal flotation device (PFD) and a wet suit all reduce the risks associated with capsizing in cold water.

- *Risks can be accepted* and we can take responsibility for them. For example, paddlers accept financial risk by acknowledging that gear will be damaged and lost during normal use.

Paddlers use all these strategies to manage safety. At times, multiple strategies are needed to reduce the risk from a single danger; the residual risk must be accepted.

The winds, currents, and rebounding waves associated with headlands pose real dangers to paddlers. A pre-trip risk assessment will identify these dangers. Traveling down a coast, the risk posed by headlands cannot be avoided, so other strategies must be considered. Choosing to round a headland on a calm day with little tidal activity can reduce the risk. If there exists a large sum of human and environmental dangers, the group must make some important decisions about managing those dangers or accepting a high potential for an incident or an accident.

Risk cannot be eliminated from sea kayaking and we cannot anticipate all the risks we face. Safe paddling experiences are enjoyable but not risk free. People who enjoy sea kayaking must also enjoy accepting some risk. For instance, there is always a risk of being caught out in bad weather. Learning about weather and local geography will reduce, but not eliminate, that risk. And there is always a risk of damaging your kayak and flooding a compartment. You can lessen the severity of that outcome by packing gear in dry bags.

The good news is that sea kayaking is a relatively safe sport. There are no high-frequency risks with high-severity outcomes associated with sea kayaking. Paddlers should focus their safety efforts toward the more common high-frequency risks with low-severity outcomes. Some effort must also be directed toward the low-frequency risks that have a high-severity outcome, such as a dislocated shoulder. But it is evident that dislocated shoulders, broken bones, severe hypothermia, and drowning are not lurking behind every wave. We should concentrate a good portion of our effort on managing the risks that frequently lead to low-severity injuries like annoying cuts, strains, and sprains.

All paddlers should be clear on the day's plans. Most decisions about planning and navigation should be made on the beach before you leave.

Reflecting on Outcomes

Reflection allows paddlers to use the clarity of hindsight to consider the merits of their risk assessment and risk management. An unexpected event should encourage reflection in an attempt to understand why it occurred (*direct learning*). Narratives that relate the misfortunes of others offer another opportunity to reflect on safety practices (*indirect learning*). These stories are common in sea kayaking magazines and in travelogues. Personal experiences and the stories of others offer excellent opportunities to improve safety practices.

It is easy to dismiss another paddler's foolishness from the safety of an armchair, but the capacity for human error rests within us all. Paddlers should take these lessons seriously and look for similar patterns in their own risk assessment and risk management. Evaluate these experiences by identifying the human and environmental dangers. In this way, reflection is structured, and lessons are learned and integrated into your judgment.

Severe accidents are rare and provide few opportunities for reflection. Kayakers should also reflect on their successes. Successes are more common and have important lessons for safety. A safe and successful outcome can be credited to good risk assessment, good risk management, skill, luck, or some combination of these. It is important to reinforce successful strategies and to replace unsuccessful ones.

For example, after a successful five-day trip in the Bay of Islands, New Zealand, a group of paddlers used reflection to identify several important safety issues:

- The weather deteriorated rapidly toward the end of the last day, and the paddlers just managed to get off the water ahead of a storm. They had not packed any extra food. Upon reflection, they realized that if the weather had hit a day earlier, they might have been stuck for an extra day with little or no food. They decided that on future trips, they would carry at least one extra day's worth of food.

- They agreed that their route planning was excellent and that the demands of the trip were appropriate for the level of skill and knowledge of the group.

- The group's weather interpretation anticipated the storm, and the paddlers made an excellent camp well ahead of it. But they realized that they had cut the line quite close, and that a couple of hours' delay could have put them in danger from the storm. They agreed in the future to be more conservative in their estimation of the weather and to continue to work on developing their weather knowledge.

Leadership

Leadership can be defined as a group's ability to set goals and to make decisions toward achieving them. Throughout a trip, groups require effective leadership, in the absence of which goals are often poorly defined and not well understood. Sometimes group members hold contradictory goals, and these contradictions can cause poor decisions. In times of trouble, contradictions and misperceptions become exaggerated, preventing an effective response to a problem. Leadership helps groups resolve conflicts, identify shared goals, and work cooperatively to achieve them.

With effective leadership, a group can:

- Focus on its goals.
- Maintain safety.
- Mobilize effective rescues.
- Maximize the rewards of the trip.

The Nature of Leadership

Leadership is commonly understood to reside in a single person, and in many cases this is true. On guided sea kayaking trips and courses, leadership clearly resides with the paid leader.

But this understanding needs to be expanded to include shared leadership. In practice, many formal groups pass the leadership roles among designated members, who often will take a collective leadership responsibility. The situation is more complex in informal groups, where leadership can be said to emerge from the interactions among group members. Often it remains diffused throughout the group according to skill, interest, and ability. Responsibility is then difficult to identify, and in matters of safety, timely and positive decisions can be difficult to achieve. Nevertheless, informal groups have safely spent many days and weeks on the water without formal leadership.

Problems can arise whether a group has designated or emergent leadership. The authority of the leadership can be challenged, or its decisions may create unease in the group, leading to disruptive behaviors and divisions that compromise safety. To some extent, tensions among group members are a normal part of the paddling experi-

The accessibility of some landing sites is dependent on good weather.

ence, but without effective leadership to cope with these issues, the experience can become unsafe.

Most recreational paddlers organize themselves into groups that share leadership, delegating responsibility as needed based on identified skills and need. For example, a person will be charged with organizing dinners or arranging to rent kayaks because these things need to be done. On the water, the group may defer navigational decisions to an individual with an obvious proficiency, but leave campsite organization to everyone and food preparation to the cook. If the group is operating within its competency, leadership can be shared. As the group faces challenges that they are not able to address with confidence, a designated leader needs to emerge.

Group Structure (Leadership)

Throughout the planning, implementation, and reflection of a trip, the group must accomplish many tasks. The group structure will determine how tasks will be accomplished and who will accomplish them. A group can structure itself in a variety of ways depending on the needs and preferences of group members, their skills and experience, and the demands of the trip.

Going It Alone

In this structure, each person takes responsibility for most aspects of planning, implementing, and reflecting on a trip. This is an easy structure to follow in that tasks do not have to be assigned, and each person can work on an individualized deadline. This does not negate the need for clearly articulated expectations about the kind of equipment, skills, and preparation that is appropriate. One person's errors and omissions have a direct impact on the others in the group.

This structure can detract from a trip, placing unnecessary burdens and duplication on each member. This is especially problem-atic in groups of people with disparate skills and knowledge, placing less-experienced members at a disadvantage and limiting their ability to learn valuable lessons in preparation and organization. In such a situation, a strategy of shared responsibility will often be more effective.

Shared Responsibility

This is perhaps the most common structure used by recreational paddlers. Each person shares responsibility for planning, implementing, and reflecting on a trip, adding individual strengths and helping where appropriate. The challenge with this approach is to make sure the important tasks are completed on time and in an appropriate manner. This works well if the group takes the time early on to make a plan and assign individual tasks.

Designated Responsibility

In this structure, responsibility is clearly invested in one or a few group members, who direct other members in accomplishing tasks as needed. This model works well if the other group members are willing to surrender most of their responsibility. This is an efficient structure because decisions can be made quickly, and duties can be clearly identified. It can also lead to conflict if the person or persons put in charge adopt a dictatorial manner and fail to listen to the needs of other group members. But used with compassion, the structure of designated responsibility can work effectively.

Blending Structures

The above models of group organization fall along a continuum. These structures can be blended to create a more sensitive and responsive group where each member is aware of his or her individual responsibilities. Depending on the demands facing the group, one particular structure may work better than others. It is best to remain flexible and modify the structure as needs change.

Leadership and Decision Making

Regardless of the structure of the leadership, appropriate decisions need to be made by the group to ensure their safety, enjoyment, and comfort. The leadership starts the decision-making process by defining a problem and stating a preferred outcome. From there, the leadership must gather a wide range of possible options, evaluate those options, choose the most appropriate option, act on that decision, and finally, reflect on the outcome of that action. All decisions follow the same process regardless of the situation.

In the normal run of tripping, the leadership is under minimal time constraints to make decisions, stress levels are low, and the consequences of error are minimal. Most of these decisions will focus on the overall safety of the group, ensuring only a reasonable amount of risk. In times of trouble, decisions are bounded by the need for fast, timely action that will minimize the potential for harm. During a rescue, decisions are made based on the immediate threat to the safety of the group and its members, with considerations of comfort and enjoyment secondary. This is what distinguishes decision making during tripping from decision making during a rescue.

Consider the following situation. It is dusk, about an hour before dark. As you paddle toward the small beach, you see four kayaks hauled up on the logs. You and your friends were hoping to have this beach and its small campsite to yourselves for the next few days. The next campsite is about an hour and a half away, and you have already had a long day, beginning at 6 A.M. with a drive to the put-in. You organized this trip, encouraging your two best friends to come along for a weekend away from it all. They are grumpy and turn to you for a decision. After weighing the options, you decide to land on the beach and talk to the other campers. They understand the situation and are willing to share the site for the night. They tell you that they

are moving on the next day. The next night, you and your friends are enjoying the beach and a fancy dinner. As a group you reflect on the previous day, remembering how everyone was very tired. On reflection, it was clear that the extra paddling to another campsite would have exhausted everyone and threatened the safety of the group. The three of you decide that the decision to stay at this site was a good one.

Decisions directly related to the safety of the group must be made clearly and with as much information as possible. When all is going well, the demands on leadership are at a minimum and shared leadership works well. When trouble arises, there needs to be more structure and direction. The leadership needs to make decisions quickly and communicate efficiently to the group. This has obvious implications for rescue. As the challenges mount and paddlers experience stress, there is less time for two-way communication. Under stress, the leadership may be unable to choose among options. Furthermore, some practical options may be overlooked. The group will be better able to meet and adapt to the challenges facing them if in advance there is agreement on who will take responsibility for leadership during a rescue.

Setting and Achieving Goals

The primary function of the leadership, regardless of where it resides, is to set goals and to help the group achieve them. In the context of sea kayaking, this may seem self-evident. Groups of paddlers come together to paddle. But this is an oversimplification. There are underlying goals that must be agreed upon. For example, the key questions of how and where to paddle should be clearly defined by the leadership during planning. Individuals enjoy paddling for different reasons. Partners may both enjoy paddling, but one partner seeks the physical challenge of the sport and looks to paddle in demanding conditions,

When Leadership Fails

We were heading back along a rough and exposed stretch of coastline with limited landing options. There was a broken 6-foot swell and winds were blowing 20 to 25 knots from the stern. Everyone had lots of experience, and many of us had paddled together before. We had reviewed and established some basic safety guidelines including paddling partners, paddle signals, and radio protocols.

The group stayed together for most of the trip back, but one paddler became seasick and required assistance. At the same time, a squall hit, increasing the winds to a speed of 25 to 30 knots. In less than a minute, the group fell apart.

The largest part of the group was supporting and towing the seasick paddler. Meanwhile, one paddler moved off closer to shore, and two were left behind. The leadership style up to this point was fairly relaxed. Unfortunately, it meant that the group fell apart once the winds picked up. At the end of the trip, we had to land through some large surf. Despite the fact that we had practiced landing and launching through the surf several times on this trip, the lack of leadership meant that our well-established procedures didn't hold up. As a result, several paddlers capsized and swam on the way in, and it took a long time to get everything and everyone back together safely on the beach.

On reflection: the loosely organized leadership was unable to mobilize an effective response to these challenges. Effective leadership would have put greater emphasis on the need to communicate if conditions became difficult. VHF radios on hand could have been used, or simple paddle signals could have brought the group together prior to moving in through the surf zone.

—*Michael Pardy*

while the other prefers paddling the coastline and viewing the flora and fauna. These are difficult goals to reconcile on a trip. Effective leadership will help them resolve this potential conflict and achieve their apparently conflicting goals. Solutions will include paddling separately for a portion of the time, and scheduling trips that meet each of their needs. In this way, they will both continue to enjoy paddling with each other.

Leadership will help the group identify a common set of goals. Individuals must consider their personal goals in relation to the common goals and decide if their goals are compatible. In many situations, an institution or formal leader determines the goals. Kayak clubs and other formal kayaking programs usually have established goals for each of their activities. Informal groups usually don't have clearly articulated goals. Leadership requires that the group take the time to identify goals so that they are more likely to achieve them.

Setting goals need not be arduous or time consuming, and it will greatly benefit everyone. The leadership should take the time to establish goals as a part of the trip planning process. On short excursions, the process may simply be a brief conversation about purpose. On longer trips the goals should be discussed, clarified, and written down in the paddler's logbook.

Health and Fitness

2

The paddler's body is the kayak's engine; it needs to be well fueled and well maintained. Skill and technique must be paired with strength and fitness. In difficult situations, your body has to perform at high levels of output and efficiency. Every kayaker needs a plan for regular maintenance (exercise and skill development), systems monitoring while on a trip (nutrition, hydration, temperature), and damage control (first aid) when there is a breakdown.

Fueling a Human-Powered Craft

Food

To fuel a human-powered craft, you need food, water, and oxygen. Sugars (simple carbohydrates) supply short-term energy but fail to sustain lasting effort. Starches (complex carbohydrates) are a fuel better suited for an effort sustained over several hours. Your body can store enough ready energy for about two hours' worth of paddling. While carbohydrate-rich snacks can keep you going through the day, you will still need to maintain a diet higher than usual in fat and protein, especially when paddling in cooler climates. Save the higher fat and protein snacks and meals for the end of the day when they can be digested and metabolized over a longer time. Plan your meals over a cycle of two or three days and assure that all dietary needs are considered.

The brain requires fuel and water like any other part of the body; mental processes decline in a manner similar to physical fatigue. Impaired judgment and fatigue is a lethal combination. Proper nutrition and hydration provide the fuels for your brain, your organs, and your muscles. Your body also must maintain a proper temperature to function properly. Metabolic processes that turn food and water into energy depend on quite precise thermal regulation.

Water and Other Fluids

Good hydration is necessary for the body to turn food into fuel, transport the fuel to organs and muscles, and burn that fuel to create energy. Thirst is a poor and late indicator of dehydration. While paddling steadily, we must drink steadily. It sounds simple, but at times of high demand, when conditions become difficult (commonly late in the day), paddlers will neglect to drink. Early in the day, leaving the beach in good weather, well rested and nourished, everything is fine; it is later in the day, tired and hungry, that we are most likely to have a "near-miss" incident. We need energy to keep ourselves out of trouble and to get ashore for a rest and a meal. Drinking and snacking throughout the day help keep our bodies ready for work. In hot environments, we may need twice the normal intake of water and an increased consumption of salty foods.

Here are some guidelines for daily fluid consumption while on a sea kayaking trip. Monitor your consumption so you know just how much you are drinking. Fluids include water and other liquids, such as tea, milk, and flavored drinks.

- Half a liter (about half a quart) first thing in the morning.
- A quarter liter (about 8 fluid ounces) every 30 minutes of steady paddling.
- Something to drink with every meal and snack.
- Two to 4 liters (about 2 to 4 quarts) total each day.
- Fluids are supplied in part by consuming soup, fresh fruit and vegetables, rice, pasta, and other foods.

Methods for Treating Water

Many diseases are spread by drinking water contaminated with microorganisms (bacteria, viruses, and parasites). There are numerous causes for contaminated water. In populated and industrial areas, chemical contaminants from lawn fertilizer and manufacturing processes cannot be filtered out. In these areas, use an established source of public drinking water. In wilderness areas, natural pathogens such as giardia can cause serious infections that may not present symptoms until weeks after ingestion. This incubation time is usually longer than the length of the trip. Rainwater is a clean source of drinking water, but bird droppings and other contaminants can infect runoff collected from tree branches, rooftops, or tarps.

You should disinfect your drinking water if you are using water directly from a stream, lake, or shallow well. Also plan on disinfection if you are traveling in a region or a country where water may not be adequately treated. Anyone with a weakened immune system should routinely disinfect water before drinking it. To remove or kill disease-bearing microorganisms, water collected in the field can be boiled, filtered, or purified.

Boiling

Boiling is the best way to kill microorganisms. A full boil for at least 1 minute is recommended. To remove the flat taste of boiled water, leave it in a clean, covered container for a few hours or pour the cooled, boiled water back and forth several times from one clean container to another.

Filtering

Many manufacturers offer small, lightweight filters that can remove pathogens from water. Filters must be regularly dried and cleaned. The filters are only as good as the user's personal hygiene. Handling the filter or the receiving container with soiled hands can contaminate otherwise clean water. Store the dry filter in a clean container, and minimize cross-contamination by separating the intake hose from the outlet hose. Familiarize yourself with the filter while at home, learning how the unit works and how to troubleshoot in the field.

A variety of filter types are available:

- *Simple filters* are designed to eliminate only the largest sediments and microorganisms and will not remove all contaminants.
- *Microfilters*, generally more expensive, eliminate more organisms, but they are not effective against viruses, such as those that cause hepatitis. However, viruses are unlikely to be encountered in wilderness camping or from natural water sources.
- *Filters* or *purifiers* have a silver nitrate or iodine matrix that eliminates viruses, in

addition to giardia and bacteria. If the filter has a charcoal element, it also will get rid of the taste of iodine and other chemicals.

Still water is easier to filter than water agitated in streams and rivers because it contains less suspended matter. If possible, keep the prefilter at the end of the intake hose off the bottom to avoid drawing sediment directly into the filter unit. In heavily sedimented water, a disposable coffee filter wrapped over the prefilter will add a level of coarse filtration. Alternatively, let some water sit overnight in a clean cooking pot, then gently filter water from the top of the container.

Chemical Treatment

Water purification tablets kill most waterborne microorganisms. The tablets contain various disinfectants, with some having objectionable odors or tastes. Read the packaging information carefully and closely follow the manufacturer's instructions.

Power and Endurance

Power is the body's ability to put energy into action. You need lots of power to paddle a fully loaded kayak out through a surf zone or to paddle hard through a tide rip. Frequent vigorous paddling is a good way to increase power reserves.

Endurance is the ability to sustain power for an extended time. Your training should include efforts sustained over long periods. At the end of a blustery day, you may have to paddle energetically for a couple of hours to return to calm waters. Paddling, hiking, vigorous walking, swimming, and jogging are among the activities that can help you develop endurance.

Fatigue waits at the end of endurance. It is one of the most significant hazards you will encounter during sea kayaking. The quality of

your technique and your judgment will decrease as you become fatigued. Kayakers seldom get themselves into trouble when they are well rested and have recently had a good meal.

To build power and endurance, go paddling a lot; practice the entire range of skills. Your body will adapt to the demands of the activity. In a rescue, tipping the water out of a loaded kayak by lifting the bow takes some strength. Assisting an injured paddler back into a kayak also requires strength. An exercise plan that includes strength training and a lower body workout is a great supplement in the off-season.

Fitness

Before beginning a new exercise regime, consult a physician. A certified fitness instructor will help you get the best results from an exercise program.

A balanced fitness program develops both *aerobic* sources of energy—those that demand good utilization of oxygen—and *anaerobic* sources of energy—those that kick in when the body can no longer get enough oxygen.

Aerobic sources of energy are sustainable for long periods. When your breathing rate is raised but still controlled, when heart and lungs are working hard but without great effort, your body is receiving sufficient oxygen to maintain the workload. This is an aerobic energy level, in which the body uses fat as fuel. Even lean, fit people have plenty of fat to keep them going for a long time.

When your energy output increases to the point of labored breathing, your body is getting less oxygen than it needs. In the absence of sufficient oxygen, the body will take fuel supplies directly from muscle tissue. This anaerobic energy production quickly leads to fatigue.

For sustained activity in adverse sea conditions, you want to work at the top of your aerobic energy level without shifting gears into the anaerobic energy system. But for short bursts of power—to break through a line of surf, cross a current-swept channel, or catch up to a paddler in need—anaerobic energy is necessary.

Paddling frequently and energetically will train your body to delay switching up to the higher gear of the anaerobic energy system. The ability to work at moderate to high levels of exertion while staying within the limits of aerobic exercise is important to your safety. To train for those days of demanding sea conditions, you can paddle energetically when you don't need to. Over several weeks, as your fitness improves, you will be able to exercise longer and harder without labored breathing and fatigue.

Leave plenty of time for leisure—rest and refuel.   (GREG SHEA)

You can train your body to deliver both long-term aerobic energy and short-term, high-level anaerobic energy.

Aerobic Training

Some good activities for improving your aerobic fitness:

- walking for 30 to 45 minutes (swing your arms to get your heart rate up a little more)

- jogging

- cycling

- swimming (go at a speed that you can maintain for at least 30 minutes)

- paddling for 30 minutes at a steady touring speed of 3 knots or a little better (keep your stroke rate up to about 30 strokes per minute, counting one side only)

Anaerobic Training

The following activities will help improve your anaerobic fitness.

- While paddling, speed ahead very fast for 10 paddle strokes (counting one side only),

then paddle normally until fully rested—two or three minutes at least. Then sprint ahead for a count of 15. Once again, paddle normally until fully rested. Then sprint ahead for a count of 20, rest; then sprint ahead for a count of 15, rest; then sprint for a count of 10, and you are done. As you gain power with continued training, increase the number of sprint strokes. The rest phase is important in training your body to deliver extra power on demand and to then recover quickly, ready for the next challenge.

- When out for a walk or swim, add time for anaerobic training. Sprint (or walk very fast, swinging your arms) for 30 seconds or more and then slow down to recover. Go through the sprint-and-rest cycle for 15 to 20 minutes, in a pattern similar to that just described for anaerobic paddling.

Confidence

Confidence is the grease that makes the human machine run smoothly. Confidence allows us the presence of mind to venture into reasoned risk-taking, giving us the courage to explore outside our comfort zone and venture

Paddler's Fatigue

We left the beach early in the morning to take advantage of a slack tide. Soon after, the winds came up stronger than expected and we continued to paddle on into the wind for the next several hours. By lunch, everyone was ready for a snack and a rest. We stopped, had a break, ate some food and drank some water; but, the wind was building and there was no space for camping on our lunch beach. The next closest available camping site was 5 miles farther down the coast. We set out knowing it was going to be a long haul. We finally got to the campsite about two hours before dark. As we landed and checked the site over, a mother black bear and cub came out of the woods. We tried to shoo them away, but they showed no fear of us. Reluctantly, we decided to paddle to the next campsite a couple more miles down the coast. We left the beach with everyone cold, tired, and hungry. We rafted up, put on dry clothes, and had a snack before heading on. Soon the wind was blowing a steady 15 to 20 knots and we were paddling straight into it.

The 2 miles would have taken us less than an hour in the morning, but late in the day it turned into a two-hour ordeal. Several group members were reaching the limits of their endurance. We plodded along and took turns towing the weaker paddlers to keep the group together. By the time we landed, it was dark, and we had been on the water for over 12 hours.

On reflection: The decisions made later in the day were sound, and we did the best we could with these challenges and few options. The problem was not reviewing our initial plan when we first encountered stronger than expected winds. There was no rush, we could have waited for calmer winds, or stopped to camp before lunch as the wind was building.

—Michael Pardy

into new experiences. A lack of confidence holds us back from practicing our skills and slowly erodes our abilities.

Confidence and skill are essential in meeting the demands of wind, wave, and current. Our confidence and skill improve when we overcome a challenge. Surpassing our expectations, we discover that we have more in reserve than we anticipated. But be careful to take on new challenges a little at a time. Confidence develops slowly with a levelheaded understanding of abilities. If we outstrip our physical and mental abilities, the resulting failure can eat away at our confidence. How far we push our limits determines whether an adventure is productive.

A paddler's confidence varies over the years and from day to day. In the natural flow of human endeavors, confidence can vary for no readily obvious reason. Temporarily stepping back, taking a day off to rest, can be sufficient to renew vigor and self-assurance. After a deeply stressful incident, a paddler can be traumatized. It can take a long time to rebuild confidence to former levels. Practicing familiar and achievable tasks at ever-increasing levels of difficulty can restore diminished confidence.

Medical Conditions

Before a sea kayak trip, the medical needs of the group must be taken into consideration. Group leaders need to know which people are taking medication for conditions such as asthma and how their health could change during the trip. Leaders should also be made aware of latent conditions such as food allergies and allergic responses to insect bites. It is also important to know the human resources of the group: some will have first-aid or leadership training; others may be expert at camping or possess skills that can be essential during a medical emergency.

A good first-aid kit and the knowledge to use it promptly when needed is a vital part of sea kayak touring. A painful sliver in a hand with no tweezers to remove it, or an upset stomach with no analgesic to relieve the distress, can bring a kayaker's progress to a halt. During the trip it is important to report and treat wounds, infections, digestive upset, or any other medical condition or injury (see First-Aid Kit in the appendix). Beyond the basic first-aid kit, you may need to create needed equipment from the contents of your kayak or from the surrounding environment. Improvisation can be the key to a successful wilderness rescue.

Simple medical events can become emergencies when the nearest professional help is hours away. A short kayak trip to an offshore island may mean that a patient must be treated on site before being evacuated. An essential principle of first aid is to guarantee your own safety and the safety of your group; in trying to help the sick or injured person, do not create another victim. Meeting the group's basic needs becomes a concern if evacuation is delayed and extended patient care is necessary. Set up shelter, and keep the patient and the group warm, rested, and nourished.

Conditions at the scene may be harsh. Bad weather, big waves, strong currents, and severe heat or cold will affect all members of the group. If one person is hypothermic, the others are likely as well to be cold. Deal with immediate problems first, then make a plan for evacuation. The patient may need to be moved to a location accessible to emergency medical help.

Proper training and preparation are basic to safe, enjoyable outdoor activity. Regular sea kayak training should be supplemented with a course in wilderness first aid that includes cardiopulmonary resuscitation (CPR). Good training and good judgment will help in the early detection of problems and quick remediation. During the trip, be aware of the resources that may come into play during a medical situation. If a member of your party carries epinephrine for use in treating allergic reactions, know where it is kept and how to inject it; know where the inhaler is for the person with asthma. Have a VHF radio, cell phone, or other communications equipment and know how to use it.

Repetitive Strain Injuries

Good paddling technique allows for thousands of repetitions per hour without undue strain, but small errors in technique can lead to debilitating repetitive strain injuries. Wrist and shoulder injuries are the most prevalent. Poor posture can aggravate lower back problems. Once encountered, repetitive strain injuries usually require a long rest and a change in technique. It is easier to take the steps necessary to avoid the injury in the first place. This becomes particularly important during a multiday trip.

To help prevent repetitive strain injury:

- Maintain good paddling technique.
- Before sitting in the kayak, warm up your shoulders, wrists, and lower back, moving all joints through a full range of motion.
- During the early stages of a trip, paddle shorter distances, stopping frequently to rest and stretch; build up distance slowly over a few days.
- Incorporate rest days into a traveling cycle.
- After sitting in the kayak, take a walk.
- Act before a repetitive strain injury becomes chronic: treat such an injury with

In the Wake of an Accident

Conditions were a little rough, but nothing that concerned Tony and Tom, two highly experienced paddlers. As they skirted along the shoreline, the breeze and incoming waves pushed them two or three yards closer to the waves breaking on the rocky shore. At that moment, the wake of a passing freighter swept into the two kayaks, picking them up and throwing them onto the rocks. Both kayaks took the impact full-force, sideways.

The boats slid down the rocks as the wake-wave receded. Tony pulled the buckle on his quick-release belt, went into a high-brace maneuver, then broached on another wave onto the rock; he managed to escape and paddle away. Tom took the brunt of a couple more large waves full broadside. His stern was catching high on the rock as the wave receded, and he was unable to get turned seaward.

Tom's full attention was on maintaining an extreme high brace and keeping the protection of the kayak's hull between his body and the rocks. Finally, with a timely push from a kayaker on shore, Tom paddled back out to calmer waters. It was a fantastic example of excellent high-bracing skill and grace under pressure.

Moments later Tony approached our small, sheltered beach. His left hand was covered in blood. On first impact, his hand had been crushed between his kayak and the barnacle-covered rock. In the rush of the moment, he had not noticed the injury. But as soon as the bow of his kayak touched shore, his face grew pale and his legs went weak. We treated and bandaged Tony's hand, then gave him some hot chocolate and a sandwich.

When Tony was feeling better, our entire group got together to review what had happened and to plan for getting Tony home. We were on a small island about a mile and a half from the mainland. The sea was choppy, and the tide runs swiftly between the island and the main shore. Tony couldn't grip a paddle with his stiff, swollen hand. We decided to tow him in his kayak. Three paddlers, pulling in a line, towed as another paddler rafted-up with Tony. It was a quick and uneventful trip back. Tony's hand was cut and bruised but did not require any further treatment, and he was soon back to paddling.

On reflection: Keep an eye out to sea for unusual incoming waves. Conditions can be just right one moment and desperate the next. A moment of inattention almost turned a pleasant day into disaster. A little less skill on the part of the paddlers—a capsize between kayak and rocks—and the outcome could have been grim.

—Doug Alderson

rest, ice, compression, and elevation (RICE); change your paddling style or use a different paddle.

Hypothermia

Hypothermia results from the body's inability to replace heat lost to the environment; untreated, it can kill. The first stages of hypothermia are feeling cold and shivering vigorously; we have all been mildly hypothermic at some time.

If a person falls into cold water, hypothermia can have a rapid onset. Or it can be brought on slowly by chronic exposure to a cold environment. In both cases, hypothermia is a progressive condition that is often preceded by a sequence of events: a cold night in a damp sleeping bag, a poor breakfast, a long and tiring day of paddling.

Prevention

To prevent hypothermia, you have to actively prevent heat loss in advance of getting cold. Keys to prevention are heat manufacture and retention. You need adequate protective clothing, food, water, and activity to generate sufficient heat.

It is important to depart camp warm, fueled, and in good health. Seated in the kayak, most of your body is sheltered and you are busy; you are insulated and producing heat. It may be a different matter when you return to shore. Some members of the group may have become cold and may already be at a low level of hypothermia. On shore, where you will be exercising less than when you were paddling, heat retention becomes more important. Change into dry clothes. Eating a snack and having something to drink will keep you warm and will help in digesting the larger meal to come.

Wear clothing in easily removed layers so that layers can be added or removed to suit changing conditions. The outer layer needs to be wind resistant. In order to create insulating air spaces, each layer should fit loosely over the layer beneath. Clothing dampened from the inside by sweat or from the outside by rain loses much of its insulating ability and increases evaporative heat loss.

Warning Signs

A person's initial response to cooling is mainly an effort to restore normal body temperature. As hypothermia develops, body functions become slower and less efficient. Blood thickens and muscles become stiff. A

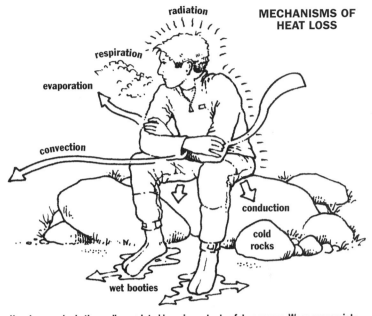

MECHANISMS OF HEAT LOSS

radiation
respiration
evaporation
convection
conduction
cold rocks
wet booties

Keeping your body thermally regulated is an important safety concern. Wear appropriate clothing, and respond quickly to changing environment conditions.

person will experience problems with physical coordination, and may shiver uncontrollably. As body core temperature drops, shivering tapers off to a point where it stops entirely. The absence of shivering further reduces heat production and begins a critical spiral of further heat loss. The person's skin may feel cold and stiff, and appear pale or slightly bluish. The body's priority is to preserve vital functions of the core and head. As hypothermia progresses, these vital systems are affected.

Hypothermia is a progressive disorder. A typical progression of signs and symptoms might look like this:

- Feeling cold.
- Skin numbness.
- Shivering.
- Loss of fine muscle control, especially in the hands.
- Slowed pace; slow paddling or walking.
- Mild confusion and apathy.

- Loss of gross motor control; stumbling or falling and inability to use hands.
- Slowed thought and speech.

Signs of *severe hypothermia* include:

- Cessation of shivering.
- Inability to stand or walk.
- Lowered level of consciousness.

Watch both yourself and the people with you for signs of hypothermia. Children and the elderly are more likely than others to develop hypothermia. If one member of your group is hypothermic, you can assume that others in the group are nearly as cold.

Treatment

A person experiencing mild hypothermia is readily treatable. As soon as the signs are recognized by the sufferer or by others, see that he or she is made dry, is kept insulated from the cold by dry clothing, and remains out of the wind. The person needs to have something to drink and should remain active.

As hypothermia progresses, these same steps can be followed for rewarming a victim, but they become increasingly more difficult and take longer to be effective. Early intervention is both easier and more successful. A person suffering from severe hypothermia requires medical treatment and evacuation. A wilderness first-aid course with emphasis on treatment of hypothermia is strongly advised.

Heat Exhaustion and Heat Stroke

Heat exhaustion and heat stroke are manifestations of hyperthermia, a medical condition that results from overheating and the body's inability to cool itself. Untreated, severe hyperthermia can kill. Heat exhaustion and heat stroke are preventable disorders.

You can help avoid the ill effects of overheating by taking a few simple precautions:

- If you know you'll be exposed on the trip to greater heat or humidity than normal, try to acclimatize by spending some time in similar conditions before the trip.
- During the trip, drink plenty of cool water—before, during, and after paddling. Even when you're not thirsty, your body is losing fluids that need to be replaced. Plain water is excellent, but it has been shown that people drink considerably more if the beverage is flavored. Sports drinks are suitable and contain electrolytes lost during sweating.
- Eat plenty of fruits and other good snack food.
- Take frequent breaks.

The signs of *heat exhaustion* include:

- Flushed skin.
- Perspiration.
- Nausea.
- Dizziness.
- Impaired mental function.

Heat exhaustion is a serious condition that needs to be carefully monitored. Treatment involves getting the sufferer to cool shade, placing cool cloths on a number of different areas of the body, and replacing fluids and electrolytes (such as those found in sports drinks).

Signs of the more serious *heat stroke* include:

- Hot, dry skin.
- Elevated pulse and respiration.
- Lowered level of consciousness.

Heat stroke is a medical emergency, and professional help is needed as soon as possible. The victim's body is unable to regulate temperature, and he or she must receive immediate first aid to relieve the body of excessive heat. Move to a cooler area and soak the person with cool water; use a fan or cold

Quick Passage into Danger

The initial crossing to Denman Island, off British Columbia's Vancouver Island, was uneventful for our five-person kayaking group. But passing between Denman and Chrome Island, the seas worsened significantly. The islands had been sheltering us up to this point. The seas were mixed and breaking, with rebounding waves from the nearby shore.

Mike strongly advised we turn around, but I wanted to proceed. Soon, however, I agreed with him and we turned toward a sheltered beach. Paul and Julie turned around with me to travel the quarter-mile to calmer waters, with Mike and Alan following behind. But when I looked back to check on them, I saw that Alan had capsized. Mike was assisting him.

Paddling out to assist, I came upon what appeared to be a successful rescue, with Alan back in his kayak. Alan's kayak was swamped and he seemed unsteady. Since he had a wet suit on, I asked him to go back in the water so that I could drain his kayak over the bow of my boat. We did this successfully. On regaining his boat, Alan seemed coherent and did not complain of being cold. He said he was fine, so I let him go. He immediately capsized again.

By this time we were being blown close to a rocky lee shore where a landing would have been destructive. I knew Alan had to be towed to the sheltered beach, with someone in another kayak rafted with his kayak to support him, but none of us had a tow rope.

I sent Mike back to retrieve the tow rope on Paul's kayak. With Mike heading for shore, I had to keep us off the rocks. Initially I told Alan, who was still in the water, to swim as he pushed his boat clear of the rocks. But he quickly complained of feeling cold, so I helped him back into his boat. Alan was very unsteady. I knew if I let him go, he would again capsize.

Mike returned with the tow rope, and I towed both kayaks to the beach, with Mike struggling to steady Alan all the way. By the time we arrived, Paul and Julie had a fire going. We piled clothes on Alan and soon he was back to normal. We all felt immensely relieved.

On reflection: Hypothermia sets in quickly. Cold water rapidly robbed Alan's body core of heat. Reduced physical coordination, which is a symptom of hypothermia, soon followed.

—Don Lockwood,
adapted from WaveLength Magazine,
www.wavelengthmagazine.com (July–Aug. 1994)

packs if available. Keep the victim lying down, with feet raised.

Sunburn

Sunburn is a universal and potentially harmful medical condition. Individuals vary widely in their sensitivity to sunlight. Gradually increased exposure that permits natural tanning and thickening of the skin will help decrease your sensitivity to sunlight, while protective clothing and proper use of sunscreen will protect your skin. Two thirds of the sun's radiation comes between 10 A.M. and 2 P.M.

To treat sunburn, remove the person from the sun and treat as a burn, cooling the affected areas and rehydrating the victim. If the burn blisters and breaks, treat as a small wound, covering the broken skin with a sterile dressing to minimize the risk of infection. If the burn covers an extensive area, consider evacuating the individual.

Environment

3

To travel by kayak is to be on intimate terms with the natural environment. While the open sea with its absence of shelter is more intimidating, the greater risks are near shore. A kayaker's refuge is a campsite on an exposed beach.

A kayaker's interactions with weather, geography, and tides bring with them an essential need for understanding and awareness. Weather systems are fickle, tides are relentless, and coastal geography interacts with waves, wind, and tides to create a dynamic and challenging obstacle course. Your understanding of the coastal environment needs to be an equal partner with your boat-handling skills. Safe travel depends on your ability to make reasonable judgments about wind, waves, rain, sun, fog, air temperature, water temperature, tides, and the shape of the land.

There are many ways to get the weather information we need. Satellite pictures have given greater accuracy to published multiday forecasts; obtain your local forecast before any outing, no matter its duration. Back on earth, we may get glimpses of high-altitude clouds on the leading edge of a storm, and there is predictive power in the understanding of local weather patterns born of experience.

Coastal geography has a profound influence on local weather. As systems cross the boundary between land and sea, they change in speed, direction, and strength. Local small-scale effects add to the nearly endless list of considerations. Considerable artistry is needed to judge how incoming weather will manifest locally. Choosing to pick up the pace and pass a prominent windy headland before the wind rises and the tide turns is a common kayaking decision. Incoming wind waves and

On calm days, both kayaker and wildlife take a pleasant break.

swell are also modified by the shape and depth of a shoreline. Along complex coastlines, tidal currents opposing wind waves create steep, dangerous seas. The interaction of wind waves and tidal currents can be responsible for some of the more dynamic sea states a coastal kayaker will encounter.

Weather Systems

It is useful to think about the effects of weather in terms of *scale* and *duration*. The scale of weather phenomena varies from the global circulation of air known as a jet stream to weather systems that cover hundreds or sometimes thousands of miles, to the often dramatic local influences on the inshore weather experienced by sea kayakers. Durations range from seasonal trends, to storms that may last for days, to the squall raining on your campsite for only minutes. These concepts of scale and duration help us sort through the often confusing information on weather.

A meteorologist's air-pressure map looks much like a cartographer's elevation map. The cartographer's map shows the height of land; the meteorologist's air-pressure map shows the weight (pressure) of the atmosphere. Contour lines that describe the ridges and troughs of the atmosphere connect points of equal pressure and are known as isobars. Wind is air moving from a ridge of higher pressure to a trough of lower pressure. A difference in pressure from one location to another creates a pressure slope. Wind strength results from a combination of pressure difference and pressure slope. Storm winds are born where there is a large pressure difference and a steep pressure slope, as depicted on a weather map by tightly bunched isobars.

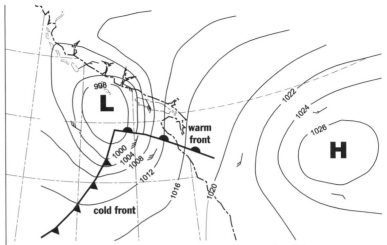

A meteorologist's weather map gives mariners a basic understanding of the movement and the strength of weather systems. The numbered lines are isobars. This map shows a low-pressure system offshore and a high-pressure system inland.

High-Pressure Systems

Air has weight, and when there is a lot of it on top of us, we have higher air pressure. High-pressure systems are ridges of air that are trying to flatten themselves out. Air from the upper atmosphere is pouring downward and outward into the lower atmosphere, and as it sinks it warms. Since warmer air can hold more moisture, the air in a high-pressure cell is always relatively dry, and the skies are usually clear. High-pressure systems can be made up of either cold or warm air masses. In a high-pressure system, the air flows clockwise in the Northern Hemisphere (counterclockwise in the Southern Hemisphere) and out from the center. The strongest winds occur at the outer edges of the system, where the air has had a chance to pick up speed as it moves down and out toward adjacent lows.

High winds and improving weather are associated with the leading edge of a high-pressure system. As the leading edge approaches and passes overhead, the wind shifts clockwise *(veers)* in the Northern Hemisphere. A veering wind generally heralds improving weather and lighter winds.

In the Northern Hemisphere winds blow clockwise and outward around areas of high pressure and counterclockwise and inward around areas of low pressure.

Low-Pressure Systems

Low-pressure systems are the real weather makers of temperate latitudes, generating strong winds, rain, hail, thunder, and lightning. For planning a safe passage, kayakers must be able to anticipate the weather phenomena associated with these systems. Low-pressure systems are atmospheric troughs that draw air from regions of higher pressure.

In a low-pressure system, the air flows counterclockwise and inward in the Northern Hemisphere. As a system approaches, the wind shifts counterclockwise (*backs*). A backing wind is generally associated with deteriorating weather and strengthening winds. In low-pressure systems, the winds are strongest near the center of the trough. The air has been drawn from regions of higher pressure and has had a chance to gather speed as it travels downward and into the low point. The approach of a major low is a good reason to postpone or cancel a trip.

Lows With Frontal Systems

Midlatitude, or temperate-zone, low-pressure systems contain warm and cold fronts separating warm and cold air. This is because lows develop on the boundaries between cold and warm air masses—typically beneath the upper-atmosphere jet stream—and as the low deepens, cold and warm air are entrained in its rotational circulation. Typically, a wedge of warm air is trapped between masses of cold air. The warm air gradually tries to ride up and over the cold air ahead of it, even as it is undercut by cold air overtaking it from behind. The resulting pattern of weather is more or less predictable and is obvious on many pressure maps as the characteristic V formed by a warm front and a cold front, with its apex at the center of the low. The fronts associated with lows have characteristic wind and cloud patterns that can be recognized by observations from the ground. More important than a momentary inspection of the sky, observations taken over a few days or just a few hours reveal changes in the pattern. Changes observed during the recent past provide valuable information about the coming weather.

Warm fronts are the leading edge of a warm air mass pushing against a mass of colder air. The warm air rising over the colder air mass cools, and as it cools the moisture in it condenses, first as clouds and then as precipitation. Near the front, high-level cirrus clouds are followed by midlevel altostratus clouds and finally thick, low-level stratocumulus clouds with rain. Winds increase and shift counterclockwise (back). Behind the front, the region of warmer air, winds shift clockwise (veer) and the weather improves slightly.

Cold fronts are the leading edge of a mass of cold air. The weather associated with a cold front is more severe and changes more abruptly. The cooler air travels quickly and the resulting front is steep. Updrafts are pronounced and the weather tends to be vigorous. In its most pronounced state, cold fronts produce the distinctively ominous cumu-

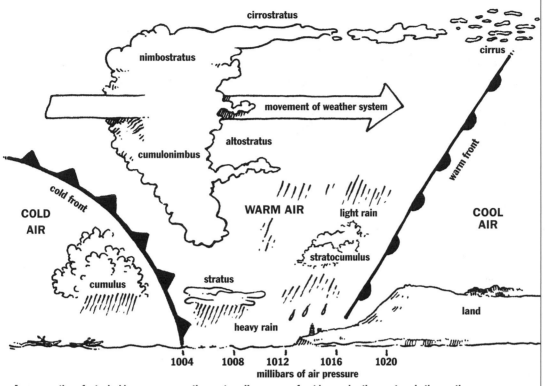

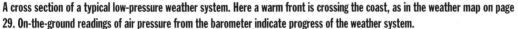

A cross section of a typical low-pressure weather system. Here a warm front is crossing the coast, as in the weather map on page 29. On-the-ground readings of air pressure from the barometer indicate progress of the weather system.

lonimbus clouds—the anvil-topped thunder and lightning clouds. Cold fronts can produce hail and sudden, heavy downpours. The wind veers, and squalls are common. A cold front passes quickly, and the severe weather does not usually last long.

As a typical low approaches, the observer on the ground experiences cool temperatures, increasing cloud cover, a lowering cloud ceiling, and a backing of the wind that is often accompanied by an increase in velocity. A distinct warming and veering in wind direction indicates the arrival of the warm front. The wedge of warmer air is a sign of worse weather to follow, however. The strongest winds can be expected behind the impending cold front. An observer near the center of the system will have very little time to take shelter, and a sudden and severe change in

weather can be expected. Farther out from the center, the distance between the warm front and the cold front is greater; thus there is more time to respond and a less severe change in the weather. Keeping a weather log that indicates the movement of weather systems relative to your position will help you plan a safe trip.

In the later stages of a storm's development, a frontal occlusion may occur. Cold fronts usually travel faster than warm fronts, and therefore at some stage, the cold front catches up with the warm front. In cross section, the warm air is lifted right off the ground, so that the observer on the surface misses the warm air mass. This is known as an occlusion or occluded front. In most cases, this is an indication of a mature weather system that is weakening.

Gale Rising to Storm Force

"Gale warning for this afternoon rising to storm force this evening."

The forecast was threatening (a gale-force wind is 28 to 55 knots, while a storm is 56 to 63 knots), but we thought we could stay in the shelter of the bay. The winds were not predicted till later that day. The bay was breezy and the water was a little choppy. The island half a mile up the open coast was within easy reach. Outside the bay, along the coast, the wind waves were 2 feet with low swell, and the wind was easterly at 10 to 15 knots. The sky was overcast, with a cold, continuous drizzle.

We paddled to the island, then found a lunch stop on its sheltered side. The sky cleared and the wind stopped. After lunch we paddled around the island and looked out to the rocky islet and its lighthouse, another 1.5 miles offshore. The crossing was well known for being current swept and rough. But at the moment, conditions were wonderful. It became so warm before our crossing that I went ashore to remove my paddling dry-top.

We crossed over to the lighthouse and spent time watching the seals, sea lions, and elephant seals; it was sunny and very warm. I had a niggling anxiety about the stark difference between the severity of the weather forecast and the fine weather we were experiencing—in a spot notorious for its bad weather, strong currents, and tragic accidents.

The lighthouse had once been manned but was now automated. Twenty years earlier I had come ashore at this light to be greeted by the keeper. Stepping out onto the concrete ramp, I had asked him what the weather was going to be like. "How the hell should I know?" he had barked. "I just report what I see. It could be blowing a gale and raining in 20 minutes for all I know!" Prophetic words.

So there I was, two decades later. After 45 minutes of watching the wildlife, we started back across the open water and made it to our previous lunch stop. We now had a mile to travel along the coast before we were safely back in the bay. The cool wind had returned and backed to the southwest, and I wished I had kept my paddling jacket on. Within 10 minutes, the weather forecast came true. The weather station at the lighthouse later reported southwest winds at 55 knots. Without realizing it, we were very close to the center of the storm. The warm front had only briefly preceded the violent conditions behind the cold front.

With only 500 yards to some shelter and a better heading off the wind, we could make no further progress. We turned downwind and came to rest in a small, remote cove on the mainland, in the shelter of the island. With the VHF radio, we called for a truck to come pick us up.

On reflection: we were very lucky. The lull in the wind contradicted a stern warning of very strong wind in a region of fast moving tidal current. We were complacent, narrowly dodging very dangerous sea conditions. Heed all weather forecasts that approach or exceed the limits of safe conditions.

—Doug Alderson

Sources of Information

Weather information comes from weather reports, weather forecasts, and personal observations. Weather broadcasts include reports of the recent past and a forecast for the future. The kayaker needs to observe the weather conditions of the moment. Like weather itself, information about the weather comes in different scales, covering areas that range from an entire continent or more down to a 100-mile section of coastline or a single coastal inlet. That information also may span an entire season, a week, or only the next 24 hours.

No single source gives all the information available. Sources include newspapers, television, radio, the Internet, marine VHF radios, weather radios, local knowledge, and personal observation. Your local radio station will tell if it is going to rain and will help you determine what the road conditions are like on the way to your launch site. The marine report will give you wind speed, wind direction, and wave heights. At the dock, an angler might tell you about the effects of a north wind at the nearby headland. Listen to the weather reports and forecast for information on medium-scale weather conditions. For indications of small-scale weather, use personal observation: look up to see the dark cloud about to rain down on your head; look out to sea and notice the squall approaching.

Weather Broadcasts

Marine weather broadcasts are available on VHF radio frequencies and other specialty weather stations. In North America, the broadcasts are continuous and are updated on a regular basis. Weather broadcasts are intended for large geographic areas, and they provide different information depending on the intended audience. Land-based reports and forecasts tell of rain and temperature. Marine reports and forecasts are centered on wind speed, wind direction, and wave height. (The Beaufort Scale, provided in the appendix, defines some of the terms used to describe heavy weather in marine weather broadcasts.) Weather forecasts reliably predict patterns over large areas. Errors in forecasting tend to be made with regard to timing and intensity at the local level. The local weather is directly affected by local geography.

Weather broadcasts are divided into *forecasts* and *reports*. A weather forecast is a prediction for the general weather in a large region over the course of one or more days. A weather report gives the true conditions at a singular site at a given moment. A weather report from one specific site may be 6 hours old, and the accompanying forecast for the region may be for 24 hours ahead. Time differences and local weather effects can be responsible for a forecast that remains consistent while local reports exhibit significant variations.

Personal Observation

The activity that ties the reports and forecasts together is personal observation. Observation allows the kayaker to evaluate the local accuracy of the weather broadcast. The kayaker needs to gather information on wind speed and direction, cloud cover, and air temperature. A hand barometer provides useful information on trends in changing air pressure.

Publications

You can find many books that describe weather systems and the daily weather cycles that form small-scale effects such as sea breezes and fog; most of these are available from commercial publishers. State and federal governments produce any number of pamphlets and handbooks to aid in understanding weather; many of these are available through government publishing houses, public libraries, and the World Wide Web. One useful resource is the series of books called *Coast Pilots*. They are detailed accounts of local weather, water, terrain, and navigational hazards and are available for most regions of the world. Though written for commercial shipping, they contain much of interest to kayakers. (See the Resources appendix for a list of useful books.)

The World Wide Web is a source for weather reports and forecasts, weather maps, and background information. Current reports from offshore weather buoys are available online, as are live video images that permit you to check the weather at a variety of sites around the world. Cameras located at popular surf beaches are a convenience for surfing enthusiasts. (See the Resources appendix for information on World Wide Web sites.)

Local publications are another good source of information. Many weather patterns are limited in area and duration and are not forecast by national meteorological offices but will be provided by local newspapers and radio and TV stations. Local guidebooks may also provide weather information and may contain a list of resources to help in your research.

Local weather phenomena are also recorded in the personal knowledge of mariners. At the marine store or the dock, it's not hard to start a conversation about the weather. Chances are you'll soon have a bunch of boaters giving you a wide range of advice. Take the time to listen to the advice, and then cautiously test their wisdom through your own observations.

Personalized Weather Forecast

To create your own personalized weather forecast, keep a *weather log* and use it to record weather reports, forecasts, and observations. Continually monitor the weather, watching for changes and detecting trends that might affect your paddling plans. Comparing the present weather with past reports can indicate future trends. At a minimum, record information once a day in your weather log. If the weather is changing quickly, record the information more often.

Urban living and the shelter of living indoors dull our sense of the weather. Jumpstart your weather sense by logging weather information for a few days in advance of a trip. During a multiday trip, especially after the first few days, your awareness of the weather will improve. It is unwise to rely on official forecasts without comparing the information against real-time weather observations.

In making your own weather forecast:

- Listen to the past.
- Observe the present.
- Predict the future.

As you create a personalized forecast:

- Remember that published weather *forecasts* are generally predictions for a wide area over an extended period of time and are prone to errors of timing and intensity.
- Remember that published weather *reports* are statements of past conditions at specific locations and times, and by themselves have no predictive value.
- Consider the scale of the information you receive from forecasts and reports—whether it covers a large or small scale of time and area.
- Keep track of the weather in a log.
- Consider how the weather that is forecast will shape your paddling environment.
- Compare the forecast and reports to what you see across the deck of your kayak.
- Know the local weather patterns.

Learning to interpret changes in air pressure, cloud types, and wind direction and strength allows the paddler to balance weather observation with broadcasts and other weather data. The table on page 36 provides some general indications of the approach of high- and low-pressure systems.

Notes taken during a weather broadcast and recorded in a weather log. The following information is found in notation form in the log:

June 11, 9:30 P.M.

SECURITE
(see page 118)

REPORTS at 10:40 P.M. At Leonard Island Lighthouse, visibility is 12 miles, and the wind is from the northwest at 5 knots with a 1-foot chop and a low southwesterly swell. The barometric pressure is 1017.9 millibars, steady.

JUNE 11   21:30
✱ SECURITE
SYN N/S R (H) → THUR
WAKE T (L) → WASH.
    TO VIs.
ST - G NW , N

REPORT   22:40
LEONARD LT VIS 12 NW5
1 FT CH   LOW SW SWELL
1017.9 ↔

WCVIS FORECAST 24 HRS
VAR 5-15   2.3m
O-L L-MOD   W

SYNOPSIS, a north-to-south ridge of high pressure is building through Thursday. In the wake there is a trough of low pressure approaching Washington State and Vancouver Island. Strong to gale force northwesterly to northerly winds.

The forecast for the next 24 hours: In the vicinity of West Coast Vancouver Island South will be variable wind at 5–15 knots—combined wind wave and swell height 7 feet. The outlook for the next 24 hours is light to moderate wind from the west.

Local Weather Effects

Some weather effects operate locally and alter the intensity and character of larger systems. Local effects can also occur without the presence of larger systems. Local effects may last for only an hour or so and be confined to a bay, headland, or strait. Because published forecasts usually cover a wide area, they do not provide sufficient detail for the coastal kayaker to rely solely on them for a safe trip. Local knowledge and a detailed study of maps and charts can provide important clues to improve the detail and accuracy of forecasting local weather. Reading several days of your weather log will often reveal local weather patterns. For instance, winds may rise and fall on a daily cycle and interact with daily tidal currents.

Thermal Effects

Many coastal features cause significant local temperature differences. Colder air falls, warmer air rises—in either case creating thermally generated winds that are usually nothing more than light breezes. But when confronted with complex coastal geography, thermally generated winds can increase notably in speed.

Sea Breezes and Land Breezes

Sea and land breezes occur during periods of general calm and warm weather and are caused by differences between daytime warming of air over the land and warming of air over the sea. During the day, the land warms faster than the sea. As the heat on land rises, cooler air from over the water rushes in, creating an onshore circulation—a *sea breeze*.

SIGNS OF APPROACHING HIGH- AND LOW-PRESSURE SYSTEMS

	Approaching High Pressure	Approaching Low Pressure
Pressure	Increasing pressure. Rapidly increasing pressure can be an indication of high winds.	Falling pressure. More than 3 millibars/hour is an indication of an approaching gale.
Cloud	Clouds lifting. Decrease in precipitation until sunny. Cumulus clouds an indication of a stable high-pressure system.	Sun and moon halo. Clouds lowering and thickening. Increased precipitation.
Wind	Wind direction veering (clockwise). Strongest winds at the outer edge of the high-pressure system.	Wind direction backing (counter-clockwise). Strongest winds near the center of the low.

As the day becomes warmer, the wind speed increases. Daytime sea breezes commonly rise to 10 or 15 knots and may veer through the day as the wind strengthens.

Later in the day as the sun sets and temperatures drop, the land cools faster than the sea. The wind subsides and changes direction, creating a breeze off the land. This *land breeze* is usually weaker than the sea breeze, but again, local geography can concentrate the effects. In areas where the wind is funneled by local straits or inlets, the wind speed can rise dramatically.

Anabatic and Katabatic Winds

Anabatic and katabatic winds—also known as valley breezes—act much like land and sea breezes and for much the same reason: differential heating and cooling of the air. *Anabatic winds* occur during the day as valleys warm up and the heated air rises upslope into the mountains. The differential heating that causes land and sea breezes is accentuated by the geography of coastal valleys and steep sided inlets. The funneling effect of the valleys further in-

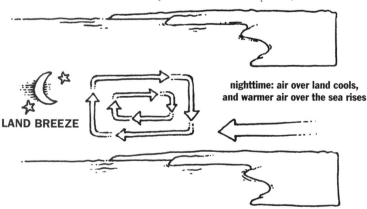

SEA BREEZE

daytime: air over land warms and rises

LAND BREEZE

nighttime: air over land cools, and warmer air over the sea rises

During periods of good weather, strong winds are caused by temperature variations throughout the day and night.

Advice from a Stranger

Not long after I started kayaking, I attempted to lead my girlfriend and my two young nephews on a four-day trip in the San Juan Islands of Washington State. I had no training and little experience, but I was brimming with confidence.

As we started loading the two double kayaks at the put-in, a middle-aged paddler approached to ask about my trip plans. I told her we intended to make the 1-mile crossing to a nearby island. She warned me that the winds were particularly fierce right then and that I should wait or consider an alternate plan. I balked immediately. Who was this person to tell me what I could and couldn't do! But she was persistent and finally persuaded me to call off the crossing for the sake of the kids. In the end, we set up a base camp and took day trips along the shore. The boys had a blast.

A decade later, the roles were reversed. I had been camped on the shores of Bahía de los Angeles in Mexico's Gulf of California for several days in late December and had watched a strong El Norte wind pattern develop. Every morning started perfectly calm, but at 8:45, a line of black water became visible out in the bay, immediately followed by a wall of wind whipping up a sea of whitecaps. In 20 minutes, the bay was awash.

On the third day of this weather system, a pair of kayakers arrived around 7:30 A.M. and began loading their boats for an extended trip to another bay, Bahía de los Ánimas. I went down to say hello and explained to them that it might be best to delay their departure until the winds stopped. "What winds?" they asked. A few minutes later, Beach Bob, a retired American who lived nearby, offered the same warning to the couple. By this time, the woman was willing to consider the warnings, but the man was undeterred.

They launched about 8:15 and headed due east across the mouth of the bay toward Punta Rojo. I followed them with my binoculars out to the middle of the bay and watched as the winds struck right on schedule. The kayakers continued to angle eastward against the northerly onslaught, but soon had to turn into the wind to round a point. After an hour of hard paddling they may have achieved a quarter-mile of forward progress, and they had yet to round the point, known for severe tide rips. Eventually I lost sight of them in the waves and spray thrown high against the cliffs.

On reflection: Taking unsolicited advice is never easy, especially from a stranger. Moreover, the advice will not necessarily be correct. But let me offer my own unsolicited advice: keep an open mind and listen to what someone tells you. Don't be offended; the stranger is just trying to help. In the end, it's your decision. Make that decision with an open mind.

—John Montgomery

creases local winds. The effect is magnified by the area's daytime sea breezes. Wider south-facing valleys have the greatest exposure to the sun and generate the strongest anabatic winds.

Katabatic winds occur in the evening as air in the mountains cools and sinks, beginning a flow of wind back down the valley and, aided by land breezes, out to sea. Katabatic winds are usually stronger than the daytime anabatic winds. A campsite along shore near the head of an inlet can become gusty and uncomfortable in the middle of the night from the sudden, dangerous appearance of strong katabatic winds, caused by cold mountain air moving downhill and out to the coast. The steep sides of the coastal inlet can confine and direct a katabatic wind, sometimes causing it to accelerate to speeds in excess of 70 knots.

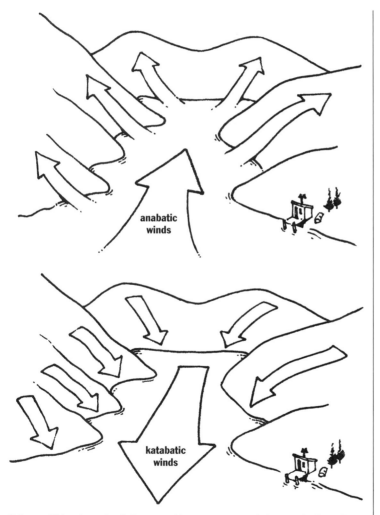

Valleys and inlets focus the air flow caused by temperature variations and increase the wind speed. During the daytime anabatic winds race into inlets and up mountain slopes, and during the night the wind flows back down the slopes and out to sea. Winter katabatic outflow winds in mainland coastal inlets of British Columbia are commonly at 40 mph and have been measured at over 100 mph.

Fog

Sea fog is formed when warm, moist air moves in over colder water and the moisture in the air condenses into water droplets. The formation of fog can be demonstrated by breathing out on a cold day. Contrary to common sense, sea fog will persist with strong winds. A warm wind blowing over cold water can cause fog. Sea fog will also form without a noticeable breeze as long as warm, moist air settles over colder seawater. Sea fog can be dense and persistent, sometimes restricting visibility to near zero. It often can be seen forming offshore before moving in toward the land. If the wind is blowing and the fog persists, it is sea fog. If you observe sea fog moving in, take careful note of your position and plot a course to a safe destination. If you're uncomfortable paddling in low-visibility conditions, get to land before the fog arrives.

Radiation fog forms over land during the early morning and is usually a problem for paddlers only in estuaries, harbors, or other inland bodies of water. Although a land breeze may move radiation fog out to sea, this fog will usually dissipate as the sun rises and the day warms up.

Effects of Topography

The speed and direction of the wind is altered by interactions with the coast. Friction between the wind and the ground slows the wind in some areas but speeds it up in others. A twisting inlet or river valley will cause the wind to shift and bend as it works its way through. Steep cliffs can cause a complete reversal of the predominant wind flow.

waters churned by gales—the potential energy of the wave form is translated into kinetic energy of tons of white water tumbling down the wave face, posing extreme danger to any kayaker.

Marine weather broadcasts forecast and report on wave heights. In the United States, reports are given separately on the swell height and the wind-wave height; the overall sea state results from a combination of both types of waves. In Canada, wave heights are given as combined swell height and wind-wave height.

Wind waves quickly spread out from their point of origin; as they do, their height subsides and their energy reorganizes into recognizable long-length waves called *swell*. Traveling over great distances, swells transfer energy from one wave to another, causing the formation of sets of similar-size waves. Swells that have traveled hundreds, possibly thousands, of miles arrive on shore in clearly defined sets. Popular notions that every seventh wave is larger or that waves come in sets of five are not true. The waves do, however, reflect the variety of wave heights and the organization of long-lasting swell into sets.

Cross Seas

Cross seas form when two wave patterns intersect. The sea state resulting from a cross sea appears chaotic and rough and may have no recognizable pattern. Cross seas can develop when storm winds change direction—after a low passes overhead, for example—creating a new pattern of waves atop a previous

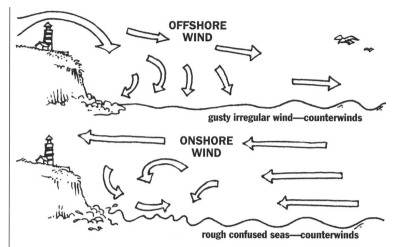

Close to cliffs the wind can change direction, creating difficult paddling conditions. Both onshore and offshore, breezes create counterwinds along the base of the cliff, resulting in confused seas.

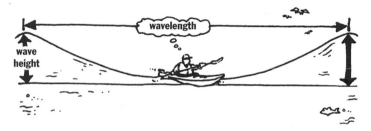

As wave height increases, wavelength also increases, and waves move forward at greater speed.

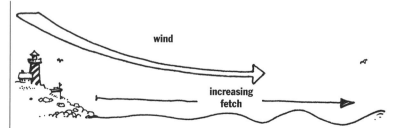

Fetch is the distance the wind blows across the water, from the same direction and with a constant speed. Fetch has a great impact on wave height.

pattern. This effect can be most dramatic when waves from two different storms intersect at a large angle.

Cross seas commonly occur when a

storm creates wind waves in an area where swell waves already exist. Swell direction is independent of local wind direction. Wind waves superimposed on swell produce waves of mixed height and shape. When wave peaks coincide, a new peak forms with a height that is the sum of the two individual waves. The encounter of a 4-foot swell and 2-foot wind wave produces some peaks 6 feet tall.

In these cases—with waves of different sizes and shapes, traveling at different speeds, crossing at an angle to each other—the resulting double wave exists for only an instant and is shaped more like a pyramid than like a regular progressive ocean swell. When by a rare coincidence of weather the converging waves are the same size and shape and traveling in the same direction, the resulting double wave can last as long as several minutes.

The joining of wave heights by two patterns of large waves can result in dangerously high seas. Kayakers face a significant safety concern when a strong wind creates new waves in the same direction as, and over the top of, an existing large swell. When sea conditions exceed the paddler's ability (see Environment and Paddling Levels table in the appendix), the situation becomes precarious. As the seas rise or the paddler begins to deteriorate through fatigue or anxiety, the situation quickly becomes unsafe.

Tides and Currents

Twice a day the gravitational pull of the moon, aided or opposed by the sun, creates a tide wave on earth that is about 18 inches high. The sun exerts much less tide-generating force than the moon because, although enormous by comparison, it is about 400 times as distant from earth. The twice-daily tide wave travels around the globe at 400 miles per hour. Each day around the Atlantic Ocean basin, there are generally two equal high waters and two equal low waters. This is the most common type of large-scale tidal pattern throughout the world. The shape of the Pacific Ocean basin alters this regular pattern, and Pacific tides typically do not have the same regularity as those of the Atlantic.

The tides follow a lunar cycle of *spring tides*, which have a maximum range, and *neap tides*, which have a more moderate range. Spring tides occur around the times of new and full moon, when the gravities of the sun and the moon pull in line with each other and are therefore additive. Neap tides occur at the first and third quarters, when the sun and moon pull at right angles and partially cancel each other.

The moon's orbit is elliptical, and over the course of a month its distance from earth

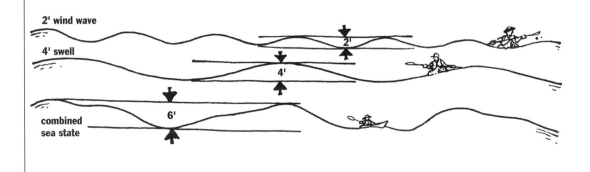

Waves newly formed by wind are overlaid onto swell, creating irregular and sometimes confusing sea conditions. In this example the 2-foot wind waves combine with a 4-foot swell to create a rough sea with occasional 6-foot wave peaks.

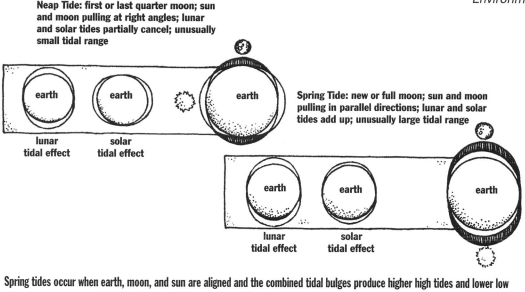

Neap Tide: first or last quarter moon; sun and moon pulling at right angles; lunar and solar tides partially cancel; unusually small tidal range

earth

earth

earth

lunar
tidal effect

solar
tidal effect

Spring Tide: new or full moon; sun and moon pulling in parallel directions; lunar and solar tides add up; unusually large tidal range

earth

earth

earth

lunar
tidal effect

solar
tidal effect

Spring tides occur when earth, moon, and sun are aligned and the combined tidal bulges produce higher high tides and lower low tides. Spring tides coincide with the new or full moon. Neap tides occur when the earth, moon, and sun are at right angles to one another and tidal bulges do not combine, producing a smaller tidal range. Neap tides coincide with the first quarter or last quarter moon.

varies. When the moon is closest to earth (apogee), tides are slightly larger than average. When the moon is farthest away (perigee), tides are slightly smaller.

Complex coastal geography dramatically alters the regular pattern of the tides. The tidal range experienced at any one location depends on local geography, time of the month, and time of the year. A tide wave rises in height as it runs ashore. In a number of locations, the 18-inch tide wave can rise to more than 40 feet as it comes ashore. Tidal patterns of the inland waterways of Alaska and British Columbia are particularly intricate and defy simple prediction. The Atlantic basin also is not immune to local anomalies. The Bay of Fundy between Nova Scotia and New Brunswick has a tidal range of 50 feet, while 250 miles to the southwest, Nantucket has a range of only 2 feet. Tidal range should decrease with increased latitude, but Frobisher Bay in the Canadian Arctic has a range of 35 feet.

The rise and fall of the tide creates a corresponding horizontal current. Within the more sheltered and restricted coastal passages, tidal current is at its most pronounced

and is most difficult to predict. In a slow-moving sea kayak, an understanding of tidal current is of fundamental importance. A well-planned trip should take full advantage of the positive effects of tidal currents and avoid its hazards.

No simple relationship exists between the rise and fall of the tide and the flow of tidal current. Tidal currents are exaggerated locally and complicated by irregular coastlines—the same complex coastlines that are most attractive to sea kayakers. Under the constraints of narrow, twisting passages and shallow, irregular bottoms, the placid shape and regularity of the tidal bulge changes into strong and sometimes chaotic currents. At their most fearsome, tidal currents run 16 knots, tidal bores are 15 feet high, standing waves reach 10 feet tall, and whirlpools are 60 feet across with 3-foot-wide voids at the center.

Tidal currents usually reverse direction four times each day, creating complicated changes in the sea state. On an open coast these reversals often proceed in a regular clockwise (or counterclockwise) pattern of *rotary currents* (see diagram). In some locations,

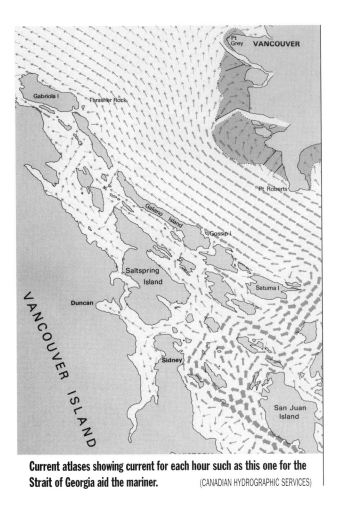

Current atlases showing current for each hour such as this one for the Strait of Georgia aid the mariner. (CANADIAN HYDROGRAPHIC SERVICES)

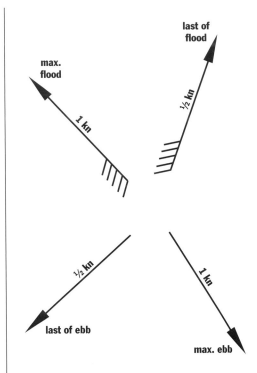

In open coastal areas the direction of tidal currents rotates with only a moderate change in speed and may not show a significant slack period. Current diagrams show the usual pattern of the current during mean tides over a large area of coastline.

however, geographic features can produce a steady current in an unchanging direction during the rise *and* fall of the tide, a nonintuitive flow that may occur at infrequent times of the monthly tidal cycle. In other places, the shape of the shoreline can entirely redirect a current, causing it to turn a full 360 degrees.

Back eddies form along irregular shorelines, their size determined by the size of the features that created them. Back eddies can be minuscule or they can be miles long. You can make good progress paddling against a main current by carefully observing and using a back eddy. But you must take care, because tide rips form at the upstream end of the back eddy where its currents reenter the

main flow, further complicating the already tangled wave dynamics.

In some regions, tidal patterns are accurately recorded and current tables and atlases are available. The sea kayaker must still look over the edge of the kayak and observe the reality of the moment. The predominant flow in a main channel will predictably follow the tide data. However, the kayak's diminutive size and shallow draft allows us to paddle into waters that can't be accounted for in the detail provided by tables and atlases. Kayakers often seek out back eddies that flow in complete contradiction to the predominant flow. In areas where there are no published tide or current data, your general understanding of the

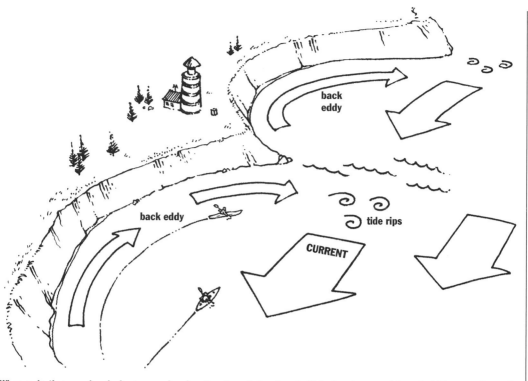

When navigating a sea kayak along a complex shoreline, the safest and most efficient route may not be a straight course. Areas of back eddies and tide rips can help or hinder progress. Here the kayaker who hugs the shore—instead of bucking the current in the channel—may make better time. (BASED ON ART BY SEAN WILKINSON IN "SEA KAYAKER MAGAZINE", JUNE 1997)

cycles of the moon, coupled with good observations and a daily log, will go a long way toward predicting water movements.

Tide Rips and Overfalls

The surface turbulence known as a tide rip forms where tidal current is restricted or forced to sharply change direction. A tide rip can form offshore where a current flows over a shallow reef or where two tidal streams intersect. Waves formed in areas of tide rips can vary from an irregular chop to large standing waves.

Tide rips pose the greatest hazard where a tidal current flows in opposition to the wind. In this situation, with current and wind colliding, waves decrease in length and increase in height, creating steep and potentially per-

ilous sea conditions. Tide rips commonly form at prominent headlands where the current is compressed and forced to change direction. Wind energy also concentrates near

In short, choppy waves the kayaker plants the paddle fully into the water to move forward and to maintain balance.

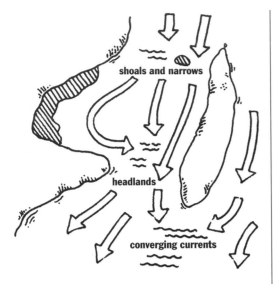

Typical areas that experience tide rips are shoals, narrows where back eddies reenter the main current, and where current streams converge.

headlands, and the combination of stronger wind and stronger current makes headlands a consistent concern for kayakers.

An *overfall* is turbulence, usually in the form of a breaking wave, caused when a strong tidal current passes through a shallow spot and suddenly drops into deeper water. This dangerous standing wave breaks upstream, back toward the tidal current. A kayaker who is paddling downwind with a following sea, but against a current and into a tide rip or overfall, cannot see the full extent of the turbulence.

Local Wave Effects

Choosing a safe route requires careful consideration of local wave effects. For the touring sea kayaker, the safest route might be well outside the influences of the shoreline. As winds and waves meet the shore, an increasing number of variables govern the sea state. Paddling near shore is not always the quickest or safest route.

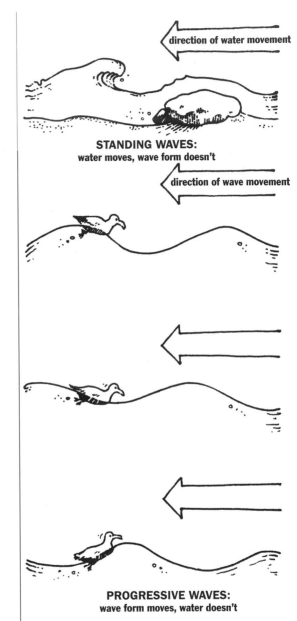

STANDING WAVES:
water moves, wave form doesn't

PROGRESSIVE WAVES:
wave form moves, water doesn't

In a tide rip (top), a standing (stationary) wave is created as the water moves over an obstruction on the bottom. In deep water (bottom), in contrast, water particles travel in a circle and do not move forward with the wave. These are known as progressive waves. (BASED ON A DRAWING IN LANGE, "WIND CAME ALL WAYS")

Going with the Flow

With some trepidation, I packed the kayak and launched into the outer reaches of Current Pass at the northeast end of Vancouver Island, British Columbia. The tide and current tables and the *Coast Pilot* warned of 7-knot currents, frequent strong eddies, and heavy tide rips. Marine publications are understated almost to the extreme. Use of such adjectives as *frequent* and *heavy* is to be respected.

Predicted slack water would last only 20 minutes, and my route through the passage would take an hour to complete. I would paddle into the last of the ebb tide and reach the area of strongest flow just before slack water. The point of no return would come when the current reversed, hopefully at a controlled rate, and pushed me through the rest of the pass.

Anxious to see what I was up against, I left shore a full hour early. If the ebb current was too strong, I could always find a kayak-size nook and wait for it to slow down. The entrance to Current Pass was visible around the first corner. Ripple Reef was evident as violent 4-foot overfalls covering the middle of the channel. A commercial salmon boat was bucking into the short, steep seas. I figured the boat's big diesel must be powered up, pushing at 8 knots against a 6-knot current. White plumes of sea spray launched off the bow and cascaded over the wheelhouse.

Two hundred yards away, close under the shore where the depth was less than 10 feet, I paddled in calm water. Much to my surprise, I was making better progress than the fish boat. Evidently, very close to shore a long, quiet back eddy had formed, flowing in my favor. I made a steady 4 knots under hand power as the fish boat made just 2 knots beneath a cloud of smoke and sea spray. I approached the predicted point of no return almost two hours ahead of the slack, closer to maximum contrary current, and I was still able to sneak comfortably along the shore.

I made it all the way through the pass against the prevailing current without ever encountering a problem.

On reflection: The microenvironment near shore can be better or worse than offshore. Confirm your predictions by taking a look.

—Doug Alderson

The shape of the shoreline and the profile of the bottom have a dramatic effect on waves and on your choices for a safe passage. Determining the best route to follow involves a balance between the effects of the shoreline and the desires of the paddlers. Paddling along a supervised surf beach in a short plastic kayak is much different from landing a fully loaded touring kayak on a similar beach in a remote wilderness. A thrill seeker might choose to paddle close in, near breaking waves, skirting in and out around the rocks, but doing so requires a high level of skill and acceptance of additional risk.

Effects of Currents

Waves are greatly altered by the presence of a current. The movement of a modest 1.5-knot current against an equally modest 15-knot breeze will result in a decrease in wavelength and an increase in wave height. These steeper waves will tend to break more frequently and can create difficult or dangerous paddling conditions. Conversely, current moving in the same direction as the wind will result in an increase in wavelength and a decrease in wave height, bringing a flatter, more comfortable pattern of waves.

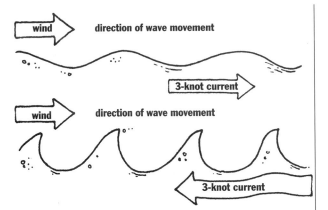

Wind blowing with the current (top) flattens the sea, making for easier passage. Wind blowing against the current (bottom) causes the waves to become shorter and higher. The larger, steeper waves can break violently, creating dangerous sea conditions. Moderate sea conditions can turn quickly dangerous when the tide reverses direction.

steep crest. The crest will rise and break when the depth of the water is approximately three-quarters of the swell height. A 4-foot swell will break in water 3 feet deep. The height of the wave at the time it breaks will be approximately 1.5 times its original deep-water height. The 4-foot swell will rise to a 6-foot crest before breaking in 3 feet of water.

Surf

The slope of the bottom determines the nature of the breaking wave. A bottom with a slowly rising profile produces *spilling breakers*, with the energy of the wave slowly released. Low, flat beaches are most often made of fine sand and make for easier kayak landings.

A steeper bottom profile produces surf with an explosive release of energy, making for more difficult landings. These waves are known as *plunging (dumping) breakers*. Beaches with plunging surf are typically made up of large gravel or cobbles. A moderate-size plunging breaker releases all its energy in one moment. The falling crest of the

Your ability to assess sea state depends partly on your location on the water. In tide rips, waves break up-current, and they can look deceivingly benign when viewed from downstream. Wind waves viewed from a position upwind break away from the observer, and thus appear smaller than they really are.

Beaches

The underwater profile of a coastal beach creates imposing changes on the incoming swell. A wave begins to deform in water approximately twice as deep as the wave height. The frictional drag caused by encountering the shallow bottom slows the forward progress of the wave. The circular form of the wave distorts to form a

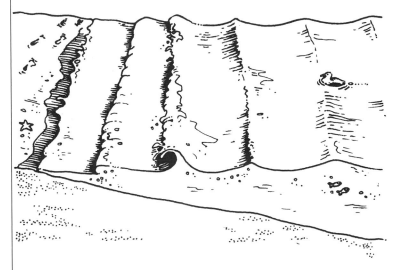

As wind waves or swells approach a slowly shelving shore the friction of the bottom slows the waves and changes their shape until they break. In some cases the circular properties of the progressing wave are evident as a plunging wave with a hollow **"pipeline" center.** (BASED ON A DRAWING IN WILLARD BASCOM'S "OCEAN WAVES" IN MOORE, "OCEANOGRAPHY")

wave penetrates down to the gravel, churning the bottom with a malevolent growl. Make every effort to avoid landing through plunging breakers on a steep gravel beach.

A third type of breaker is classified as a *surging breaker*. A surging breaker peaks close to shore, but does not break. It collapses in a forceful surge of white water up the beach. The type of breaker that forms is determined by the steepness of the beach and the steepness of the wave before it reaches shallow water.

Longshore Currents

When incoming waves arrive on a beach at an angle, currents develop that run the length of the beach: longshore currents. Most times the longshore current is of little direct interest to the kayaker. However, if you capsize in the wash zone, the longshore current will carry any floating boats, paddlers, or loose gear along the beach.

Rip Currents

Longshore currents eventually leave the beach to form rip currents. Rip currents run seaward at up to 5 knots and can present both a hazard and a benefit to sea kayakers. A deeper channel scoured by the outflowing current lessens the height of the surf and provides a point of access in or out from the beach. Unsuspecting or weak paddlers can be carried seaward against their will. Rip currents often form at points of land or other obstructions along the beach.

Reflected Waves

Steep cliffs along the shore cause incoming waves to be reflected back out. Interaction between the incoming waves and the reflected waves produces rough and erratic cross waves. Where there is deep water up to the

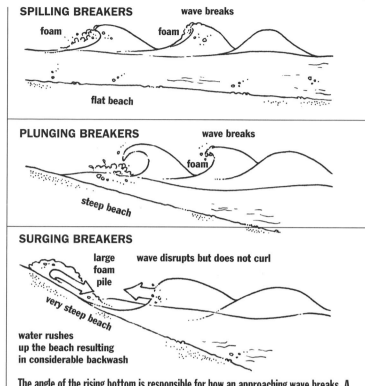

The angle of the rising bottom is responsible for how an approaching wave breaks. A slowly rising bottom allows the energy of the wave to be released slowly and safely over a considerable distance, in waves known as spilling breakers (top). A steep bottom profile causes the wave to unleash its considerable energy in one explosive plunge. The resulting plunging (dumping) breaker curls over with a single violent release of energy (middle). A surging breaker peaks and surges up the beach with a considerable foam pile (bottom).

shore, waves reflect back out with little loss of energy. Reflected ocean swell can create hazardous wave patterns for considerable distances offshore.

Effects of Headlands and Bays

Headlands have a great effect on nearby wind, waves, and current. A headland bends waves and concentrates their energy. The headland does the same thing to wind and current, creating a triple hazard for sea kayakers. In an opposite manner, bays distribute incoming wind, wave, and current energy to produce a calmer sea.

As a larger set of swell comes near shore shallow rocks or ledges can create occasional, large breaking waves. Keep a lookout well ahead and watch for signs of shallow water.

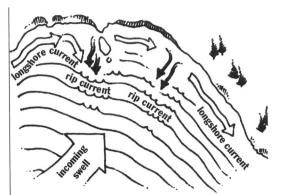

With waves breaking on shore, longshore currents run laterally along the beach. Tide rips will form where longshore currents encounter an obstacle or where piled-up water rushes back to sea. Once such a rip current scours a channel, it will become semipermanent and localized.

Effects of River Mouths

River mouths are places of steady currents that often flow over sandbars and create pronounced local changes in the sea state. The combination of shallow water, incoming swell, and outgoing current generates hazards.

Forecasting Sea State

The result of the interaction between wind, waves, current, and geography, sea state is the measure of the roughness and complexity of the surface of the sea. A forecast of the sea state must take into account these factors.

The often-cited Beaufort wind scale (see appendix) provides a means to approximate wind speed and assumes an unlimited fetch. The sea kayaker in coastal waters must consider additional local factors of, current, swell, and geography to determine sea state.

Local factors work to change the shape of the waves. It is predominantly the shape of the waves that creates risk for the paddler. Increasing wave heights or decreasing wavelengths will create steeper more challenging sea states.

Increasing wind speed, fetch, duration, current, and the presence of swell create challenging paddling conditions. Combinations of factors can have compounding effects that can rapidly change a moderate sea state to a dangerous sea state. There is a natural difficulty in describing a rough sea state; the skill level of the paddler is the benchmark. For a novice, 2- or 3-foot tall breaking waves in 15 knots of wind would be difficult and rough, but for an intermediate paddler the same sea state is entirely comfortable (see Environment and Paddling Levels table in the appendix). The table on page 52 can be used to assist in determining sea state.

Campsites

Once the challenge of making it ashore safely is complete, the kayaker has to deal with all the risks and responsibilities of camping. It is fortunate that beach locations sheltered from the wind and rain are also likely to be partially sheltered from the full impact of the waves.

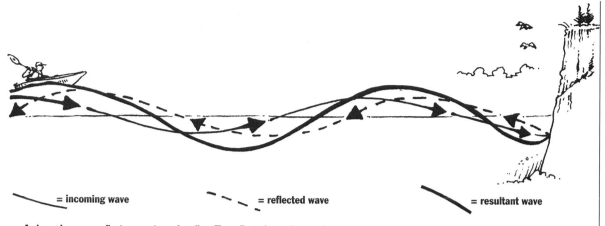

= incoming wave   = reflected wave   = resultant wave

An incoming wave reflects on a steep shoreline. The reflected wave is superimposed onto other incoming waves, producing choppy irregular waves. The resultant wave form changes constantly as the incoming and reflected waves interact.

At the end of the day, paddlers are often cold, wet, tired, thirsty, and hungry. If anyone in your group is seriously cold or injured, there is little time to waste in securing a good camp. A temporary shelter can serve as a place to change into dry clothes and have something to eat and drink. A snack and a few moments of rest to collect your thoughts will improve your judgment. Make a camp so comfortable that you will be sad to leave when the weather improves. Discomfort and an unwarranted urgency to leave camp can lead to a bad decision to leave a safe camp for an unsafe voyage.

Shelter from the wind is a principal ingredient for a comfortable campsite. Avoidance of wind is key to avoiding hypothermia. Strong winds bring the hazards of falling tree branches and blowing sand. At your campsite, make a secure area for kayaks and gear. Tie down all kayaks, paddles, and PFDs.

Choose a tent site high enough to be above the highest possible tide. River mouths, estuaries, and low islets are subject to flooding.

Runoff will raise river levels in only hours. Be sure you have access to high ground.

In stormy weather, a storm surge can substantially raise the sea level. Storm surge is water that is pushed toward the shore by the force of storm winds and the influence of low atmospheric pressure. This advancing surge can combine with waves and tide to

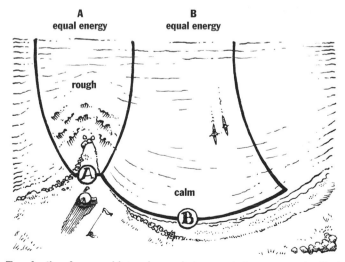

The refraction of waves arriving on shore works to concentrate energy near headlands (A) and dissipate energy in a bay (B). The same principles apply to wind and current, making sea conditions near headlands some of the most demanding.

(BASED ON A DRAWING IN "OCEANOGRAPHY")

FACTORS THAT INCREASE THE SEA STATE*

Increased fetch

Increased wind strength

Increased duration

Current direction changing to oppose the wind direction

Current speed increasing in opposition to wind direction

Swell direction in opposition to direction of current or wind

*i.e. increase the wave height or decrease the wavelength

raise the water level as much as 15 feet or more, causing severe coastal flooding. The slope of the shoreline partially determines the effect of the surge. A shallow slope allows the surge to rise higher and run farther inland. A small storm surge can swamp an unwary kayaker camped on a beach at the end of a shallow inlet.

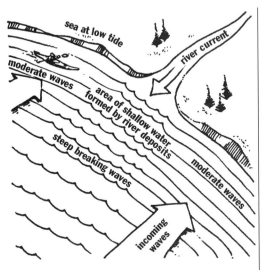

River mouths can pose significant hazards for the sea kayaker. When incoming waves encounter shallow water and an opposing current, they slow down and rise up, forming breakers.

Survey your camping area for signs of wildlife trails. Animals use open beaches as walkways, so place your tent away from their morning route. All wild animals can be dangerous if not treated with respect. Campers are visitors in the home environment of animals that might include bears, wolves, cougars, raccoons, coyotes, ravens, mice, scorpions, or snakes—and local people and their dogs.

Here are a few additional suggestions for your camping safety and enjoyment:

- Camp where you have a good view of the water for assessing sea state prior to leaving.

- Determine an alternate route home by land in case dangerous weather or sea state keeps you from paddling back out to sea.

- Find the nearest source of fresh water; in bad weather, you may be at the camp for a few days.

- Find a place to hang all food, cosmetics, toothpaste, chocolate bars, and other tasty, aromatic items, to keep them out of the hands (and mouths) of the mice and the bears. (Don't leave food in your kayak in bear country; they can rip open a kayak like a teenager tearing into a bag of chips.)

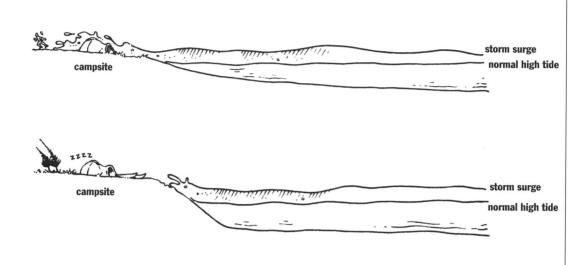

campsite — storm surge / normal high tide

campsite — zzzz — storm surge / normal high tide

Storm surge is caused by the combination of storm-pushed seas and the rising of local sea level caused by the reduction in atmospheric pressure that accompanies most storms. Along a slowly shelving shore (top), large storm waves will run up and break dangerously high on the beach. A steeper beach (bottom) offers protection from the rising sea level and does not allow the waves to run up excessively high on the beach.

- Situate your cooking area 100 yards from your tent site and preferably below high tide, so that any crumbs or smells attractive to animals will be washed away.
- Pack out everything that you paddled in with.
- Know the insect pests in the area, and make camp after inspecting for signs of the little creatures. Keep your tent door closed at all times.

- In camp, close your kayak with a cockpit cover to keep out stowaways, like bees, snakes, and slugs.
- Always travel with a friend, both while kayaking at sea and while hiking on land. You are more likely to suffer an injury on shore than you are while paddling.

Safety and Rescue Gear

4

It is common knowledge that no amount of gear or physical preparation can make up for a lack of skill or judgment. It is also true, however, that good gear and well-considered preparation can turn a potentially slow, wet, and unsuccessful trip into a pleasure to remember.

Much of the gear we carry contributes to our safety and is useful or vital for rescues. The best gear serves more than one function without compromise, saving space and money. This chapter describes gear pertaining to safety and rescue in a wide variety of sea conditions. Techniques for the use of this gear are covered in other chapters.

Rescue gear needs to be secure from accidental loss, accessible when needed, and reliable. Personal preference has a great deal to do with where you keep each piece of gear. Whatever storage plan you use, practice accessing the gear in a variety of conditions so that you can reach it quickly in an emergency.

The two most important pieces of gear are your brain and the group you are paddling with. Before heading out, make sure everything, and everyone, is in working order.

How to Choose Gear

There are so many products claiming to enhance sea kayak safety that a peek into your local paddling store or a browse through the ads in a paddling magazine can be intimidating. You will hear numerous and often contradictory arguments for carrying a certain piece of gear or leaving it behind, and each style and brand claims advantages over the others, ad infinitum. Some gear will be needed not only because it promotes safety but also because it is required by law; some gear fits a special need; other gear is just great fun. Sorting through legal requirements, your own needs and preferences, and manufacturer claims can fill as many winter evenings as you care to let it.

Here are a few simple guidelines for selecting gear:

- Do your homework before you buy. Read the magazine reviews, talk to other paddlers, and consult the staff at your paddling store. You want to get a sense of the kinds of products available and their features. With this information in hand, it is much easier to whittle down your choices.

- Keep the distinction between *features* and *advantages* in mind. Features are the dis-

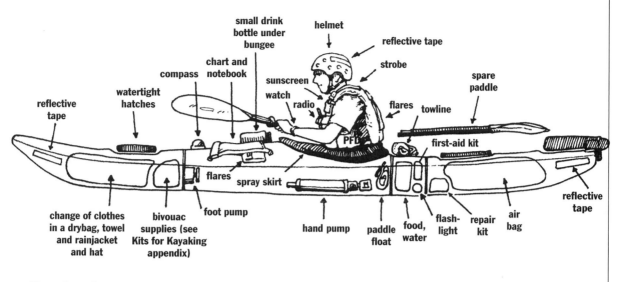

small drink
bottle under
bungee
helmet
reflective tape
strobe
chart and
notebook
spare
paddle
compass
sunscreen
watch
flares
towline
watertight
hatches
radio
reflective
tape
first-aid kit
PFD
flares
reflective
tape
spray skirt
change of clothes
in a drybag, towel
and rainjacket
and hat
bivouac
supplies (see
Kits for Kayaking
appendix)
foot pump
hand pump
paddle
float
food,
water
flash-
light
repair
kit
air
bag

Most safety and rescue gear needs to be accessible for ready use. A day hatch behind the cockpit is convenient for many items. The decision to put a particular item on the paddler, on the deck, in the cockpit, or below deck is very much a matter of planning and preference.

tinctive parts or qualities of each product; advantages are those features that are actually meaningful to your kayaking. Take, for example, a kayak that is light, thanks to Kevlar construction. Is this an important advantage for you (making the kayak easier to carry across a beach or to lift onto a roof rack)? Does this advantage justify the additional cost of space-age Kevlar fabric?

- Decide what you want the product to do. Before shopping for a radio, decide if you want to use it for two-way communication on multiday trips or simply to receive weather information closer to home. You can then concentrate on comparing such features of similar products as battery life, waterproofness, and durability.

- Test your gear. Harshly. Replace it if it does not fulfill its function. If your towline is not easy to deploy and gets tangled, modify or replace it.

There is no single list of the right safety gear always to bring along. Such a list could be so extensive that the sheer volume of resultant paraphernalia would create a hazard.

Your needs change over time; your preferences change; your skills develop and so does the gear that is available.

Any list of safety gear has to be adaptable. For example:

- The best gear for a skilled paddler may not be sufficient or appropriate for a novice. Why carry a towline if you haven't learned how to use it?

- The same paddler on different trips needs different safety gear. If a trip includes surf landings, for example, you will need a helmet.

- Each member of a group does not require every piece of gear required by a solo paddler. In a group of five, two or three stoves may be sufficient.

- Some wise choices are not necessities. Paddling a temperate coast, it is wise but not essential to bring a tarp.

When gear does not meet your needs, modify or replace it or design your own. Gear is constantly being improved, and novel paddling adventures require new or modified gear. You may find yourself continually experimenting with gear—making, adapting, and buying new products in a never-ending search for the perfect towline or combination of paddling clothing.

Kayak Safety Features

Kayak safety features can be divided into two catagories. Integral features built into the kayak at the time of manufacture, and supplementary features that can be added after purchase. Integral features such as cockpit size and the quality of the seams and hatches cannot easily be changed. Supplementary features such as perimeter lines, end toggles, and rudders can be added to augment safety.

Integral Safety Features

Some features are designed and built into a kayak. These features had better be there when you buy the boat because they're difficult or impossible to change after manufacture.

Cockpit Size

For safety in landing on a surf beach, the cockpit opening should be long and wide enough to permit easy entry and a quick exit but narrow enough to permit a paddler to grip the under-deck with knees and thighs. A large opening requires a large sprayskirt to complete the cockpit seal, and the substantial surface area of such a skirt makes it susceptible to implosion from waves breaking over the cockpit. Further, a large cockpit will hold more water in a capsize.

It is possible to reduce cockpit volume by installing a custom bulkhead, which also adds volume to the adjoining storage compartment. The bulkhead may also be useful as a foot brace (footrest), eliminating the need for separate braces. Some manufacturers will install a custom bulkhead at the time of manufacture; otherwise the owner will have to install it. It is also possible to reduce cockpit volume by using a sea sock. This is a popular alternative for kayaks without bulkheads.

Flotation and Watertight Integrity

Kayaks must meet one primary safety criterion: they must float even when the cockpit is fully flooded. All other considerations come second to staying afloat. "Afloat" means more than simply not sinking. With the paddler in the cockpit, there must be sufficient buoyancy to permit the water to be pumped out. Designers meet this need for buoyancy through a variety of features, such as bulkheads and double-walled hulls. Owners can help with supplementary flotation, including sea socks and float bags.

Bulkheads are the most common means of ensuring reserve buoyancy, and should be placed so as to minimize the amount of water that can get into the cockpit. Bulkheads that

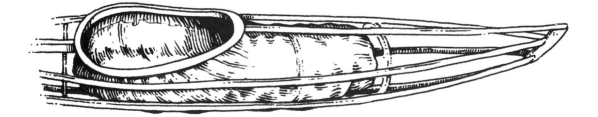

A sea sock is an alternative to a custom bulkhead. A sea sock is a cockpit liner that attaches to the coaming, creating a cocoon for the paddler's legs, and limits the amount of water that can flood into a cockpit.

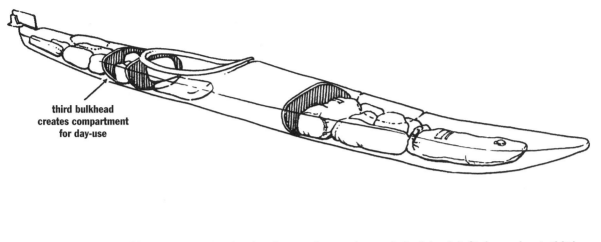

third bulkhead
creates compartment
for day-use

Bulkheads provide watertight storage compartments and ample reserve buoyancy in case of a flooded cockpit. Storing gear in watertight bags will not only keep your gear dry, it will also add redundant buoyancy in case of leakage from a loose hatch or damaged hull.

are too far forward or too far back don't leave the reserve buoyancy needed in the ends of the kayak to keep it afloat when the cockpit is flooded.

Some kayaks are manufactured with three bulkheads instead of two. This third bulkhead creates a smaller watertight compartment within reach of the paddler, a space usually reserved for items regularly used while paddling. If flooded, the small volume of this day-use compartment does not seriously compromise the stability of the kayak.

In decked sea kayaks, a sprayskirt keeps the water out of the cockpit. In rain, wind, and waves, the skirt is an important piece of safety equipment. The seaworthiness of your kayak is compromised if the seal leaks or the skirt becomes unattached.

Novice paddlers may prefer a looser-fitting skirt, which is easier to remove in case of a capsize. Skirts that fit the coaming snugly are a boon in rougher waters, staying attached even in breaking waves, but are also harder to get off when you want to exit. As with any piece of safety equipment, practice using it in a variety of conditions.

The watertight integrity of the kayak is only as good as the hatch covers, bulkheads, skeg box, skirt, and the seam between hull and deck. Check the seams, hatches, and flotation of your kayak on a regular basis. If leaks are found around the deck seam, the cockpit coaming, or bulkheads, patch them at once. Get professional help if you are not familiar with the adhesives and materials used in kayak construction.

Supplementary Safety Features

A variety of supplementary features that contribute to safety are standard from some manufacturers. If not, you can add them after purchase.

Perimeter Lines

As the name suggests, perimeter lines are a length of cord secured around the perimeter of the kayak, and these facilitate a rescue by providing multiple handholds for swimmers and rescuers. If your kayak does not have perimeter lines, you should add them.

Quarter-inch braided polyester (Dacron) line serves well for perimeter lines. It is abrasion-resistant, stands up well to the sun's harmful rays, and does not stretch. It also feels good in the hand. Avoid thin lines and lines (such as cotton and nylon) that stretch under load or when wet.

To distribute the sometimes heavy load imposed during a rescue, perimeter lines need to be secured at multiple points around the hull. Deck fittings should be strong enough to withstand the considerable forces applied during rescues. If your deck fittings are too narrow to accept quarter-inch line, replace them with wider ones.

Deck Rigging

Deck rigging—consisting of short straps, cords, or line—is standard issue on most kayaks. Unlike perimeter lines, deck rigging is not designed as a secure holding point for swimmers or rescuers. Rather, it provides points of attachment for a variety of gear. Charts and water bottles are conveniently held under deck rigging on the front deck. Spare paddles are often stored under deck rigging on the back deck.

Some paddle-float rescue techniques require deck rigging on the back deck. Many manufacturers install bungee cords for this purpose. Make sure it is thick and stiff

enough so that it does not stretch too much during a paddle-float reentry. Deck rigging made of nylon webbing fastened with clips provides a low-stretch alternative to bungee deck rigging. Practicing in rough conditions will reveal if the fittings and the straps or cords are strong enough to stand up to rugged use.

Be conservative in the amount of gear held by deck rigging. Excessive gear stored on deck is prone to being lost overboard. Gear strapped on top of spare paddles can make the paddles hard to retrieve when they are needed. Gear on deck can foul towlines, and it can create a hazard during rescues.

End Toggles

End toggles are installed at each end of a kayak to provide handholds for swimmers. The rope attachment must be short enough to prevent finger entrapment and twisting, but long enough for the swimmer's hand to clear the end of the kayak. Kayaks with rudders don't accommodate end toggles on the stern.

End toggles are often confused with the toggles used for lifting and carrying a kayak; lifting toggles have longer rope and are often positioned away from the ends of the kayak.

Perimeter lines go along both sides of the front and rear decks and provide a secure handhold during rescues.   (GREG SHEA)

Visibility Aids

Visibility of the kayak is a key safety feature. Luminescent hull colors such as white, yellow, and robin's egg blue make a kayak more visible to rescuers in a boat or a helicopter. You can also use reflective tape on the hull, reflective lines on deck, and reflective strips.

Skeg or Rudder

A skeg is a fixed or retractable fin that is designed to minimize weathercocking (the tendency for a kayak to turn upwind when making a course across or down-

In a rescue, you can secure any loose paddles under a heavy bungee located forward of the front hatch. A wooden bead will lift the bungee off the deck without scratching the gel coat.

Purpose-built deck rigging and straps made of nylon webbing hold a paddle-float outrigger firmly in place.

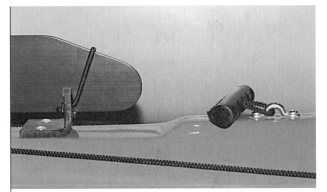

Lifting toggles are positioned in front of the rudder. To create a short leash for a swimmer, a length of line or webbing can be attached to the perimeter lines or the lifting toggle.

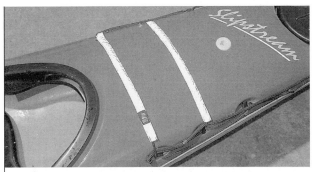

End toggles provide a safe handhold for a swimmer. They should be just long enough to grab and present no danger of entanglement. End toggles can be the only safe place to hold onto a kayak in breaking waves or strong current.

Hollow nylon tubing with reflective fabric sewn on can add considerably to the visibility of a kayak in low-light conditions. There is also reflective tape on deck underlining the name and on the side along the hull-to-deck seam.

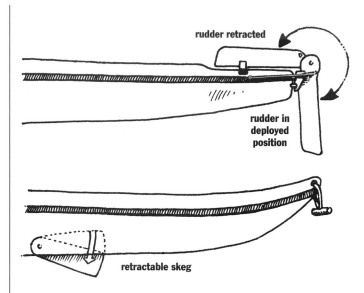

rudder retracted

rudder in
deployed
position

retractable skeg

Retractable rudders (top) are controlled by cables that can both turn the rudder and lower and raise it. Retractable skegs (bottom) are also controlled by cables that allow the paddler to adjust the depth of the skeg.

wind). Retractable skegs have control cables or lines running from the skeg to the cockpit enabling the paddler to adjust the depth of the skeg to suit different conditions.

A rudder is a movable and retractable fin designed to minimize weathercocking and for holding a course in wind, waves, and current. Retractable rudders have control cables or lines running from the rudder to the cockpit enabling the paddler to deploy them. In addition, control cables run from the rudder to the interior of the cockpit allowing the paddler to adjust the angle of the rudder by means of moving their feet.

Most skegs and rudders are installed during manufacture, but some can be installed by the owner. Either is a useful piece of equipment in a variety of situations, including towing.

On most kayaks with a skeg or a rudder, it will be the only moving part, and it is susceptible to failure. As an important safety requirement, you must be capable of paddling

in adverse conditions without relying on a skeg or rudder.

Paddling Gear

Paddles and a personal flotation device (PFD) are essential pieces of gear that are important to our overall level of safety and enjoyment on the water.

Paddles

The paddle moves you through the water. You will swing it as many as 1,500 times an hour, holding it out in front of your body for hours and days at a time. There is no hard and fast rule for choosing a paddle. Consider material, length, and blade shape, and match them to your budget, height, kayak width and depth, and paddling style.

High-quality paddles are light and strong, ensuring many miles of use even in rough and rocky conditions. Check your primary paddle and your spare for wear, cracks, and leaking. Leaks will be obvious: as you tilt the paddle back and forth, you will hear and feel water moving in the blade or shaft. Most often, the leak occurs through the joint at the neck or through the plug in the shaft.

In rough conditions, paddle blades can break off, and shafts can snap. And without a paddle, you are up that famous creek without one. You may have the greatest roll or the most efficient forward stroke—but just try it without a paddle.

Personal Flotation Device (PFD)

Nearly all victims of drowning are found without a personal flotation device or life jacket. Technically speaking, a PFD is not the same as a life jacket. A life jacket will float you face up even if you are unconscious, which a PFD

The Sinking Paddle

I was practicing my kayak rolls, trying various techniques. As I worked out in the bay with my spare paddle, I had to make a wet exit from the kayak, and I let go of the paddle.

It didn't float. The manufacturer had failed to put the plugs into the shaft. I could see the paddle lying on the white, sandy bottom, about 20 feet down in very cold water. I had no way to retrieve it, so I learned a valuable, though expensive, lesson: not all paddles float.

On reflection: Test a paddle's flotation before it is needed.

—*Michael Pardy*

Fully loaded, leaving the swift moving tidal water of a coastal inlet, this paddler is headed out for an extended trip on the open coast. Rescue and navigation gear is on his front deck; he wears a PFD and hydration pack on his back. A helmet, parachute flare, and short Greenland-style spare paddle are on his back deck.

won't necessarily do, but the PFD's advantages are its better fit and freedom of movement, essential to the sea kayaker.

When choosing a PFD, try a number of them on to ensure a secure fit. If it fits well, you are more likely to wear it. Sit in your kayak with the sprayskirt attached and see how the PFD fits: an ill-fitting PFD will ride up over your ears or force the sprayskirt down, allowing water to pool and potentially leak into the cockpit.

PFDs are available in a variety of sophisticated designs as paddlers demand more features and greater durability. You can find PFDs with such features as pockets, attachment points for knives and other safety equipment, and loops for waist-mounted towlines. Better-quality PFDs use supple, longer-lasting materials. Some offer special adjustments to improve fit and comfort for any body type. Spending a few extra dollars here can make a big difference in your comfort and safety on the water.

Paddles come in various materials, shapes, and sizes. The top paddle has a straight shaft and a durable plastic blade suitable for general paddling. The middle paddle has a bent shaft that helps align the paddler's wrist in an ergonomic position to minimize stress on the wrists. The blade is long and narrow, made of lightweight carbon fiber and fiberglass, making this paddle suitable for long-distance touring. The bottom paddle is made of wood and has a shorter overall length and wide blade with reflective tape applied for increased visibility. The shorter length makes this paddle suitable for a smaller person with a narrow kayak. Paddle design is influenced by a great number of factors, and personal preference plays a large role in the final selection.

Most jurisdictions require paddlers to carry PFDs but do not require that they wear them. The norm in most sea kayaking groups is to wear a PFD at all times. If you choose not to wear one, make sure you do a careful risk assessment and take appropriate countermeasures. At a minimum, the PFD needs to be well secured and accessible at a moment's notice. The best case for wearing one is that it is difficult to put on a PFD while you are in the water, which is precisely when you will need it.

Helmets

Helmets are an essential piece of kit for kayakers. As we stated in the beginning, the most important piece of equipment we carry is our brain, and paddlers should take every reasonable precaution to protect it. In practice scenarios and real scenarios, there is the pos-sibility of getting hit by other kayaks, especially if you are floating around in rough water. Perhaps more importantly, the forces involved in surf landings and in paddling around rocks are such that a helmet must be worn any time you approach these potentially hazardous areas.

Helmets come in a variety of shapes and sizes. Get one designed for use in whitewater. Bicycle helmets, hockey helmets, and others offer protection to different parts of the head and are designed for different types of impacts. The helmet should fit snugly and not slide off. Adjustable fit systems will also allow you to wear an insulating cap for cold-weather paddling.

Helmets can be stored in a kayak hatch if you don't need them often on a trip. Otherwise, they should be secured to the deck within easy reach. If you plan to carry them in the kayak, make sure they fit through the hatch.

Living Dangerously

I had paddled for several hours along the inlet, toward the open coast. The day was hot and sunny, the seas calm. My PFD was tucked under the bungee cords on the back deck.

In half a mile I would leave this inlet, round the point to the west, travel a quarter-mile up the coast, and enter a smaller inlet. As I approached the open coast, I reassessed my decision to wear no wet suit or PFD; I confidently made no change.

Moments later I noticed that the coastline was zipping by more quickly than I was paddling. An ebb current was pushing me along. As I reached the corner leading into the open sea, the current met a westerly wind. In seconds I was in seas rising to 4 and 5 feet. Chaotic waves spiked up, then disappeared, leaving deep troughs. A wave rose violently be-side me; the kayak dropped vertically into the neighboring trough, leaving my stomach behind. My placid paddle trip turned almost instantaneously into an anxious struggle.

Conveniently stored within reach, my PFD may as well have been on the moon. My hands were more than busy keeping the paddle braced on the water's surface one moment, then paddling me through the tide race the next.

As a tide race is prone to do, it ejected me out the other side within a few minutes. Away from the outgoing tide of the long inlet, the open ocean swell was long and gentle, and I took the opportunity to reach back to get my PFD.

On reflection: It has been on ever since.

—*Doug Alderson*

Wear a helmet when coming in to shore through the surf.   (GREG SHEA)

Paddling Clothing

Paddling clothing must help protect you from a variety of environmental challenges, including sun, rain, snow, insects, wind, hot weather, and cold weather.

Paddlers operate at the boundary between water and air. The challenge is to balance the demands of both environments without compromising safety. The adage that says to "dress for the water" can be difficult and uncomfortable to follow on a bright, sunny day. You must exercise good judgment and choose the most appropriate clothing based on the environmental dangers as well as your skill. While we do not make specific clothing recommendations, some general advice applies to all.

Always have sufficient clothing secure and accessible in the event of a change in the environment. Assess the likelihood of capsizing or of facing inclement weather. When in doubt, dress for the worst. Regardless of your choice in clothing, change out of damp clothes and into dry when you go ashore.

Choose clothing that protects the skin from the harmful effects of sunlight. Pay particular attention to areas that are often exposed, like the back of the hands, the face, eyes, and the back of the neck. Sunglasses designed for use on the water will protect your eyes, while a wide-brimmed sun hat will keep the sun off your face, head, and neck.

On a hot day, loose clothing will permit ventilation and adequate cooling. On a cold day, the body loses heat through the head, neck, torso, and groin, and special consideration must be given to insulating those areas.

Hands lose their dexterity very quickly in cold water. When paddling, keep your hands warm by wearing gloves or mittens or by putting your hands inside the paddle wraps known as pogies. If you end up in the water, gloves are the most helpful.

The paddler on the left is prepared for warm-weather paddling with quick-dry top, shorts, hat, and footwear. He is wearing a coast guard–approved PFD with several technical features that include a quick-release belt for towing and a cow tail. A whistle is attached to one shoulder strap, and a rescue knife on a lanyard is tucked under the belt. The paddler on the right is prepared for paddling in a cold climate. A dry suit over insulating layers is augmented with a cap, gloves, and booties made of neoprene. The coast guard–approved PFD is a simple design with two large front pockets.

Rescue Gear

Reliability and ease of use is paramount when it comes to gear for rescue. A lot of rescue gear is seldom used and gets little attention. Poor-quality gear left unattended will quickly degrade to the point of being more hazard than help. Flares are a good example. Cheap flares have a short life span and some tests have shown only a 50 percent success rate for firing. When you need a flare, you want it to work right, and right now.

Rescue equipment can be loosely grouped by use into four categories:

- Gear for stabilizing a kayak.

- Gear for helping the kayaker get back into the kayak.

- Gear for removing water from the kayak.

- Communications gear.

Gear for Stabilizing

If you lose control of the angle, motion, or tilt of the kayak, you're no longer in charge of it, and a rescue may be in the offing. Gear is available to help make a kayak more stable, including sponsons and sea anchors. A tow-line can be used to stabilize and move a kayak that no longer can be effectively controlled by the kayaker alone.

Cold Hands, Warm Heart

We had been on the open coast for a couple of days and it was time to come home. Seas were windy and rough; the air temperature was 55°F (13°C) and the water temperature was 50°F (10°C). Kurt was seasick and feeling dizzy; he needed a tow.

I held onto his kayak to keep it stable as kayakers in three other boats towed us. With 18 knots of wind at our backs, 3-foot wind waves also pushing us along, and three strong paddlers towing us forward, the ride was a raucous roller coaster. My hands were constantly awash. I tried to pull my pogies off the paddle and put them on my bare hands, but in the attempt, one pogie washed away. My dry suit kept my body warm.

After an hour of towing, we arrived off our beach. Kurt was eager to make it to shore, and we were quickly into the steep surf before the beach. People on the beach later said we were in the biggest set of waves so far that day.

I rode the first two waves without broaching, but the third wave launched my kayak into a down-wave, high-speed surf ride. The wake off the bow rose past my ears as the kayak rolled right and the stern passed me by. Still trapped in the wave, my roll did not meet the challenge, and I had to make a wet exit and start swimming. Moments later during a lull, Gary came by and held my kayak as I jumped back in.

My hands were useless. Although they did not hurt, they were frozen blocks, and I could not attach my sprayskirt. My hands were so numb I could not even *feel* the sprayskirt. When the lull ended, a large breaking wave arrived. Gary and his kayak passed overhead as we capsized with the crest of the wave. Moments later on shore, I tried to pull my kayak up the beach, but my hands were so stiff I could not grasp the bow toggle. Kurt and Gary pulled my kayak up the beach.

Remarkably, my hands recovered in just a few minutes. I jumped into the cockpit, attached the sprayskirt, and launched back into the surf to help others still spilling and thrilling.

On reflection: The dry suit had kept me warm, but the peripheral circulation in my hands had shut down. With a warm body, the circulation was quick to return, but not soon enough.

—Doug Alderson

Towlines

A towline is a fundamental piece of safety gear for towing another kayak. You can use a towline to assist tired or injured paddlers and keep them moving with the group, or you can help a struggling paddler keep on course when strong winds or current make directional control difficult. In many circumstances, a tow can prevent a more severe incident.

A towline needs to meet several demanding and sometimes contradictory requirements. It must be unobtrusive but close at hand, enclosed but easy to open. In use, it has to attach easily and come off easily, but remain secure under difficult conditions. It should be of simple design but adaptable to various modes of use. It should be strong yet somewhat elastic; it must be quick to deploy in a short tether or in a long towline. It must release reliably when the user is capsized and the line is under tension. It must be usable with cold, wet hands or with gloves on.

Most towlines work fairly well in calm water, but their use near surf, in breaking waves near rocks, or in strong current can be dangerous. And it is often just such rough conditions that make a tow necessary. Rope and water make a dangerous combination. Treat rope with respect while on the water, look after it, and practice with it so that you are comfortable manipulating it under adverse conditions. If the rope gets tangled, you can use a knife to cut it free; carry a knife in a secure and accessible spot on your PFD.

For safety, any towline should be readily releasable with one hand. A towline needs to have an easy-to-use attachment clip, with no barbs or hooks to get hung up on other rope or wires. A towline should float.

Before you use a towline for rescue, learn to use it safely. Practice with your towline in a variety of conditions so that you are comfortable deploying it and understand its idiosyncrasies. Check the line regularly for wear, abrasion, and thin spots. Rope deteriorates over time—more quickly if it is stored wet.

Towlines are normally available in long

The best attachment hardware to use are stainless steel marine-grade clips (bottom) and carabiners (top). Gates should be smooth inside and out to allow for smooth operation. Both clips have enclosed ends to keep the attached line from moving around. The lower example has only two parts, a body and self-closing gate. This design omits the need for a hinge pin and a spring, which can corrode and be the source of problems. When working with cold and stiff hands, larger clips are easier to grasp and work with. The line at top is tied on with an anchor bend and whipping, and the lower line is tied with a figure-eight loop (see the appendix on knots).

Towing systems can include a belt and a bag with the towline contained. (COURTESY NORTHWATER RESCUE AND PADDLING EQUIPMENT)

A belt and cow tail provides for an effective quick-release towing system. Many PFDs are outfitted with belt loops to accept a belt. A longer line can be attached to the cow tail when a long in-line tow is necessary. (See "Towing in Assisted Rescues" in chapter 9.)

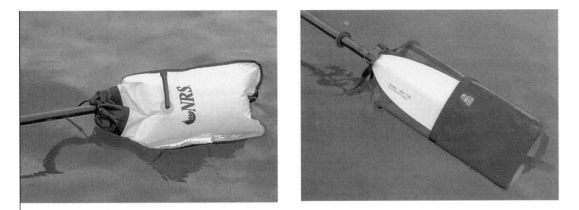

Paddle floats fit on the paddle blade to provide additional support. The paddle float on the left is inflated by mouth. The one on the right is rigid foam inside a fabric case. The paddle blade is inserted into the pocket and a strap around the paddle shaft keeps the paddle float from slipping off. Additional reflective tape enhances low-light visibility.

and short lengths. Long towlines (usually between 30 and 50 feet) are commonly used to tow over long distances. The length of line used depends on sea conditions. You want the towline to be long enough so that the kayak being towed does not surf down a wave and into the towing kayak.

Short towlines (sometimes called pig tails or cow tails) are usually between 6 and 12 feet long. They are often used to transport disabled paddlers over short distances, usually out of some immediate danger. Towlines are available that mount to the paddler, to the cockpit, or to the kayak.

Gear for Assisting Reentry

A paddler should know how to get from the water back into the kayak without use of special equipment. However, there are some valuable pieces of gear that can help the paddler and facilitate a rescue.

Paddle Float

An air-filled bladder or piece of lightweight rigid foam, a paddle float can be attached to a paddle blade to provide supplemental buoyancy for safety or rescue.

Paddle floats are either inflatable or made of foam. An inflatable float takes up little room and supports more weight, but is prone to leaking. Check it regularly to see that it holds air. A foam float is bulky and supports less weight, but cannot be punctured. Storing a foam float securely on the kayak in an accessible location can be a challenge because it takes up a fair amount of space. A foam float is commonly secured on the back deck just behind the paddler.

If your paddle float doesn't have a tether, add one to keep the float from washing away in rough water. A clip on the free end of the tether can make it easier to attach and release.

Sling

The sling is a loop of webbing or rope rigged to create a stirrup that assists a swimmer in stepping up into the kayak. In the water, use of a sling helps you lift your weight up over the kayak and onto the deck. Many paddlers can do this without aid, but others need a boost, especially if they are tired or cold or if the kayak sits high out of the water. The sling, looped around the cockpit coaming, provides this boost. A sling can easily be made at home.

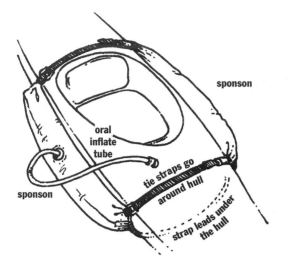

Sponsons are inflated bladders firmly rigged to the sides of the kayak.

The paddle float and sling can be used together.

Sponsons

Sponsons are flotation devices that attach to the sides of a kayak and act as outriggers, greatly enhancing stability. Most sponsons are inflatable and are attached to the hull as needed, with clips or through-hull fittings. The kayak must be rigged with these attachments in advance; check to see that these points are secure before you head out onto the water. Sponsons have a loyal following in many regions of North America and can be a useful tool for paddlers.

Gear for Removing Water

Getting the water out of a flooded kayak is a critical safety issue. The initial step, however, is to minimize how much water gets in in the first place. The dry bags that carry your clothing and other gear and supplies will reduce potential flooding and provide buoyancy. A medium-size dry bag that displaces, say, 28 pounds of water will still provide 22 pounds of positive buoyancy when carrying your 6-pound tent. If the tent was stored instead in a plain nylon stuff sack, which does not keep water out, there would be no buoyancy; in a flooded compartment, there would only be 6 pounds of sinking weight.

Empty or partially loaded compartments should have secondary flotation added, to accomplish which you can simply inflate one of the bags made for this purpose. The inflated float bag provides backup buoyancy in case of a leak. Float bags can also be added to help minimize flooding when a compartment begins to take in water, perhaps from a leaky deck seam or skeg control cable. The inflated bag will displace much of the incoming water and provide substantial buoyancy.

There are a number of ways to remove water from a flooded kayak, including simply lifting the kayak up and letting the water drain out. Under many circumstances, however, this will not work, and we need additional help; the answer, of course, is a pump. Kayakers have a choice of foot pumps, electric pumps, and portable hand pumps. The foot and electric pumps, because they are permanently mounted in the kayak, cannot be used to help pump out another person's kayak. A

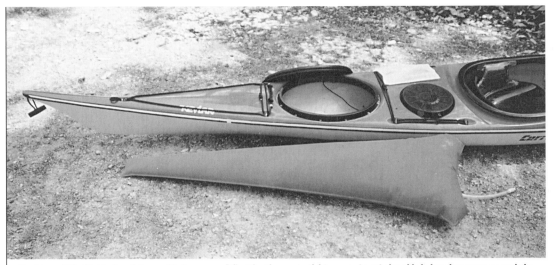

Float bags fit inside the kayak to provide buoyancy. A float bag in a watertight compartment also aids in keeping cargo securely in place.

supplemental portable hand pump can be useful for that purpose.

One type of sea kayak does not need any kind of pump. This is the design known as a sit-on-top, which, with no enclosing cockpit, is a self-bailer. The shallow pan where the paddler sits is slightly above the sea, so water simply flows back out like water off a sailboat's deck.

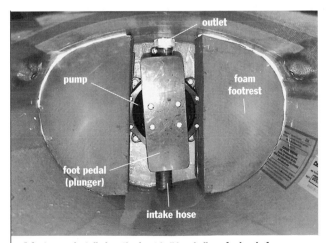

A foot pump installed on the front bulkhead allows for hands-free pumping. Foam blocks have been installed to the left and right of the pump to support the paddler's feet.

Foot Pump

The foot pump frees the hands for other duties: paddling, bracing, putting the sprayskirt back on. Foot pumps are reliable and secure. Commonly mounted on the forward bulkhead or on a movable track at the feet, the foot pump draws water up a short hose and ejects it overboard through a hull fitting. Water entering the cockpit from a leak in the coaming or the sprayskirt can be conveniently pumped as it comes in, preventing any buildup.

Electric Pump

Electric pumps are fast and efficient and permit hands-free pumping. Most run off a 12-volt battery that is commonly mounted behind the aft bulkhead, while the pump itself is mounted in the cockpit in front of that bulkhead. An activation switch is mounted in an accessible spot where it won't be accidentally turned on.

Although electric pumps are sealed and fully submersible, the marine environment is hard on the external wiring. Proper installation and

A variety of fully submersible 12-volt electric pumps are available that are suitable for installation in the cockpit of a kayak.

maintenance are essential. An electric pump can be a good choice for a double kayak because the pump is fast enough to deal with the large volume of water in a flooded double.

Portable Hand Pump

Portable hand pumps are inexpensive and easy to use. They can also break easily, and can get clogged with rocks and sand. The portable hand pump can be carried tethered on the deck or in the cockpit. Make sure it floats; add a bit of foam around the outside if necessary. Choose a bright color so it is easier to see. A hand pump is capable of moving water at a good rate, but the shaft can bend if not used carefully. A portable hand pump is useful when helping to pump out a partner's cockpit.

Communication Gear

Communication equipment can help members of a kayaking group communicate with one another, obtain vital information, and call for outside help as needed. The most important consideration is the range of the equipment—how far its signal can be detected. Satellite telephones, for example, provide almost universal coverage; cell phones work only within narrow bands along the coastline. Parachute flares can

A hand pump is invaluable for assisted rescues as a means to pump out others' flooded cockpits or compartments. A hand pump is often used as a primary pump but obviously does not allow for hands-free pumping.

be seen over many miles; most flashlights are visible for only for a mile or two. (See the section "Communicating Your Position," at the end of chapter 6 "Navigation," for more details on the use of communication tools.)

Two-Way Communication

Two-way communication is useful in many situations. It allows for accurate, timely, and subtle messaging between parties. There are a variety of products to consider as you choose the most appropriate tools for your needs and finances.

VHF Radio

VHF radios have been the standard for two-way marine communication for many years. In addition to connecting you with a network of other marine users, VHF radios provide weather information, internal group communication, and a vital link to emergency services.

VHF stands for Very High Frequency. By international agreement, radio waves are categorized into groups of frequencies with prescribed uses. In the case of marine VHF radios, these frequencies are preprogrammed into channels. Channel 16, for example, is the international distress channel, corresponding to a frequency of 156.8 MHz. Other channels are set aside for weather broadcasts and vessel traffic control, and still others are open for public use. In most jurisdictions, the radio and/or the radio user must be licensed. Check the regulations in your country or region.

VHF radios are expensive and prone to water damage. There are many excellent handheld units on the market, and a variety of bags and cases for carrying them. Most VHF radios offer basic features in common. Differences in price usually relate to size of the radio, sensitivity (ability to focus on and hold a frequency), waterproofing, and battery life. The transmission range is limited by power and by horizon distance (since VHF radio waves propagate along line-of-sight), and that effectively means a range of 5 miles for a 5-watt radio broadcasting from a low-lying kayak. Land features will obstruct transmissions, reducing that range.

Kayak groups and other users of marine VHF radios have long had the comfort of knowing that if they must send a distress signal, it will be picked up by another vessel or a ground station. With the advent of satellite communication and digital signaling has come an expansion in the emergency signaling options available to vessels. One result of this expansion is a potential reduction in the numbers and kinds of vessels and ground stations that receive VHF signals. At present there appears to be no threat to the continued surveillance of marine VHF radio frequencies, but future coverage may shrink and monitoring may be reduced.

Local services will dictate the best choice for wireless marine communications. VHF radios (left) broadcast to everyone listening on nearby marine vessels and local coast guard. Cell phones (right) provide one-to-one communication where there is cell coverage.

Walkie-talkies

Handheld citizens band radios are popular among many outdoor enthusiasts, allowing groups to split up but still keep in touch. They can be useful for groups of kayakers on the water by allowing the lead and sweep paddlers to stay in communication. They aren't much good for communicating outside the group, however, because most vessels and emergency response services don't monitor these frequencies.

The frequencies used by these radios have been put into the public domain in some countries and not others; check the regulations in your country or area. These walkie-talkies come with a variety of features and seem to be generally reliable. Range is limited by the power source and the topography.

Cell and Satellite Phones

Cellular telephones can be a valuable tool for sea kayakers if there is a receiving tower within range. Satellite phones are an excellent communication tool in remote areas away from cell phone networks. Satellite networks are similar to cell networks, but run off a series of satellites instead of a series of ground stations. Costs for satellite phones are still high; in some areas you can rent them. Satellite phones and cell phones allow for direct private communication. In times of distress, however, the wider broadcast of a VHF radio that reaches all nearby vessels has distinct advantages.

One-Way Communication

One-way communication tools are blunt instruments because you have no way of knowing if the message you sent has been received or how it has been interpreted. Nevertheless, they can provide additional levels of safety.

One-way communication tools are used to send a simple, clear message. If you receive a one-way communication, respond as if there has been an incident. If it turns out to be a false alarm, or if the situation is not as perilous as first assumed, at least you have kept up a marine tradition of vigilance and of response to a call for help.

Flares

Flares are commonly used by mariners to signal for help. Flares fail sometimes, especially the cheaper ones, so carry extras. Flares are explosives and pose a risk to users. They should be handled with care, never pointed at anyone, and launched away from the body. Distress flares are red.

Parachute flares fly up to 1,000 feet high and burn for at least 45 seconds. They are useful for attracting as much attention as possible. These are the most expensive type of flares.

Multistar flares are smaller than parachute flares, fly lower, and burn for less time. As their name implies,

they are two flares in one, with two distinct bursts. They are useful for signaling for help in areas with lots of boat traffic. In addition, they help emergency response personnel pinpoint the location of a paddler in distress. In general, paddlers should carry at least three of these.

Handheld flares are also useful for signaling for help in areas of high boat traffic and helping emergency personnel locate a paddler. These flares show up on the infrared goggles used by some search and rescue crews. In a pinch, handheld flares can be used to start a fire.

Flares are best used at night, although they are bright enough to attract attention during the day as well. Smoke flares, on the other hand, are best used during the day. Smoke flares release a dense orange smoke that can be seen for many miles on a clear

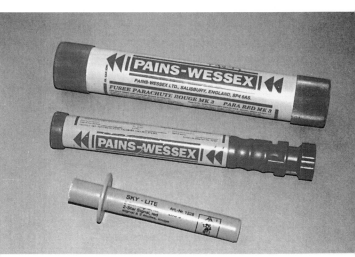

Flares come in a variety of configurations. Shown here is a parachute flare (top) that rises high into the air and descends slowly on a parachute. Because this flare is high in the sky and bright, it can be visible for several miles around. Also shown is a handheld bright incendiary flare (middle). Although they are deployed low to the water, incendiary flares are very bright and can last for a long time. On the bottom is a twin rocket flare that fires two small rockets in a low arc. Handheld rocket flares are small and convenient to carry in a PFD or rescue satchel. They are not as bright and do not last as long as either parachute flares or incendiary flares.

day. In reduced visibility such as fog, rain, and low-lying clouds, flares are less effective. Nevertheless, they are an internationally recognized means of communicating distress.

Strobes

Strobe lights are a recognized means of signaling for help. These comprise a very bright, flashing white light, operated by batteries. Strobes can be attached to the kayak or to the paddler. They should be waterproof, and the batteries should be fully charged immediately before a trip. They are particularly useful in pinpointing the location of a kayaker in the water at night.

Personal Locator Beacons

Personal locator beacons broadcast a signal on one of two internationally designated frequencies. Using satellites and ground and air stations, search and rescue organizations can identify the location of the transmission and send help. Depending on the location of the transmission, it may take as much as several hours to pinpoint the source.

Some personal locator units come equipped with GPS (Global Positioning System) capability, which speeds locating the source of the transmission. There are several small, kayak-friendly personal locator units on the market. These are fairly expensive, but will work anywhere in the world and can provide a valuable backup to other communication systems.

Other Aids

Kayakers can use a variety of other one-way communication aids. Some will be recognized as a distress signal. Others will simply create curiosity. In addition to communicating with individuals and organizations outside the group of paddlers, many of these signaling devices can be used to communicate within the group. Each group member must be clear on the intended message of each signal. The message may be one of distress, but many of

A strobe light such as the waterproof one attached to the back of this PFD is one of the most visible nighttime rescue aids available to a kayaker.

these devices can also be used to convey simple meanings such as "Come together"; "Stop"; "Toilet break"; or "I'm OK."

- *Lights.* A variety of lights can be used to signal others. Flashlights, headlamps, and glow (cyalume) sticks are a few of the lights useful to the sea kayaker. Most lights used by kayakers are not very powerful and are only helpful over short distances. Signals might include making a circle of light, meaning "I'm OK"; a vertical movement meaning "Come together"; and a horizontal movement meaning "Stop." These motions correspond to commonly used hand and paddle signals.

- *Sounds.* Sound signals include air horns and whistles. The sounds these tools make should be louder than the human voice so the sounds can travel farther and attract more attention. Recognized signals include a single blast to attract attention and three blasts to indicate distress.

- *Large bags.* A large orange or yellow garbage bag or bivy sack can be used to make a simple distress signal. By trapping air in the sack and sealing the end, a large buoy is made that can be tied to the kayak or held by the paddler. These bags are easily carried in a pocket, are inexpensive, and are visible for a couple of miles on a clear day.

- *Paddles.* Paddle signals are useful for communicating over short distances with other vessels and members of your own group, and a variety of signals can be used. You can wave a paddle over your head to attract the attention of other boaters. Because kayaks are low in the water, the waving of a paddle can help other boaters identify your kayak and steer clear of it.

- *Mirrors.* Specially designed signaling mirrors that focus a beam of light can be used to attract attention over several miles on a bright day. They are finicky to use at first, so practice using the mirror before an emergency. They are small, waterproof, and fit into a pocket on a PFD.

Additional Safety and Rescue Aids

Kayakers have a variety of other powerful safety and rescue equipment available to them.

GPS Unit

A portable GPS (Global Positioning System) unit can be an important piece of safety equipment. The unit pinpoints a kayaker's location and provides navigational bearings to previously programmed locations (known as waypoints), such as campsites, water sources, and put-in and takeout points.

The GPS unit does not replace chart and compass work in navigation, but it does provide an accurate backup. This is particularly useful on longer crossings to small targets, while navigating in fog and at night, and for logging trip information such as distances, speeds, and places of interest. As with all electronic equipment carried on a kayak, a GPS

unit must be treated with care and protected against immersion.

Barometer

A portable barometer can provide some of the current, local weather information so important to the safety of kayakers. Barometer readings can supplement information from weather broadcasts and personal observations.

A barometer measures the atmospheric pressure, which is an indication of the expected weather. A downward trend in barometric pressure is usually an indication of deteriorating weather; an upward trend can be seen as an indicator of improving weather. Portable digital barometers usually provide a graph of pressure trends over a period of time. Trends are less readily discerned with an analog barometer; these instruments must be checked regularly and their pressure readings recorded in the trip log.

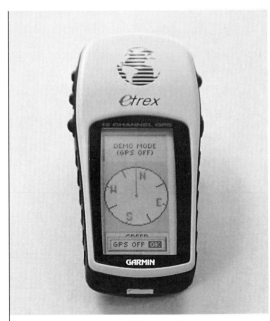

Global Positioning System (GPS) navigation devices provide accurate navigational information. Handheld GPS units like this one are available in portable waterproof versions that are especially useful to sea kayakers.

Duct Tape to the Rescue

The two of us were on a multiday trip in a double kayak when the storm hit. We settled into a reasonably sheltered site, battened down the hatches, and prepared to wait it out. During the very windy night we heard a loud crack and a boom. A tree branch had fallen onto our kayak, crushing it across the bow! Disheartened, we returned to our tent to wait until morning.

In daylight, the kayak looked as bad as we feared. The seas were still rough and the winds still strong, but at least the rain had stopped. We pooled our resources and decided we had enough duct tape to possibly tape the bow back together. We removed the branch, reshaped the bow as best we could, and began a long and careful process of taping the bow back together. We reinforced the bow by shoving an inflated float bag wrapped in duct tape up inside, then wrapped a lot of tape around the outside.

It wasn't pretty, but it turned out to be watertight. We were able to paddle out the next day.

On reflection: Some things cannot be anticipated. A lot can be done with a little creativity, persistence, and duct tape.

—Liam Edwards

First-Aid Kit

First-aid kits vary with the particular needs of each group and of each trip. Each kayak group should carry a first-aid kit appropriate to its needs and to the training of its members. For packing and for use, it helps to think of your medical supplies as falling into three categories of need: traumatic injury, illness, and everyday use. Categorizing the supplies gives you some flexibility in how to pack. Everyday items should be close at hand; medications and supplies for illness and injury can be packed away with less emphasis on immediate accessibility. (See the appendix section, First-Aid Kit.)

Repair Kit

A flexible, well-considered repair kit provides for important repairs in the field, maximizing safety and comfort. The exact contents of a kit depends on the length and remoteness of the trip and the equipment that could potentially need repair or maintenance. Most minor repairs can be left until after the trip, but some are essential to safety. Structural damage to a kayak, a broken rudder or skeg, or a nonfunctioning stove pose threats to health and safety. The repair kit needs to reflect these priorities. (See the appendix section, Repair Kit.)

Bivouac Kit

A bivouac kit provides enough gear, such as a light plastic tarp, fire starter, and extra cord, to handle an unexpected overnighter. A small, durable kit should be part of the standard supplies for any day trip. (See the appendix section, Bivouac Kit.)

Paddling Technique

5

Efficient paddling techniques that use the least amount of energy are essential for sea kayaking safety. In adverse sea conditions, the capable paddler remains in control and on course, with sufficient energy in reserve to deal with worsening conditions. When temporarily taken off course by a strong wind, capsized by a wave, or held back by a current, the capable paddler is safe and is able to independently regain control.

There is a natural difficulty in describing adverse sea conditions; the paddler's skill level is the benchmark. (See also Environment and Paddling Levels in the appendix.) For a novice, adverse conditions may include the wavelets that arise before whitecapped waves appear. For a more skilled paddler the same waves are hardly noticeable. An intermediate-level paddler will be our benchmark.

The capable intermediate paddler has a complete set of paddling and recovery strokes. Strong forward and turning strokes are backed up with effective bracing skills. Our capable paddler can make comfortable, steady progress while paddling in conditions that can include whitecapped waves up to 3 feet, wind up to 18 knots, or current under 3 knots. Combinations of wind, wave, and current can certainly create more than our capable paddler could manage comfortably.

Knocked over, our capable paddler will recover with a spontaneous low or high brace.

Adequate Reserves

The sea has no regard for how much you have given—only how much you have left to give. Safety demands that you keep adequate energy in reserve to meet unexpected demands. When assessing the risks of a long crossing or paddling against a strong headwind you must consider how to spend your limited energy budget. Against a 10-knot headwind a paddler may be able to make 3 knots for 3 hours and retain an adequate energy reserve to cope with an unforeseen surf landing or unexpected current. To maintain a similar reserve in a 25-knot headwind, however, the same paddler may be able to paddle at only 1 knot, and only for 1 hour. Frequent eating and fluid intake is essential to maintain adequate reserve energy.

Once ashore, there is still a camp to set up and meals to prepare. An exhausted body does not function well, and the ability to make good decisions is seriously impaired. Poor energy management often prefaces serious incidents. It is not surprising that a large proportion of accidents and incidents occur late in the day after a strenuous paddle and an unexpected demand on energy.

Along with maintaining adequate energy reserves, paddlers must maintain adequate skill reserves. As the wind, waves, or current increase, a higher order of skill is needed to match them. When the difficulty of the conditions exceeds your skill level, you have crossed the line into unacceptable risk.

Skills

A capable paddler has equally developed mental and physical skill so the mental skills of judgment, risk assessment, and risk management must be on a par with the paddling skills and the demands of the paddling environment. A no-nonsense understanding of your own skill level is fundamental to the good judgment necessary for safe paddling.

Coaches, instructors, and leaders are useful for more than just abetting skill development. They will select the conditions necessary to challenge your abilities and provide for the practical application of paddling skills. They will assist you in learning how to judge what constitutes a safe yet challenging paddling environment. To learn the paddling techniques necessary to keep you safe at sea takes time, persistence, and a little help. Take courses, paddle with people of greater skill than yourself, and practice in safe yet demanding conditions. Physical skills develop slowly and need to be practiced in a variety of sea conditions. To keep your skills up, paddle regularly in the relevant conditions. After taking long periods off, your skills and confidence will decline and will have to be revived.

Equipment plays a role in how we paddle. Some sea kayaks are narrow, with a long and level keel line. These kayaks tend to track straight, keeping to a consistent heading, but can be difficult to turn when off course. Shorter and wider hull designs with more of the hull out of the water—more rocker—will slide off course but are easy to turn. Your choice of paddle design is influential in propelling and controlling a kayak. A widebladed, 70-degree feathered paddle offers less resistance paddling into the wind but can be difficult to control when crosswinds lift and spin the windward blade. A smaller blade and shorter paddle shaft may permit a higher stroke rate and provide better acceleration.

Nuances of paddling style and equipment need to be overlaid on a solid foundation of efficient technique. Efficient paddling technique serves two masters: the mechanics of a paddle and the capabilities of a human body. The human body is part of the equipment necessary to propel a sea kayak, and it comes in as many shapes and sizes as kayaks and paddles. Part of the joy of paddling is the opportunity to develop an individual style.

Sea kayakers need to acquire good basic techniques and then learn to modify them to suit changing conditions. Being able to safely land on a surf beach or make a steady course across a fast-moving tide rip can keep you out of trouble and away from having to use your rescue skills. To get home on time, paddling upwind requires an efficient and sustained forward stroke. Traveling across the wind, efficient turning strokes are necessary to keep the kayak on a steady heading. Downwind, pushed before a steep wave with a strong wind at your back, the ability to maintain directional control is a primary safety concern. Towing a disabled partner back to camp can be a long and arduous effort. Conditions certainly exist that no amount of skill can overcome, but a skilled and experienced paddler can maintain reasonable control in quite awful sea conditions.

Forward Stroke

Paddling forward consumes more time than any other skill. A good forward stroke propels the kayak at the best speed with the least effort. Subtle improvements in technique can make major improvements in forward progress. Each little improvement is multiplied by many hundreds of paddle strokes per hour. Two paddlers can reach the same destination at the same time; one, cruising comfortably, arrives fresh and ready to continue, while the other, exerting a maximum effort, arrives exhausted.

Efficient forward paddling technique draws energy from the body at a steady, sustainable rate—exerting enough energy to keep the kayak moving forward while keeping some energy in reserve. Excessively slow progress exhausts a paddler by requiring too long to reach a destination. At the other extreme, too high an average speed prematurely exhausts the paddler before reaching the destination.

Paddling forward consumes most of our energy when sea kayaking. Sit up, reach well forward, and keep the paddle blade in the water near the kayak.

The last leg of a day's journey often includes a surf landing, a contrary current, or a building afternoon breeze. Efficient technique allows you to make good speed upwind in order to pass a headland before the tide turns, or to paddle hard upwind for an hour and a half to get to the beach before the tide turns against the wind and the sea becomes a roller coaster. The efficient, capable paddler claims no special ability and makes no great exertion. Against the wind, rounding the headland before the turn of the tide, this paddler arrives at the destination to comfortably ride a 4-foot breaking wave to shore and make camp well before dark. Each of the 3,000 strokes made in the preceding 2 hours produced a maximum of propulsion with a minimum of effort. The capable paddler does not paddle hard for a long time; this kayaker actually paddles easier for a shorter time.

The forward paddle stroke has four phases: setup, plant, power, and exit. Throughout the stroke, the paddle should be held loosely, with hands slightly more than shoulder width apart and an equal distance in from each end of the shaft. Keeping a relaxed grip on the paddle will help with an efficient stroke as well as help to reduce the possibility of repetitive strain injuries such as wrist tendinitis.

Sitting correctly in the kayak allows for an efficient transfer of energy from body to kayak. An upright posture is fundamental to good forward paddling. Knees should be braced under the deck and the balls of the feet should be in contact with stable foot braces (footrests). Sitting up, reaching well forward, the bottom arm should be straight, with the torso slightly rotated. This sets up the paddle to be planted cleanly into the water as far forward as comfortably possible.

For most people the blade enters the water somewhere near the feet. Then the power phase pulls the blade through the water, near the kayak. To complete the stroke, the blade exits the water somewhere near the hips; the setup for the opposite stroke has already begun. An appropriate paddle length permits a forward stroke near the kayak with the blade fully immersed.

The position of the lower body, hidden inside the kayak, is as important as the more visible upper body posture. In calm water, the feet are steady on the footrests, but when extra power is required, it is important to know how to bring them into play. You should be pushing with one or both feet during the power phase of the stroke.

To reduce fatigue, forward paddling technique needs to utilize the larger muscle groups. The technique is difficult to explain but relatively easy to do. A coach or mentor will ask you to rotate your torso and keep your paddle out in front while paddling forward. When they demonstrate, the technique is subtle and its effect is not immediately apparent, but when repeated 1,500 times an hour, the outcome is obvious.

Paddling with both a relaxed grip and a relaxed fluid motion allows the body a micro-rest during the setup phase of each stroke. The micro-rest is exceptionally brief. To take advantage of thousands of micro-rests each hour, you need to remain relaxed while also putting out substantial effort. The muscles are given a chance to relax and at least partially recharge, extending the limits of endurance. Torso rotation comes from reaching well forward with an extended arm and shoulder and some twist at the waist. The paddle is drawn back by pulling with the arm, unwinding the shoulders and torso, ready to reach forward on the left. This motion brings many muscle groups into play and aides greatly in power and endurance. Micro-rests aid in conserving and restoring energy reserves.

Stroke Rate

Stroke rate is a key element of forward paddling technique. There are many variables to take into account, such as

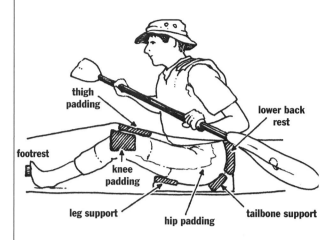

Fitting comfortably in the cockpit with good contact at feet, knees, thighs, and hips helps with balance, control, and efficient paddling technique.

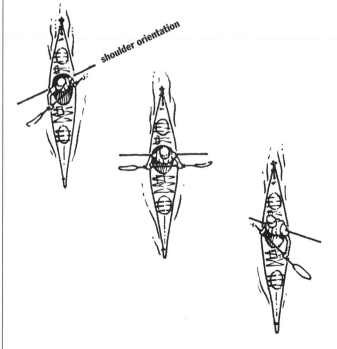

In a forward stroke, rotating your torso by twisting at the waist incorporates large muscle groups, making a strong forward stroke easier to maintain over a longer time.

paddle length, body size, wind strength, sea conditions, and speed through the water. The body is most efficient when required to do more repetitions at lighter effort loads. For general traveling, a quick rate of about 25 paddle strokes (counting one side only) every minute is common among accomplished touring sea kayakers.

It is important to note that a consistent energy output is required to propel the kayak forward at a given speed. Slow or quick stroke rate, vertical or horizontal paddling style, the kayak requires exactly the same amount of energy. An improved stroke technique is more efficient, directing the greatest portion of the human effort to propelling the kayak. When a consistent amount of energy is put into a forward paddling stroke, the more efficient stroke will move the kayak forward at a faster rate. A good analogy is bicycling uphill. A higher gear requires fewer but harder pedal cycles. A lower gear requires more pedal cycles, but each cycle requires less effort. In each case, the simple mechanical system requires the exact same amount of energy.

It requires less energy to keep a kayak moving at a steady rate than it does to speed it up. Paddling with a quick stroke rate keeps the kayak moving more steadily forward than does a slow stroke rate. With a quick stroke rate, the paddle is in the water a good percentage of the time. With a slow stroke rate, the kayak slows down between each stroke. A glide degrades forward momentum and reduces speed, so the paddler has to recover from the loss of speed by accelerating the kayak slightly during each stroke. A quick stroke rate is energy efficient: you can paddle quickly and easily, maintaining good speed with little loss of energy. With a quick stroke rate, the amount of effort for each stroke can be less.

There are times when it is necessary to vary stroke rate. To speed up, you should increase the stroke rate: paddling faster is more efficient than paddling harder. To make progress against a brief current, it may be necessary to use a short flurry of paddle strokes. Long-lasting headwinds call for a comfortable and sustainable stroke rate. The need to tow another kayak sharply increases the power required, and stroke dynamics will change once again.

There is no one best style of forward paddling or one best paddle blade or paddle length. Personal preference plays a considerable role in your choice of equipment and technical style. However, good technique always includes the ability to adapt. A capable paddler varies the stroke to suit the conditions. When you are paddling slowly downwind with lots of time to reach a destination, there is little demand on technique. But getting to a rescue quickly, paddling hard into waves, or crossing a strong current requires performance paddling. Traveling many miles in fair weather can also make a high demand on technique. Getting to the destination on time with energy in reserve is the final measure of an efficient forward-paddling stroke.

Brace Strokes

Brace strokes are quite different from the other strokes that deal with maneuvering a kayak. Brace strokes are used to support the kayak in a steady position or to recover from a knockdown. One good brace can prevent the need for a difficult rescue. Good bracing skills prevent a full capsize and the difficulties that follow. After a partial capsize, recovery brace strokes return the kayak to an upright position. A recovery from a capsize that wets only one ear can be called a brace. If both ears get wet, we can call it a roll. Think of a successful brace as an understated self rescue.

Learning to use recovery strokes presents a circular problem. You need good recovery strokes to be confident in rough water, and you need to be confident in rough water to develop good recovery strokes. Skill with recovery strokes develops with experience paddling in a variety of demanding conditions. Start in calm water and then progress out into the wind and the waves. Good judgment is required in choosing conditions that are safe, yet demanding enough to provide a useful learning environment.

Boat Control and Balance

Controlled tilting (edge control) and an understanding of balance are fundamental to efficient maneuvering and bracing. Balance in a kayak has more to do with control of boat tilt and body lean than with support from the paddle. Balance includes sitting upright with the kayak level in flat water and tilted in rough water. Tilting the kayak improves its maneuverability and can add stability when paddling in waves or current. The absence of good edge control makes the paddler reliant on using the paddle for stability and balance. The boat should support your weight, and the paddle is best used for propulsion and turning.

The kayak is stable as long as the weight of the paddler is centered over the hull. The capable paddler can hold a considerable tilt while keeping the kayak stable. Practice making paddle strokes on both sides of the kayak while balanced and tilted. This is not intuitive or comfortable. There is a strong tendency for paddlers to lean outward to tilt the kayak.

Near-capsize Recovery

Recovery brace strokes are used to regain lost stability. A kayak brace stroke is a dynamic action that involves the entire body, the kayak, and the paddle. From head to foot, the actions of your body make the brace work. The kayak must fit you well, so that it responds to your actions. The paddle provides sufficient lift and support when body and boat are working together. For the paddle to provide lift or support, either the paddle or the water must be moving. With the correct posture and a

This paddler does not need the paddle to remain upright. Instead, while sitting up, he is lifting with the upper knee and simultaneously shifting his weight onto his lower buttock and hip. With his body centered over the kayak, the paddler and kayak remain stable and upright.

In a low brace turn, the paddler tilts the kayak on edge by means of hips and leg control and uses the backside of the paddle blade to assist in the turn.

In a high brace turn the paddler tilts the kayak on edge by means of hips and leg control and uses the power face of the paddle blade to assist in the turn.

Poor bracing technique can be responsible for serious injury. There is considerable momentum in a loaded sea kayak pushed by a modest wave. Bracing into a breaking wave, the paddler must balance a heavy, loaded kayak against the considerable force of the wave. A loaded kayak with paddler can easily weigh 300 pounds. To reverse a capsize and return to an upright position is almost effortless when done correctly. It is difficult and hazardous done incorrectly. Good technique will keep your shoulders in a strong posture and prevent excessive strain or even a shoulder dislocation.

Several aspects of good technique are important to remember:

cockpit that fits the paddler, very little lift or support is required from the paddle.

Once stability is lost, the kayak begins to rotate, taking the kayaker into the water. The correct response is to move your hips, changing the pressure from the upper knee to the knee that is lower, and to move your head toward the water. Done quickly, this motion of the hips and head is called a hip flick. For the beginner, it seems entirely illogical to move your head toward the water in order to prevent a capsize. Although the head is influential and readily visible, the trick is primarily in the use of the lower body and good contact between the under-deck and the knees. A change of head position allows a change of knee pressure, and very often this alone can be enough to return the kayak to a balanced position. There is minimal support needed from the paddle. Without a change of head-tilt and knee-lift, recovery is nearly impossible. An overemphasis on the action of the paddle detracts from learning the less visible, but more efficient, actions of the body.

- Keep your elbows bent and near your body.
- Keep the paddle blade in front of an imaginary line drawn through the shoulders.
- Keep your forearm at 90 degrees to your paddle shaft.

Skill with a high brace will prevent most capsizes. Keep elbows in close to body, forearm near 90° to the paddle shaft, and paddle shaft in front of the body.

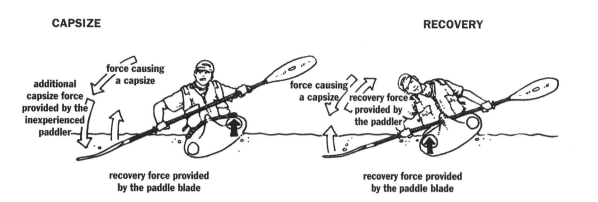

CAPSIZE

force causing a capsize

additional capsize force provided by the inexperienced paddler

recovery force provided by the paddle blade

RECOVERY

force causing a capsize

recovery force provided by the paddler

recovery force provided by the paddle blade

Learning how to keep a kayak upright is an invaluable safety skill. When the kayak becomes unstable the untrained kayaker (left) will tilt his head away from the direction of the capsize. The upper knee will lift on the deck, contributing to the capsize. There is also a natural reaction to sit upright. This raises the center of gravity and adds to the instability. Continued effort to keep the head away from the water increases the lifting force of the knee and a full capsize becomes inevitable. The kayaker has a sense of being locked in place, unable to move. Capsize recovery (right) can be made with a quick change of posture. This change of posture is not intuitive and needs to be learned through training and practice. The correct response to an imminent capsize is to tilt the head toward

the water; lifting the lower knee which contributes to righting the kayak. Leaning forward, with the head moving toward the lower knee and closer to the kayak, will lower the center of gravity, adding to stability.

Inside the kayak, the hips and knees move very little. When the paddler fits properly in the cockpit, the actions of the hips and knees are efficiently transmitted to the kayak. The kayak moves in response to the action of the lower body. Hips and legs impart a force that moves the kayak. The head and upper body move to enable the movement of the lower body, lower the center of gravity, and provide a counterweight to the action of the lower body.

Low Brace and High Brace

A low brace is done with the back side of the paddle blade, and the hands are lower than the elbows. The grip on the paddle shaft does not change. A spontaneous low brace is the quickest response to momentary upset. The low brace blends easily into the end of a forward stroke.

A high brace is done with the front side of the paddle blade, and the hands are higher than the elbows. The grip on the paddle shaft does not change. The high brace blends easily into the beginning of a forward stroke.

Either a low brace or a high brace can be used for support or re-

The low brace should be a first line of defense against a capsize. Note that his forearms are near 90° to the paddle shaft and in front of his body. The head has moved down toward the water as the kayaker completes a hip snap and the kayak comes upright.

covery. In rough seas, subtle braces blended into a strong forward stroke will help keep a kayak balanced and upright.

Supportive braces also help keep the kayak tilted and balanced, as in the case of brace turns. Brace turns are particularly useful when paddling in current or breaking waves. A brace turn provides maneuverability and support at the same time.

Before a trip, practice bracing in sea conditions at the upper level of what can be expected, or beyond. The expression that says "the more I practice the luckier I get" has a measure of truth. Having practiced and developed confidence in rough water, the capable paddler is prepared to place a preemptive recovery stroke into a threatening wave.

Sculling Brace

Sculling can prolong the effectiveness of a brace. Sculling is the back and forth sweeping of the paddle. Like spreading icing on a cake, the angle of the blade is critical to success.

Sweeping the paddle back and forth is the motion necessary to create lift. A single sculling stroke at the end of an almost successful brace can add the last bit of lift and support to complete the recovery. When fully capsized, but not inverted, sculling can provide momentary support until you have time to do a high brace and return to an upright position.

Paddling in Wind and Waves

Breaking waves will often turn a sea kayak sideways to the wave. Lean toward the wave and brace firmly. Leaning away from the wave will result in a near-instantaneous capsize.

A sculling stroke can halt a capsize at the surface, before the kayak is fully inverted. A high-brace recovery will have the paddler back upright.

Much of our sea kayaking is done when weather and sea conditions are fine. Many of us paddle for several seasons and never encounter conditions that demand the most of our skills. The impression we get is that we are doing just fine and our skills are more than good enough—until an unexpected change of weather or an error in judgment has us paddling frantically for shore. To prepare for the rougher-than-planned day, we need to practice the very best technique on the gentle days. To test our technique, we need to get out and practice on a few of the rougher days.

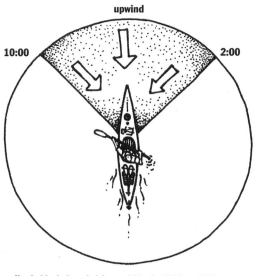

Upwind includes wind from within the 1000 to 0200 arc on a circle.

Paddling Upwind

Paddling upwind is about forward paddling technique, power, and endurance. Most kayaks will track into the wind, and keeping a steady heading is easy. The paddler's job is to move the kayak forward, putting shoulder and back into a good stroke. Such an energy-intensive task requires efficient paddling technique that wastes as little energy as possible. That technique must also suit the human body's ability to deliver power to each stroke. Power consumes energy, and the body has a limited capacity to replenish energy reserves. An efficient forward paddling stroke uses energy only slightly faster than the body can regenerate it. We need to arrive at our destination before energy reserves are exhausted.

Simply paddling more quickly against the wind has a definite ad-

vantage. You expend less energy if you minimize the time spent fighting the wind. Speeding up saves time and energy. Arriving at your destination on time is more than convenient. Navigational plans may include critical times to avoid tidal currents or daily thermal winds. Having the strength and the technique to sustain good speed around a windy headland, or upstream against the beginnings of a tidal current, is much better than having to perform a rescue in a maelstrom.

A crossing that takes less time will generally result in navigation that is more accurate. When navigating by dead reckoning, the accuracy of time and distance estimates becomes poorer as more time is spent on the water. Longer time spent trying to keep a compass course can result in greater errors.

Take a look at the table on the next page for dramatic confirmation of the time saved by speeding up under three different wind conditions: calm; against a little opposition (a 15-knot breeze or 1-knot current); and against a lot of opposition (a 22-knot wind or 1.5-knot current).

For a 6-mile crossing against a 22-knot wind, the difference between speeding up

A good forward stoke is necessary to move effectively through turbulent tidal waters. The paddler is sitting upright and reaching well forward to plant his paddle out in front for a full length of stroke.

(GREG SHEA)

PADDLE HARD TO SAVE ENERGY

The table compares the results of paddling hard or slowing down against the combined opposing forces of wind and current. Speeding up a little is an effective way to save energy and minimize the time that the wind and current can push you backward. In this example, there is a significant difference in time taken to travel 6 nautical miles. In the windiest of conditions shown here, if you paddle as little as ½ knot slower (2.5 knots instead of 3 knots), it will take you 2 hours longer to make the crossing, increasing paddling time for the 6-mile crossing from 4 hours to 6 hours. Speeding up by just ½ knot will save a full hour, allowing you to cross in only 3 hours.

BOAT SPEED (KNOTS)	COMBINED EFFECT OF WIND AND CURRENT (KNOTS)	RESULTANT SPEED MADE GOOD (KNOTS)	DISTANCE (NAUTICAL MILES)	TIME (HOURS)	TIME SAVED OR LOST
Calm					
slow to 2.5	0	2.5	6	2.4	lose 24 min.
3	0	3	6	2	
speed up to 3.5	0	3.5	6	1.7	save 17 min.
Moderate 15 KN Wind or 1 KN Current					
slow to 2.5	1	1.5	6	4	lose 60 min.
3	1	2	6	3	
speed up to 3.5	1	2.5	6	2.4	save 36 min.
22 KN Headwind or 1.5 KN Current					
slow to 2.5	1.5	1	6	6	lose 120 min.
3	1.5	1.5	6	4	
speed up to 3.5	1.5	2	6	3	save 60 min.

your paddling by half a knot and slowing it down by half a knot is 3 hours of paddling time.

Paddling across the Wind

When making a course across the direction of the wind, it can take considerable effort to keep the kayak on a steady heading. Turning strokes are used to change heading and to hold a straight course when the wind contin-ually tries to push the kayak off a desired heading. In calm conditions, sweep strokes and brace turns work well. But when the wind blows, some strokes work more efficiently than others. In choosing which stroke to use, it helps to understand the forces that push a kayak off course.

Weathercocking

The difference in water movement around bow and stern causes a kayak to deflect its

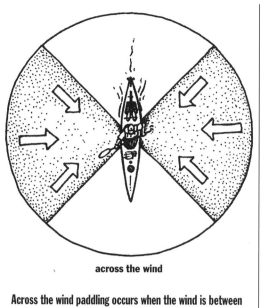

across the wind

Across the wind paddling occurs when the wind is between the 0200 and 0400 and 0800 and 1000 arcs in a circle.

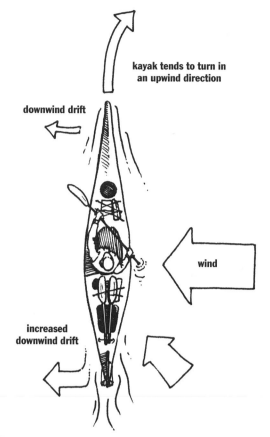

kayak tends to turn in an upwind direction

downwind drift

wind

increased downwind drift

A crosswind or quartering wind creates forces that cause the kayak to turn upwind. As the kayak moves forward the resistance of the water around the kayak changes and the effects of the wind will change. Turbulence at the stern creates a region less resistant to drift, resulting in increase downwind drift of the stern and a tendency to turn upwind (weathercocking).

course in an upwind direction. As a kayak travels forward, the bow cuts cleanly through the water. The water smoothly separates, creating a path for the widest part of the kayak. As the kayak passes, the water begins to close in again as it approaches the stern. Unable to conform perfectly to the shape of the kayak, the water forms turbulence near the stern. This turbulence provides less grip at the stern than at the bow, where the water flow is smoother. Because of the dissimilar water flows between bow and stern, a crosswind tends to push the stern farther downwind than the bow. The net effect is that the kayak tends to turn upwind—an effect called weathercocking. As the paddler moves the kayak faster forward, the turbulence at the stern increases and the weathercocking effect increases, deflecting the kayak even more upwind.

Other forces generated from the shape of the hull above and below the waterline combine to moderate or amplify the effects of weathercocking. Consequently, different hull designs vary in how much they tend to weath-

ercock. A kayak designed with a deeper stern will probably suffer less weathercocking (but will also be more difficult to turn). Loading a kayak with heavier gear in the back, so the kayak sits deeper in the stern, will also aid in reducing weathercocking.

To keep a kayak on course in a crosswind, you can tilt the kayak into the wind. The natural tendency of most hulls is to turn away from a tilted edge. This effect helps to counteract the effects of weathercocking. The forward paddling stroke can be modified for a wider sweep stroke on the upwind side and a stroke closer to the hull on the downwind side.

Rudders and skegs are a great help in dealing with weathercocking and keeping a kayak on a steady heading. The stability of foot braces (footrests) in a rudder system is an important consideration, since good boat control requires firmly positioned braces. In short, steep waves, the rudder can rise out of the water, providing inconsistent control.

A drop-down skeg controlled from in front of the cockpit is simple and effective in adjusting the heading of a kayak in windy conditions. When lowered, the skeg helps counteract the effects of wind and waves pushing the kayak off course. On a steep wave, a skeg is less likely than a rudder to rise out of the water. Be aware that the skeg box can interfere with packing the stern compartment, however. To avoid leaking, the control cable must be securely fastened into the skeg box.

Consider a rudder or a drop-down skeg as a convenience and not a necessity. Learn to paddle in all sea and wind conditions without rudder or skeg. Regular maintenance of your kayak will keep you shipshape and under way. Speeding down the face of a 6-foot wave is one of those times when you want all systems to work well. You could be in trouble if the rudder cable comes loose as you ride this big wave.

Turning in a Crosswind

In a strong wind, making a turn to change course can be difficult. The kayak will find a point of balance between the effects of weathercocking and the added action of the waves. At times, it seems exceedingly difficult to change that course and turn the kayak. The external forces acting on the kayak can be used to assist, however.

In a crosswind, not all turning strokes are equal. The stroke known as the stern rudder (not to be confused with a mechanical rudder) is the best choice for turning a kayak from broadside to the wind to a downwind heading. The stern-rudder stroke on the downwind side impedes the drift of the stern while allowing the bow to drift downwind. Tilting the kayak into the wind will complement the turn and angle the stern to slide easily across the water.

In waves, a rudder (top) can temporarily rise out of the water, losing some control. The deeper and more forward position of a skeg (bottom) keeps it in the water in most situations.

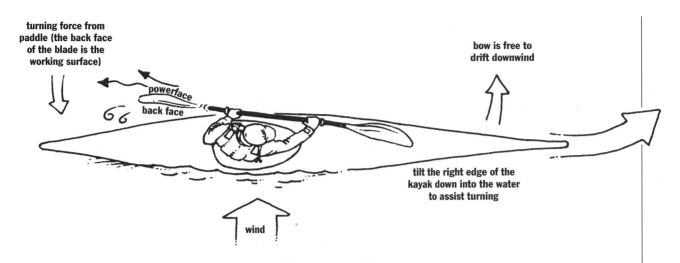

turning force from paddle (the back face of the blade is the working surface)

powerface

back face

bow is free to drift downwind

tilt the right edge of the kayak down into the water to assist turning

wind

The stern rudder is preferred when turning the kayak toward a downwind course. The paddle remains still for a rudder strike. The momentum of the kayak moving through the water provides the force. The paddle blade's placement and angle of attack create the desired turning effect.

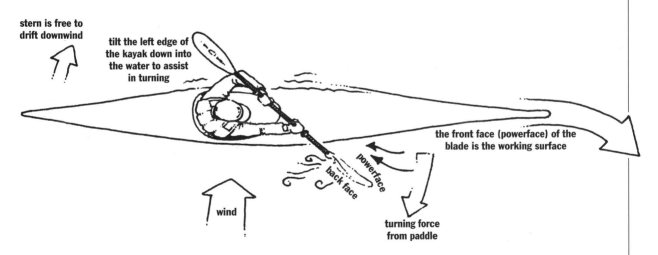

stern is free to drift downwind

tilt the left edge of the kayak down into the water to assist in turning

the front face (powerface) of the blade is the working surface

powerface

back face

wind

turning force from paddle

The bow rudder is preferred when turning the kayak toward an upwind course. The paddle remains still for a rudder strike. The momentum of the kayak moving through the water provides the force. The paddle blade's placement and angle of attack create the desired turning effect.

The stroke known as the bow rudder is a good choice for turning a kayak from broadside to the wind to an upwind heading. The bow-rudder stroke on the upwind side impedes the drift of the bow while allowing the stern to drift downwind. Tilting the kayak downwind will complement the turn and angle the stern to slide easily across the water.

A capable paddler blends the best strokes in the right order at the right time. Sweep strokes, draw strokes, and brace turns will turn a kayak. Turning up into the wind, a sweep stroke on one side can precede a bow-rudder stroke on the opposite side. Turning downwind, a low brace turn can follow a stern-rudder stroke. A low brace turn downwind in steep breaking waves, however, would likely result in a stunning capsize.

Once again, the capable kayaker will seamlessly use several strokes at just the right moments to effect the best turn with the least apparent effort. Applying the best technique involves subtle expertise. Adapting and blending turning strokes to suit specific circumstance is a necessary skill that comes with much practice undertaken in a variety of sea conditions with the aid of a good coach.

Paddling Downwind

Paddling downwind demands a broad range of skills. To maintain a steady heading when paddling downwind, edge the kayak and use turning strokes. In a regular pattern of give and take, a kayak moving downwind in a moderate sea will often veer off course and then swerve back the other way. Course corrections are best made as the kayak crests a wave; anticipate and work with the passing waves.

Paddling in Tidal Current

In deep water, away from the effects of land, tidal currents are evident as moderate changes in sea surface conditions. As with paddling in wind, good technique is needed to maintain progress toward your destination. Closer to shore, currents change in speed and direction, and sea conditions become more complex.

Various tidal currents have characteristics that are of interest to sea kayakers:

- Current traveling over an irregular, shallow seafloor alters the surface of the water, producing standing waves, boils, upwelling, and whirlpools.

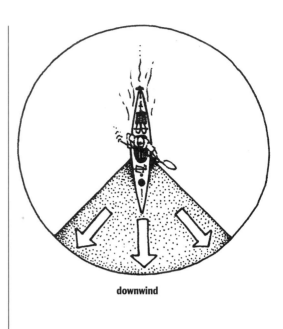

downwind

Downwind includes wind direction from 0400 to 0800 on a circle.

- Where current flows in opposition to the wind, sea conditions can become very rough.
- A current that flows in the same direction as the wind can aid in calming the sea.
- Current in different bodies of water can have different speeds and directions; where these waters meet, there can be tide rips.
- Where a current meets an obstruction, it can change direction and form eddies.

Restrictions in the depth or width of a channel increase the speed of the current, creating turbulence and wave action. In Alaska, the speed of tidal currents in narrow channels can exceed 12 knots. Skookumchuck Narrows, in British Columbia, has a standing wave that reaches 10 feet high. The Strait of Corryvreckan, in Scotland, generates whirlpools fully capable of sucking a kayak to the bottom. Tidal bores run upriver at great speed.

Surge Narrows

Near the end of a ten-day solo trip I was passing through narrow channels and some very fast tidal waters. My destination on the other side of Surge Narrows was the sheltered waters of Octopus Islands Marine Park, British Columbia. The *Sailing Directions* read (paraphrased), "Tidal streams reach 12 knots in Surge Narrows. It is the only navigable passage into Okisollo Channel and the Octopus Islands Marine Park. It has a minimum width of 200 ft. and a midchannel depth of 18 ft. Tusko Rock dries at 4 ft. on the north side of the west end of the passage. At times with the flood stream there is a wall of water 4 ft. high. The duration of slack varies from 5 to 11 minutes."

Excerpts like this really focus your attention and lead to considerable time spent with charts and current tables. It is what we call a crux move; once away from shelter and committed to the passage, bad planning or hesitation may result in calamity. Alone, without the distraction of partners, my mind tends to revisit worst-case scenarios to near obsession. The only relief is to get underway and put a well-laid-out plan into action. As I approached the narrows, the current of the flooding tide was pulling me along the south side of the passage. On the other side of the pass I could see the current flowing in the opposite direction. Slack water here means the 3-knot current travels in every direction at the same time. The most constricted part of the narrows is only visible from a few hundred feet out and as it came into view the current quickened . . . if I capsize I will just roll up . . . if I don't just roll up the current will flush me through to the other side . . . Tusko Rock must be avoided at all cost if I hit that . . . the possibilities play like a broken record through my head. In 4 or 5 knots of current I am on my way through—there is no turning back. A few whirlpools and a small wave make the passage entertaining and not at all malevolent, and I pass into benign waters on the other side.

My attention had been narrow and straight ahead, I had not seen the other kayaker following me through. As he caught up he said, "A little squirrelly through there today, isn't it?"

"You're right—not much slack water around here. Where are you headed?" I replied.

"Oh, I live on the other side of the narrows, and I'm just going to work. That's my fish-boat over there tied up on shore." He paused, twisting around to open a back hatch, and up popped a 8-month-old black Labrador Retriever puppy, happy as a kid on a fairground ride, tongue hanging out, eyes twinkling like abalone shells. "I like to close the hatch on him when we are going through rough water," he said.

On reflection: The pleasures of solo paddling include the opportunity to focus on the surroundings and the satisfaction of accomplishing something on your own. One person's wild wilderness adventure is another person's daily trip to work.

—Doug Alderson

Without a breath of wind, a 4-knot tidal current running along the shore of a steep island creates a tide rip and a safe place to practice maneuvering in current and choppy seas.

wind waves, reflected waves, and standing waves—sometimes all at once. Excellent preparation for these conditions is to learn basic whitewater paddling and rescue skills and surf-kayak techniques. Whitewater and surf kayaking are all about angle of attack, motion of the water and the kayak, tilt of the kayak, and timing. While the expert surf kayaker or whitewater rodeo paddler is a master of angle, motion, tilt, and timing, the touring sea kayaker needs to know the fundamentals.

For the most part, sea kayakers can wait for tidal currents to subside or skirt around the hazards of fast-moving water, but even the most cautious paddler must eventually submit to paddling through a tide rip. The natural environment that the sea kayaker inhabits is too dynamic and chaotic to permit perfect predictions. Plans must allow a wide margin for variability. Capable paddlers have the skills in reserve for unexpected sea conditions.

All of these extreme tidal currents attract kayak adventurers. Although most sea kayakers touring along a coast give these waterways a wide berth, there are substantial currents in many of the inland waterways most attractive to touring kayakers. The reversing nature of tidal currents means that twice a day, the current will slow to a stop and change direction. Tidal currents in a variety of popular sea kayaking destinations regularly run over 5 knots.

Currents of 3 knots or more running against winds of 15 knots will raise rough sea conditions, with the possibility of steep and breaking standing waves. Unlike the more rounded deep-water waves, standing waves in narrow passages demand excellent paddling technique, similar to that required for surf and for whitewater rivers.

The coastal sea kayaker will encounter chaotic water that includes tide rips,

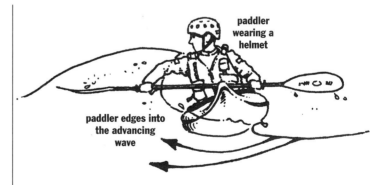

paddler wearing a helmet

paddler edges into the advancing wave

In waves steep enough to present stability problems, the forces on a kayak often turn it sideways (broached) to the wave, at which point a breaking wave will push it sideways. To maintain stability, the paddler must edge into the advancing wave. The kayak's leading edge is raised, allowing the kayak to move over the water. If a standing wave is formed by moving water, as in the case of an overfall, and the paddler is moving downstream into the wave, the response needs to be the same: edge and brace into the wave. Be assured that edging the wrong way in any breaking wave will result in a sudden and forceful capsize.

Good edge control is essential in fast tide rips. This paddler is crossing a fast-moving tide rip. The downstream edge of the kayak is tilting to allow the approaching water to flow beneath the kayak. If the upstream edge of the kayak is caught in the current, the kayak will capsize immediately.   (GREG SHEA)

Paddling in Rough Seas

When paddling in open water, you need to be self-reliant. Paddling partners may be close by, but they also must look after themselves. Open-water paddling requires a high level of competence. Unfortunate kayaking incidents often begin with boats and people prepared for a playful paddle near the beach but later finding themselves in conditions that demand more than their ability can provide.

Hazardous combinations of wind, current, and waves can come on unexpectedly. Paddling downwind in good weather, you can make a comfortable course and good speed. Changes in the weather or the sea state can quickly create an unsafe situation. An unskilled or inattentive paddler is in danger of becoming overwhelmed.

Seek out safe but rough locations and practice your techniques with skilled paddling partners. Looking ahead at a wave, the paddler is poised for a quick downstream brace.

Rough sea conditions are considered to have one or more of the following features: waves higher than 3 feet, wind speed greater then 18 knots, current faster than 3 knots. While a 3-foot swell on a calm day is barely noticeable, a short and steep, breaking 3-foot wind wave calls for a paddler's close attention. In combination, 15 knots of wind against a 2-knot current can make for very difficult paddling conditions. Having the skill and judgment to deal with sudden transitions from calm waters to stormy seas is fundamental to sea kayak safety.

Big Waves

The shape of the general wave pattern is of greater interest than the average height of the waves. A sea with long-wavelength, 4-foot swells in deep water is of little concern. A sea filled with short-wavelength, 4-foot wind waves makes for difficult paddling. A moderate 3-foot sea pushed up to 4 feet by an opposing current creates steep, threatening waves. A 4-foot dumping (plunging) breaker on shore is definitely unsafe. The waves of

The best plans and weather forecast will sometimes result in unexpectedly rough conditions. When the 2-knot current turns against a 15-knot breeze, calm seas quickly become more demanding.

concern to kayakers are waves with short wavelengths and steep faces: a steep 3-foot breaking wave can break over a kayaker's head.

In dealing with big waves, stay loose, remain confident, paddle hard, and brace confidently. Hesitation and passivity will let the wave take charge, and you may end up with more opportunities than you want to test your rolls and rescues.

Cross Seas

Cross seas develop where two wave patterns intersect. Cross seas are short, steep, and doubly difficult to handle because they arrive with no discernible pattern. Peaks can rise up without warning, only to suddenly turn into deep troughs. In cross seas, you will be bracing more and paddling less. A cool, confident performance and good balance are necessary to keep upright.

Cross seas near shore are often kicked up where waves cross at an angle to tidal currents. If you are traveling with the wind or current, you will usually pass through the area of cross seas in a short time. Knowledge of the local geography and understanding of the cause of the cross seas and tide rips will calm your nerves and help you stay loose and paddle through.

Surf

Paddlers who travel along an open coast must be able to land and launch through surf. Illness, injury, or a sudden change in weather can alter your plans for landing. No amount of planning will guarantee the destination beach to be surf free.

Handling a 17-foot kayak in surf requires an understanding of surf waves and some well-applied paddling technique. Good choice of technique and correct form is critical in the surf zone. The forces encountered with a modest 3-foot surf wave are sufficient to seriously injure a shoulder or break a boat.

Launching through Surf

It is usually easier to paddle out through the surf than to come in through it. It is also easier to see the size of the waves from the beach. Standing on the beach, the waves are not nearly as intimidating in appearance as they will be from the seat of the kayak. A 4-foot wave is at the height of your chest as you stand on the beach; it is a foot over your head as you paddle out. Viewed from onshore, breaking waves that rise up to cross the horizon are taller than you are. While on shore you have the choice to stay or paddle out. You are deciding whether to leave a position of safety to head into a position of possible risk. Judge the conditions carefully before you push off.

From shore, take plenty of time to watch the pattern of the waves. They come in sets of larger and smaller waves. Larger waves may break once farther out and once again closer

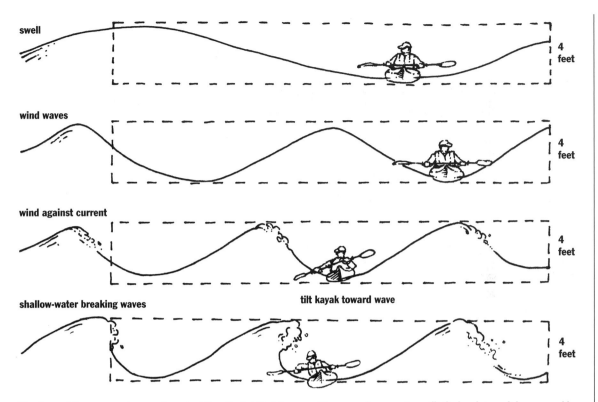

swell

4 feet

wind waves

4 feet

wind against current

4 feet

shallow-water breaking waves

tilt kayak toward wave

4 feet

The shape of the wave may be more important than the height of the wave. When waves become steep, tilt the kayak toward the wave and be prepared to brace into the wave.

Jordan River

It was one of those beautiful winter days on the ocean, clear and cold with very little wind and a clean 4- to 6-foot surf break onto a gently sloping sandy beach. We were sitting outside the break zone taking a rest when we saw it. A wall of green water was moving toward us. By the time we processed this information, we got caught in indecision. "Do I paddle out? Or try to surf in?" I decided to try surfing in.

I paddled hard toward shore to try to get ahead of the break. No such luck; I ended up in a broach surf barreling toward shore with very little control. I simply hung onto my hanging high brace and offered up what prayers I could to the deities of the great ocean. I hit bottom and stayed upright for another second before being unceremoniously left high and dry on the shore. I opened my eyes. There was a bunch of paddling gear scattered over the bay; my buddies hadn't fared so well. I ended up 15 feet past the high-tide line on the road above the beach. I got out, got my car, and headed home.

On reflection: When the unexpected happens, good technique regularly practiced will stand you in good stead. A bit of luck helps to.

—*Michael Pardy*

Launching from a rocky shore can be a challenge. A well-timed push from a buddy may be needed. The last paddler to leave has to get away unaided.

in. Sets of waves may be interspersed with periods of calm.

The shape of the surf is an important consideration. The waves known as spilling waves release their energy slowly and are easier to paddle through. A dumping wave (also called a plunging wave) of the same height releases all its energy in one short, explosive crash and can be truly dangerous. Avoid the dumping surf commonly seen on steep gravel beaches.

Look along the beach and find where the surf breaks with the least violence. Choose a path well clear of large boulders and rocky outcrops. Rip currents, consisting of water that is returning to sea after hitting the beach, create channels of deeper, calmer water that can be a preferred route out through the surf (and also back in). Choose a launch site well clear of other boaters and board surfers.

Once the decision is made to paddle out, wait for a lull between the larger sets, then paddle hard and fast, remaining in the break zone for as little time as possible. If you face a wave larger than expected, the best defense is to paddle hard all the way through the wave. As you approach the crest of the wave, place the paddle low and in line with the kayak so that the face of the wave does not drive the paddle into your body or your face. Cresting the wave, reach to the back side of the wave and take a strong paddle stroke to pull you through.

Paddle hard through big waves. Giving in to the natural urge to stop and gawk at a wall of water coming at you is a sure way to surf backward, or to flip end-over-end backward, or at least to get a remarkable amount of water up your nose. Once through the line of breakers, continue to paddle hard beyond the outer limit where the largest waves break and out to where the swell remains smooth, long, and round.

Landing through Surf

From a position in a kayak off-shore, you have a poor view for determining the size and shape of waves breaking on a beach. It is best to have some knowledge of the beach before attempting a landing through surf. An understanding of the depth profile of the beach will help in determining how the waves are breaking on shore. Study the charts and tide tables. Anticipate which beaches you will be landing on, and the type of surf you can expect to encounter. The surf at low tide may break over a steep gravel bar, but the upper part of the beach may be sandy and flat, producing a much kinder wave-shape at high tide.

Leaving the beach and paddling out through just 3 feet of surf can be a challenge. Make sure all gear is secure on deck before leaving, and paddle hard through the wave.

Even the best-laid plans change through the day, and all manner of circumstances might lead to a landing on an unstudied beach. It can be unnerving to land on an unfamiliar surf beach. But if it is late in the day, and you are tired and hungry, the desire to get ashore can be too much to resist. Before you head in, however, remember that the decision to move forward into the break zone is usually irreversible.

From a position just outside the larger breakers, study the shape of the waves and the layout of the beach. Take careful note of the timing of the wave sets. Clear loose gear off the deck; put on your helmet and your PFD. Try to time the start of your run during a lull or during a set of smaller waves. Then start paddling.

As the bow of the kayak rises with the wave in front of you, lean forward and paddle hard and fast, making all effort to stay ahead of the wave behind you. You really do not want to surf; you want to ride up on the back of the wave that is in front of you. With good judgment, good timing, small waves, and a strong forward stroke, you will arrive at the beach.

If the wave behind is larger or faster than expected, it will catch up with you and pass you. As it approaches, the stern will rise and the kayak will begin to accelerate. The conservative choice is to slow the kayak and let the wave pass beneath you. Once again, try to ride in close to the back of the new wave now immediately in front of you. If the bow begins to bury into the trough, however, the bow may suddenly stop, allowing the stern to catch up and pass over the bow in a spectacular end-over-end capsize (known as pearling). The recovery from an end-over-end capsize in deep water can be a straightforward roll after the wave has passed. (A wet exit leads to a potentially dangerous situation.)

If the wave is large, it may have too much power. You will have to turn, lean hard toward the wave, and place a strong brace into the breaking crest, bringing the kayak into a broach, broadside to the wave. A very large

When caught sideways in a breaking wave, lean boldly toward the wave and high brace. This is quite a stable position. The paddler will side-slip up onto the beach to jump out of the kayak as the wave recedes.

With a good brace, a broached sea kayak is remarkably stable. Broaching a sea kayak before a breaking wave is a commitment move; once done, it is difficult to get out of the wave before you arrive near the beach. There is limited control of a loaded sea kayak broached before a breaking wave. Hopefully your prior planning included a wide lane clear of rocks, swimmers, and other paddlers.

Once ashore, quickly exit the cockpit with paddle in hand, grab the bow line, and pull the kayak free of the water. Always exit your kayak on the seaward side. The steeper the beach, the more important it is to get out quickly. A steep gravel or cobble beach can present considerable difficulty and hazard as you try to get out of the cockpit and make your way up the beach. As you stand ankle-deep in the swash, the next wave may arrive as deep as your waist. That wave is likely to fill the cockpit and make for a very heavy kayak; it might also pick up the kayak and fling it toward you.

wave might require a high brace; keep your elbows in close to your body. With the kayak now parallel with the wave, moving rapidly sideways toward shore, continue bracing confidently onto the wave and keep the kayak well-tilted toward the wave. It will be a bouncy and frothy ride, but with good bracing and tilting technique, this is a safe procedure preferred for large waves.

Whenever you are on shore and attempting to help a paddler coming in through the

The Probe

The surf was dumping 4-foot waves onto a gravel beach. I was with a couple of friends on a short trip along the open coast. My friends had designated me *probe*, which meant that I had to check out the landing first.

All went well as I waited and timed my landing to coincide with a smaller set of waves. I paddled hard onto the beach, undid my sprayskirt, and made my mistake. I threw my paddle up on the beach, away from the water. The inertia of tossing the paddle sent my

kayak sliding backward into the dumping surf. Needless to say, the ending was spectacular, with me being ground into the stones, along with my kayak. My friends had a good laugh that evening. They had enjoyed a front row seat to my folly.

On reflection: Newton was right: for every action there is an equal and opposite reaction.

—Michael Pardy

surf, stay out of the path of the oncoming kayak. Even on a flat, quiet beach, the wake of a passing boat can create a substantial wave. If you observe this safety procedure even on the calm days, you will react that way automatically during the stress of rough conditions, when standing in the way of an advancing kayak spells real danger.

Leadership in the Surf

A system of leadership can help a group of sea kayakers launch and land through surf.

For landing, one of the better paddlers experienced in surf heads in first. Once ashore, this paddler becomes the beachmaster. Looking seaward, this person has a better view of the size and shape of the waves. The beachmaster signals the next paddler where and when to start a run into the beach. As the second paddler arrives, the beachmaster helps get both paddler and kayak safely up the beach. Other members come in according to the beachmaster's signals.

The group uses the same process to leave the beach. The beachmaster gets ready at the shore and takes a helpful push off the beach. Once outside the break zone, the paddler waits for others to follow. The beachmaster can watch for lulls in the sets and send each paddler out to the others waiting outside the surf.

Confidence and safe technique in the surf can only be gained by regular practice in gradually increasing increments of difficulty. A plastic whitewater kayak, or shorter plastic general-purpose kayak, may be the best for practice in the surf. Long fiberglass sea kayaks are not engineered to stand up to mistakes in the surf zone.

Here are some safety tips for getting through the surf:

- Wear a PFD, for flotation and for body protection.
- Wear a helmet.
- Learn to roll.
- Launch and land one at a time to avoid collisions.
- Keep the paddle low when cresting a wave to avoid shoulder and face injuries.
- Keep your elbows low and near your body to maintain strong shoulder posture.
- Clear your deck of extraneous gear.
- Clear away any loose lines and tethers.
- Always stay seaward of your kayak when getting in, getting out, assisting, or swimming.
- Be prepared to make it to shore on your own; rescues in surf are not always possible.

Navigation

6

Navigation is the art and science of keeping track of where you are and judging a safe route to where you want to be. The concerns of navigation range from the larger issues of a weeklong trip down to the immediate details of entering a busy harbor; a navigator's work is never done. The slow-moving, hand-powered nature of a sea kayak poses significant navigational challenges. Coastal navigation seldom deals with the concerns of being lost; more often it aims to identify and avoid environmental dangers.

Kayak travel and navigation is subject to the chaotic interplay of wind, current, and waves. It's as if, while you drive a car on land, the hills were to undulate and the asphalt beneath your tires glide along like an escalator. In kayak navigation there is seldom a straight course to be found. A good deal of choosing the best route lies in observing the action of your kayak and the movement of the water. Interactions of contending currents create local anomalies, as does the interplay of a current with irregular features on the coastline or the ocean bottom. Careful observation of the sea surface yields useful navigational information.

The front deck of a kayak is a poor navigational table; there is no room to deploy the basic tools. Most or all of the technical navigation must be done before leaving the beach. Once under way, the kayak navigator must rely on timely observation and ongoing reassessment of the original route plan.

Coastal navigation from the cockpit of a kayak is more refined art than technical science. Once mastered, good navigation, like good judgment, can function at an uncon-

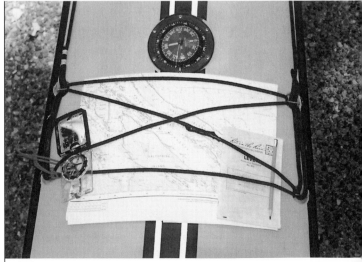

The kayak navigator has room on deck for little more than a chart, a compass, and a notebook.

scious level. As with good paddling skills, the outward appearance can be deceptive and should not be confused with intuition or good luck. The knack of knowing where you are and judging the best route ahead requires thorough planning, keen observation, and frequent reassessment.

Tools for Navigation

On the tiny wave-washed deck of a kayak there is limited space for the tools for navigation. Tools must be small, sturdy, and water-proof. The principle tools are nautical chart, topographical maps, compass, reference materials, and, increasingly, a GPS.

Nautical Charts and Topographic Maps

Nautical charts describe marine waterways and are designed specifically for marine navigation. Topographic maps describe the land. The intents of navigation on the sea and route finding on land are the same, but some of the tools and processes are different. The sea kayak travels along the border of the land and

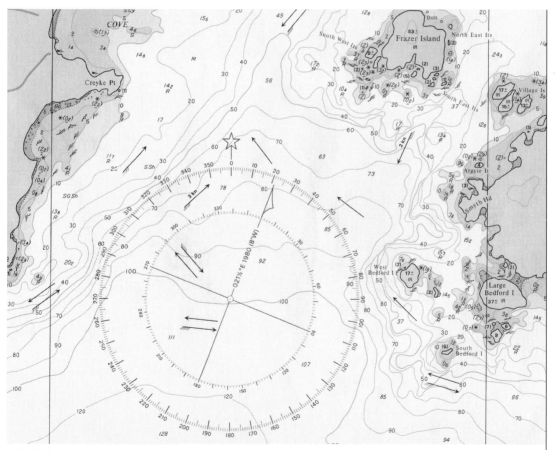

Nautical charts show both true and magnetic bearings on the compass rose. The kayaker can work with a marine deck compass and magnetic compass bearings without the need to account for local magnetic deviation (boaters call this variation) and convert to true directions. Nautical charts provide information on current speed and direction, water hazards, water depths, and a wide variety of other detailed information for the maritime navigator.

(CANADIAN HYDROGRAPHIC SERVICES)

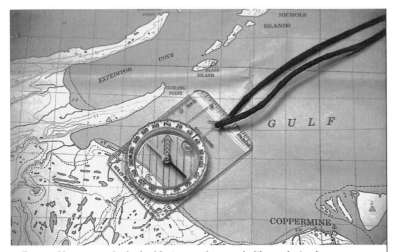

Topographic maps emphasize land features and are used with an orienteering compass.

1:80,000 covers twice the area and will not have to be refolded every couple of hours, but the detail is not sufficient to distinguish small islets or a beach just the right size for kayak camping. It is best to study the more detailed charts at home or on the beach and transfer pertinent information onto a chart that covers more area, which can then be folded on deck. Keys to topo map symbols are given on the front or back of each map. The symbols on marine charts are defined in a booklet called Chart No. 1, which is no longer available directly from the U.S. government but can be purchased in several commercial editions.

A chart's primary use in visual daytime navigation is to identify coastal land features, for which purpose a chart a few years old might suffice. However, lights and beacons and other aids to navigation can change.

the sea, so kayak navigation uses a combination of marine and land-based methods. Both nautical charts and topographic maps are useful sources of information.

Nautical charts have a compass rose showing both true and magnetic north. They also show longitude and latitude, the locations of aids to navigation, water depths, and principal heights of near-shore land features. Distance scales on the chart include nautical miles, land miles, and kilometers.

Topographic maps also indicate both true and magnetic north and give longitude and latitude. They are measured in statute miles or kilometers and show physical and geographic features. They include more information on heights of land than a nautical chart, but little or no information on water depths. The specifics of your destination will dictate whether charts, maps, or a combination of the two provide the best choice of information.

Charts and maps are printed in various scales. Typically a chart with a 1:40,000 scale shows sufficient detail for good sea kayak navigation. When folded into a watertight case on deck, the visible portion of the chart may show an area 5 miles by 7 miles. Traveling in a straight line, a sea kayaker can cross this part of the chart in an hour or two. A scale of

Study charts and tide tables while onshore. Make notes on the charts or in your notebook to review while paddling.

(DOUG LLOYD)

Looking Back

The first sea kayaking trip I took with Michael Pardy was in the Canadian Arctic. We were heading out beyond the Barrier Islands of Coronation Gulf to Klenenberg Bay. Michael is an experienced arctic traveler and guide. He has canoed a considerable number of miles of fresh water following the contour lines on his topographic maps. On the other hand, I have always lived on a coastal island, and a nautical chart has been my constant companion.

I had looked over the chart and made my usual notes and plans. We discussed the distances and the times it would take to make necessary landfalls. Likely campsites were selected, and we had good local information. Our marine VHF radios were useless; there was no one to call. With our kayaks heavily packed for many days away, we pushed off from shore. Three hours later, we were making our first landing when I noticed Michael looking back for what must have been the tenth time.

The beach was gravel and sloped up to the 15-foot summit of a flat, featureless island. From the top of the beach I looked back to see what was so interesting to Michael. It was quite a shock: there was nothing there. From our treeless island, without mountains and without any altitude to speak of, the mainland had disappeared. All references to my chart had vanished. But in the far distance, well behind the now invisible shoreline we had so recently departed, there appeared two angular escarpments. These huge features of the landscape showed clearly on Michael's topo map, though not on my chart.

On reflection: Different environments require different tools and experience.

—*Doug Alderson*

When traveling in unfamiliar or hazardous waters or making a long nighttime crossing, use the most recent edition of a chart.

Compass

A compass does much more than indicate a direction of travel. A good navigator will keep a close eye on the compass. With a watch, a compass, and a chart, a navigator can:

- Fix his or her position using cross bearings.
- Determine boat speed by measuring changes in position or changes in the bearing to a fixed object over time.
- Estimate the effect of wind and/or current by comparing his or her course (intended direction of travel) with heading (the actual direction the boat is pointing in order to achieve that course).

- Detect a change in the wind by noting its compass heading over time.
- Detect a change in the current by comparing your course and your heading over time.
- Identify landmarks by comparing his or her bearings to them with data on the chart.
- Approximate the time of day by the sun's bearing.

GPS Unit

A Global Positioning System receiver can be useful in conjunction with all the other navigation tools and techniques. The unit can pinpoint your location, and it can permit accurate measurements of speed and distance. Using GPS information, you can accurately log the locations of freshwater sources, open-water crossings, campsites, and other points of interest, and program these before your trip as *waypoints* in the receiver.

A GPS unit is subject to the vagaries of any electronic device exposed to a marine environment. The unit can be great for planning while on the beach, but it has less practical value while at sea with a paddle in hand.

Although a GPS receiver is a powerful tool, its ready use on deck is limited. A GPS receiver has particular value to the sea kayaker in low-visibility conditions, out of sight of land, along nondescript coastlines, and in high latitudes, where compasses perform poorly.

Publications

A variety of publications provide valuable navigational information. Government agencies publish books with such titles as *Sailing Directions*, *Coast Pilot*, and *Small Craft Guide*. Much of the information in these books relates to commercial shipping, but they also contain material useful to the kayaker. Regional weather patterns and hazardous sea conditions are described, along with coastal marine facilities. Government navigational publications are updated regularly. Parks departments, forest services, and other land managers produce maps and guidebooks with useful information for camping on shore. (See Resources in the appendix.)

Commercially published guidebooks for the recreational sailor, fisherman, hiker, and kayaker focus on smaller details that can have considerable value to the touring kayaker. The material in a guidebook is only as good as the author's experience and research, however, and of course the information is current only to the date of the research.

Tide and tide current tables are published for many geographic regions. Each volume contains daily tide height and time data for listed reference stations. Current tables con-

tain daily predictions for the times of maximum velocity and directions of flow.

Current atlases can be acquired for a few areas, such as the San Juan Islands of northwest Washington state and the Gulf Islands of southern Vancouver Island, British Columbia. These publications are tremendously useful, but it is important to remember that the information is based on the main flow of the current in the larger channels. Traveling close along the shore, the kayaker can encounter significant variations in the speed and direction of the current.

Aids to Navigation

An aid to navigation is any device external to a vessel intended to assist a navigator in determining position and a safe course. In populated areas there are a number of these—marine signs, beacons, buoys, and lights—to guide the passage of marine traffic. The shallow draft of a kayak means that kayakers can avoid the shipping lanes and instead navigate shoal backwaters and eddies. Paddling in the margins, you can use the beacons and lights as an aid to avoiding the hazards of fast-moving traffic and in keeping on course when visibility is reduced.

To be of use, aids to navigation must be correctly identified. Daytime aids are identified by their location, shape, color, and markings. Nighttime aids use illumination as the principal means of identification. They are known by the sequence or pattern and duration of light, and by their color.

Buoys and beacons warn the navigator of some danger or obstruction and point out the limits of safe travel. The location of each buoy or beacon indicates the direction of the danger it marks relative to the safe course. In the Western Hemisphere, green buoys mark the port side of a channel for boats returning from seaward or progressing in a generally clockwise fashion around the coast of North and

South America; red buoys indicate the starboard side. If traveling elsewhere in the world, familiarize yourself with the local system, and always use a chart as the final authority on where a hazard lies. Buoys also are used to mark rocks, shoals, islets, and other dangers in and near open sea.

Different than lateral markers that indicate the outer limits of the safe channel, cardinal buoys indicate the location of the safe passage relative to the position of the buoy. A north cardinal marker (see accompanying art) indicates that safe passage is to the north (true compass bearing) of the buoy. Cardinal buoys are used to mark offshore, rocks, shoals, islets, and other dangers in and near the open sea.

Rules of the Road

Yachts and large vessels are required to have running lights. To the observer, running lights give a good indication of a vessel's direction of travel. The rules say that if you see a vessel's red running light, you are required to yield the right-of-way. If you see a vessel's green running light, you have the right-of-way. But the practical reality is that kayaks yield the right-of-way to all craft not propelled by human power. You may have right of way under the law, but the awful consequence of a collision with almost any other vessel warrants great caution.

When you cross paths with a motorized vessel, make your intentions clear. Any

The shape of the top features on a cardinal buoy indicates the location of the safe passage relative to the position of the buoy. This west cardinal buoy (two cones in) indicates to the skipper of a larger vessel that the safe passage is to the west (true compass bearing) of the buoy. The shapes of the cones for the cardinal directions are given in the accompanying diagram.

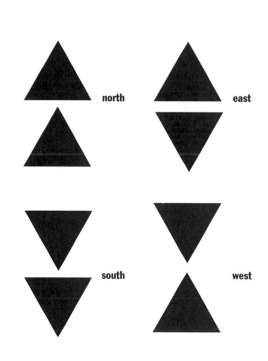

Cardinal markers indicate fair passage to the indicated cardinal (true compass) direction. The shape of the cones indicates the direction of safe passage.

Lateral markers indicate by their shape and color the outer limits of the safe passage. This marker is green and has a flat top indicating that for safe passage a larger vessel passes this port-hand lateral marker leaving it on the left (port) side of the vessel. Colors of lateral marks depend on the navigation region you are traveling in. This port-hand lateral mark is in Region B, which includes the Americas and the Caribbean.

Whales always have right of way. (GREG SHEA)

Not all marine traffic is boats. Sea planes have landing and take-off lanes marked on charts.

changes in your course should be sufficiently obvious that the captain of the vessel understands your intentions. Slowing down just a bit to let a vessel pass, for example, is not as clear and obvious as coming to a complete stop.

Dead Reckoning

Dead reckoning (DR) is the process of determining your position from a previously known position and intervening measurements of your time, direction, and speed of travel. You can use dead reckoning to estimate a present position from a past one or a future position from a present one. In either instance, a DR position is only as good as the previous position and time/speed/distance measurements from which it is calculated. It should also be noted that a DR position makes no allowance for wind or current. Careful observations and recorded notes of course and heading may reveal the effects of wind or current, which your subsequent navigation can then take into consideration. Adjusting a DR position based on assumptions about current and drift results in an *estimated position*.

When a dark night or dense fog obscures all visual references, the navigator must rely on dead reckoning. In the absence of sensitive and accurate electronic navigational instrumentation, a kayak travels an unsteady speed along a wavering course. A good paddler might be able to maintain a steady speed of 3 knots plus or minus 10 percent, and in a calm

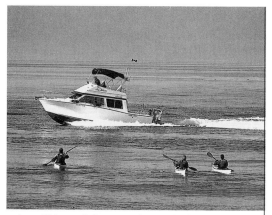

Large high-speed pleasure craft are a significant danger to anyone in a small boat. Kayaks can often travel in the shallow water out of the regular traffic lanes but cross a common route with great care. (GREG SHEA)

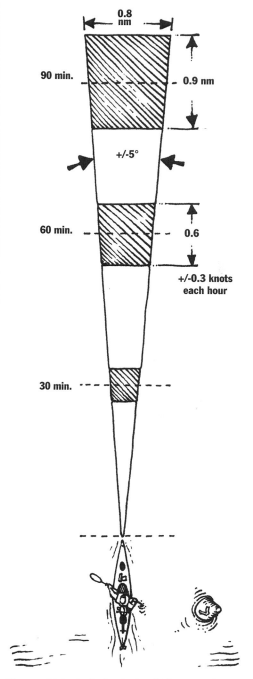

sea with a good deck compass, he or she might be able to steer a particular course within 5 degrees on either side. After just thirty minutes, the potential error in distance traveled is as much as three-tenths of a mile, and cumulative course error could be almost as high. Clearly, a paddler must take every opportunity to confirm his dead reckoning by reference to charted objects: nav aids, a bold headland, etc.

Piloting

Piloting is the navigation of a vessel in nearshore and confined waters with frequent reference to geographic features and aids to navigation. Piloting is the formal name for the usual way of getting around.

Estimating Distance

Over open water, a kayaker's horizon is approximately 1.5 miles away. The crest of a beach 9 feet above the water is just visible at a distance of 4.5 miles. During a long crossing, the elevation of an isolated island can provide information about position.

The uncertainty of a dead reckoning plot increases the longer the paddler relies on it. The shaded areas represent the increasing inaccuracy of the dead reckoning position of a paddler moving at 3 knots.

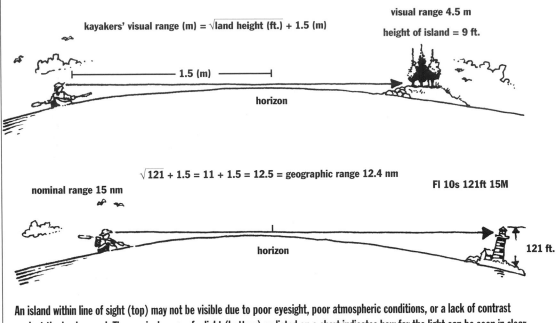

An island within line of sight (top) may not be visible due to poor eyesight, poor atmospheric conditions, or a lack of contrast against the background. The nominal range of a light (bottom) as listed on a chart indicates how far the light can be seen in clear conditions without consideration for the curvature of the earth. Fl 10s 121ft 15M indicates a light at a height of 121 ft. flashing every 10 seconds with a nominal range of 15 nautical miles. From the seat of a kayak, the light will come into view at 12.4 nm.

Visual estimates of distance across the water give uncertain results, but familiar objects such as buildings or trees can still provide helpful estimates. Atmospheric conditions such as rain, haze, or radiating heat can spoil a good guess. The best way to know how far it is to a destination is to know your position and measure the distance off the chart.

Lines of Position

When two stationary objects fall in line from your vantage point, one directly behind the other, you have established a *range*. If the two objects happen to show on your topo map or chart, your range is one example of a *line of position* (LOP). When your course keeps the two objects in line, you know you are traveling along the range line. Draw a line through the objects and extend it toward your presumed location. Your position must be somewhere along that line.

One well-chosen range may confirm a safe course into a narrow passage but is not sufficient to fix a position. A second LOP that intersects the first will establish your approximate position. Lines of position can be established not only with ranges but also by using compass bearings to charted, stationary features in the water or on shore. A hilltop, a water tower, a navigation buoy, and a headland are all good candidates for a LOP. Occasionally you'll come across special navigational ranges established to accurately indicate a line of position in a complex waterway.

Aiming Off

Aiming off is a technique used in conditions of low visibility to account for normal errors in dead reckoning that can carry you unpredictably to one side or the other of your intended destination. To aim off, deliberately set your course to miss the destination either wide

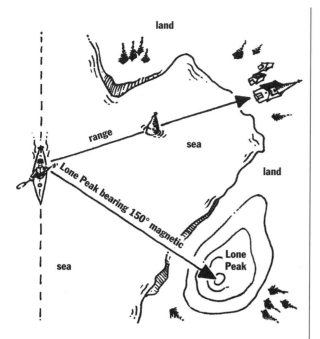

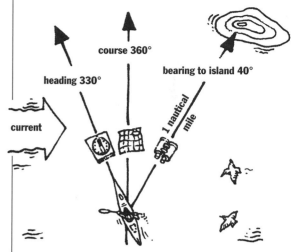

A range—one example of a line of position—can be established by visually lining up any two natural features, shore structures, or aids that appear on your chart or topo map. More generally, a compass bearing to any mapped or charted feature makes a line of position. You can fix your position by intersecting two lines of position; as here, where a range line is crossed with a bearing. If your distance from a charted feature is known, a single line of position will fix your position.

It is important to be understood clearly when communicating navigational information. The terms heading, course, and bearing have distinct meanings. The heading is the direction the kayak is pointed, the course is the direction made good as a result of all factors, and a bearing is the compass direction to any identified point of reference. In the diagram, the kayak is pointed on a heading of 330°, but pushed sideways by the current will travel on a resulting course of 360°. The bearing to the small island may be used as a line of position and will provide a fix if its distance off is also known.

to the left or wide to the right. That way, when you arrive at the shore, you'll know which direction to turn to reach your objective.

In conjunction with aiming off, determine a *backstop* that will provide a known and definite limit to forward progress—a point at which you must turn one way or the other. The shore itself commonly serves as the backstop. After turning at the backstop, the final step is to follow a *handrail* to your destination. Again, the shore often also serves as the handrail.

Collision Course

To determine if you are on a collision course with another vessel, take a compass bearing to its position. If that bearing does not change

while the distance between you decreases, you will collide.

The bearing can also be determined as the angle between your bow and the other vessel. A visual bearing, a paddle pointed in the direction of the vessel, or an outstretched arm will generally be sufficient to determine a bow angle. If the angle decreases over time, the vessel will pass in front of you. If the angle increases, you will pass in front of the other vessel. If the angle remains the same, you could collide. If either vessel changes course or speed, the potential for collision also changes.

Many ships travel at high speed and approach deceptively fast; constant vigilance is required.

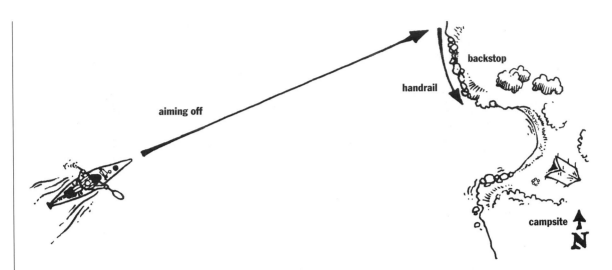

Aiming off—deliberately setting your course to miss your destination to one side or the other, and then turning toward the destination—provides a greater chance of achieving a destination than simply aiming for it. In this example the kayaker has purposefully steered a course to the north so that a right turn will lead to the campsite. Aiming off assures the campsite will be to the south. The coastline acts as a backstop—a definite limit, a place where a turn must be executed—for the paddler, and as well as a handrail—a guiding path.

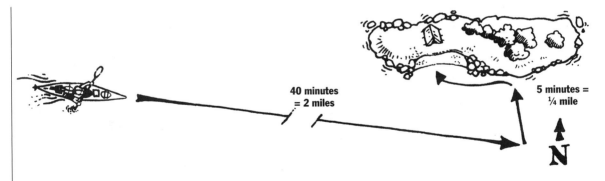

In this example the kayaker is using the clock as the first backstop and the length of the island as a second backstop. The kayaker knows it is 2 miles to the island. Paddling at 3 knots on an ESE course the kayaker needs to turn north after 45 minutes. Paddling north will bring the paddler to the coastline—his second backstop and handrail—at which time he will turn west and paddle until reaching the campsite. In very dense fog, he might miss the campsite. While following the shoreline, if his course turns to the north he has gone too far.

Navigating through Tidal Currents

The relationship between the rising and falling of the tide and the changing direction of the current is not as obvious as is often thought. The complexities of geography can have a significant distorting effect. In some locations, the incoming current can persist well after the time of high water, and in other locations, the current can persist in one direction throughout the entire cycle of high and low water. It is for this reason that tide and current tables explicitly give two sets of tables, one that gives the height of the tide, and another that gives the speed and direction of the current. The terms *ebb*

Crossing (Barely) to Safety

On a trip to Baja, I began my paddle to Isla Espíritu Santo with a 4-mile crossing right through a shipping lane that leads to La Paz, the biggest port on the peninsula. I wanted to make an early start to avoid thermal winds that might kick up later in the morning, so I was packed and on the water before the sun rose above the horizon. In a short while, I approached a buoy that marked one side of the shipping lane. The other side of the lane, about a mile away, was also marked with a buoy.

Looking southeast toward the rising sun, I could barely make out a white speck on the horizon. I didn't know what kind of ship it was, but I wasn't too worried. It would take me only 20 minutes at most to cross the shipping lane.

As I paddled, the ship grew rapidly larger to my eye. It was a cruise liner steaming full speed into La Paz. I found it difficult to tell exactly where the ship's bow was pointing in relation to where I was paddling. It seemed to be coming right for me, getting bigger all the time. By the time I reached the buoy on the far side of the shipping lane, the liner had crossed directly behind me.

On the beach that night I felt compelled to do the math. From the seat of my kayak on a bright, clear day without the sun in my eyes, a full-size ship with an upper deck 49 feet above the water will be barely visible 8.5 nautical miles away (take the square root of 49, then add 1.5 miles). If the ship is traveling at 25 knots (a typical cruising speed for such a vessel), it will cover those 8.5 miles in approximately 20 minutes—as fast as I could cross the 1-mile channel in my kayak. This was a race that I barely won.

On reflection: Big ships travel fast, and kayakers cannot see very far.

—*John Montgomery*

and *flood* can be ambiguous, and the rise and fall of the tide needs to be distinguished from the changing direction and speed of the current.

When currents occur as slow-moving, large bodies of water, the effect is to alter your speed and direction of travel. Common navigational skills for dead reckoning can measure and predict the net effect of a current. With a watch, a chart, and a compass, you can log successive positions and times, and from these compute a speed made good and compare that with your known average paddling speed. Any significant difference between these is a good sign of the presence of an otherwise undetected current.

The simplicity of kayak travel is part of its attraction, so keep your calculations for navigation simple. Approximate results are all

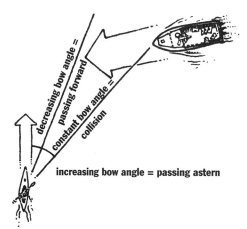

If the bow angle between your kayak and a passing vessel remains constant over time, the two vessels are on a collision course. If the bow angle decreases, the other vessel will pass in front of you. If the bow angle increases, the vessel will pass astern.

you need. Accurate calculations are not necessarily desirable and may not tell the truth. Kayaks do not travel in straight lines for long distances, and their slow pace means that tidal currents are likely to change while on the water. A kayak traveling near shore encounters currents that are highly variable in space as well as time.

50/90 Rule: Speed of Tidal Current

In confined waterways tidal currents build to a maximum velocity, then slow to a time of slack water, and then turn and reverse direction to build to a maximum velocity in the opposite direction.

In the first third of a current cycle, the current will increase to 50 percent of its maximum velocity.

In the second third of the cycle, the current will increase to 90 percent of its maximum velocity.

The current will slow down in a similar manner—first to 90 percent of its maximum, then to 50 percent, and finally to slack water before turning direction again.

For example:

Tide turns 1300. Max flood at 1600, 4 knots.

At 1400 (1300 + 1 hour) the estimated current is 0.5 X 4 = 2 knots.

At 1500 (1300 + 2 hours) the estimated current is 0.9 X 4 = 3.6 knots.

Slow-Water Rule: Duration of Slack Water

The tidal current will remain below 0.5 knots for as long as it takes the maximum predicted currents (before and after the predicted time of slack) to travel 1 nautical mile each.

For example:

Tide turns 0300. Max flood at 0900, 4 knots.

Tide turns 1600. Max ebb at 2100, 3 knots.

To estimate the duration of slack water near 1600:

Duration of slack before 1600 (60 ÷ 4 = 15 minutes).

Duration of slack after 1600 (60 ÷ 3 = 20 minutes).

Total duration of slack near 1600 (15 + 20 = 35 minutes).

Estimating the height of the tide becomes important near shallow water and when camped on gently sloping beaches. The lowering of tide height over a shallow reef or sand bar can cause waves to break where only swell existed an hour ago. In local areas where currents run in shallow water, the maximum current velocity may occur out of time with predictions for the deeper main channel. Waking in the morning on a shallow beach to find the water several hundred yards away makes for difficult launching. Camped in a small cove backed up to a steep shore, it is always prudent to estimate the height of the midnight tide as com-

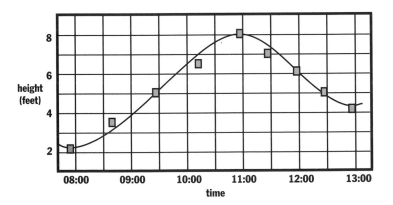

In regions of moderate tidal range, simple interpolation provides a reasonable estimate of the height of tide at any given time. (The Pacific basin has predominantly mixed diurnal tides with unequal tide heights and durations, which complicates these calculations.) The dots represent the estimates for a tidal exchange of 6 feet over 5 hours, determined by interpolating, ¼ of the tide height in ¼ of the time and ½ of the tide height in ½ of the time. Maximum error at ¼ of the cycle is less than 10 percent of the tide height.

pared to the floor of your tent. Good approximations for the height of the tide are usually quite sufficient.

Ferry Angles

To make a steady course across a current, the kayak must take a heading that compensates for the moving water. When the current is directly in line with an intended course, no compensation is necessary, and determining speed made good is a simple matter of adding the speed of the current to the boat speed if the current is going with the kayak, or subtracting it if the current opposes the kayak. But when the current is at an angle to the intended course, determination of an adjusted heading and the resultant speed requires some navigation work.

Navigating across moving tidal water may require determining a ferry angle.   (GREG SHEA)

Steering off course to compensate for the effects of current is called *ferrying*. The difference between your actual heading and your desired course made good is called the *ferry angle*.

It's impractical to figure a precise ferry angle for a kayak because the boat travels so slowly and the overriding current flow may be punctuated by whirlpools, back eddies, and boils. Furthermore, in moderate waves, a deck compass on a kayak is constantly swinging and an accurate course is difficult to maintain. An error of just 10 degrees over 3 miles will put the paddler half a mile off course. Practiced and informed judgment will make amends for many of the confounding influences, however. Regardless of the many difficulties, ferrying remains the best way of getting close to your destination.

In most cases, a kayak's ferry angle is determined using natural ranges—that is, by staying on a heading that keeps your kayak on a straight line between two stationary objects,

such as a buoy and a lighthouse. As long as you stay on this natural range, you are compensating for changes in currents.

When crossings take longer than one hour, the tidal current will vary significantly and precise navigation is difficult. Long crossings over channels with tidal current require special skills and knowledge. Most importantly, long crossings in low visibility carry a high level of risk. When visibility is reduced due to darkness or fog, more technical navigational methods must be used.

Following are two formulas that provide good approximations for ferry angles:

For a current from abeam:
ferry angle = (speed of current ÷ paddling speed) x 60 degrees.

The above formula provides a good approximation of the ferry angle where the relative angle of the current is estimated as coming from abeam. To make a course of 300 degrees into a 1.2 knot beam current coming at right angles, where the paddler is going at 3 knots:

$$\text{ferry angle} = (1.2 \div 3) \times 60$$
$$= 24 \text{ degrees}$$

To maintain a desired course of 300 degrees, the paddler must ferry 24 degrees into the current—taking a heading of 276 degrees.

For a quartering current:
ferry angle = (speed of current ÷ paddling speed) x 40 degrees

The formula above provides a good approximation of the ferry angle where the relative angle of the current is estimated as coming from the stern quarter. To make a course of 60 degrees into a 1.5-knot quartering current coming from the stern quarter where the paddler is going at 3 knots:

$$\text{ferry angle} = (1.5 \div 3) \times 40$$
$$= 20 \text{ degrees}$$

To maintain a desired course of 60 degrees, the paddler must ferry 20 degrees into the current—taking a heading of 80 degrees.

The formulas above for determining the

ferry angle are an approximation that provide good results for ferry angles less than 40 degrees. They don't provide any information about the resultant speed made good as a result of the current and ferry angle.

In most cases visual piloting methods are used to confirm and correct for errors in determining ferry angles. The increased accuracy of vector solutions may be of advantage in situations of low visibility or for long passages that span the time of significant changes in current velocity and direction. Vector solutions are also used to determine the speed made good as a result of the current and the ferry angle.

When ferrying across a current, the speed the kayak makes over the bottom is different than the paddling speed. The speed over the bottom is referred to as "speed made good." You need to determine the speed made good in order to calculate the time it will take to paddle a given distance. Use vector solutions when you need to determine speed made good and when planning a long crossing of several hours across a changing tidal current. Vector solutions can be made for each hour of a long crossing, thereby providing the paddler with new course corrections and time estimates for each hour as the current changes in speed and direction. There are no calculations for vector solutions, the method is entirely graphic.

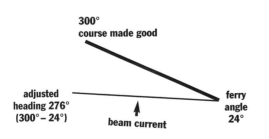

Determining ferry angles in a beam current: if you know your speed and the speed and direction of the current, you can determine a course to steer that compensates for the beam current (see text).

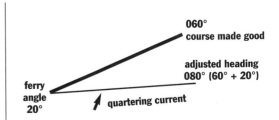

Determining ferry angles in a quartering current: if you know your speed and the speed and direction of the current, you can determine a course to steer that compensates for the current coming at your stern quarter (see text).

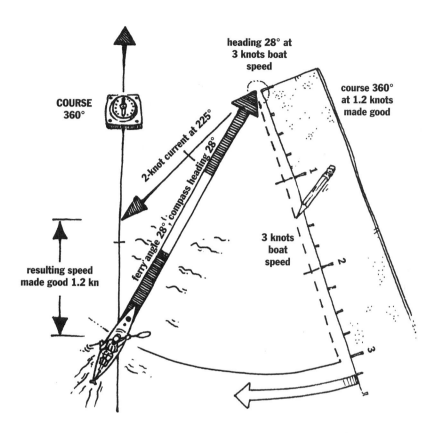

Ferry angle and speed made good can be determined using vector solutions. In this example, the kayaker is paddling into a 2-knot current running at 225°. Heading and speed are determined in the following manner. 1. Draw a line to represent the direction of the intended course. The length of the line does not matter. 2. Draw a vector at an angle and length that represents the current (2 knots at 225° in this case). The arrowhead that represents the current direction touches the course. 3. From the tail of the current vector, swing a vector that represents the paddling speed (3 knots in this case) until it meets course line. 4. The length of the resulting third side of the triangle represents the resulting speed made good (1.2 kn). 5. The direction of the boat speed vector (28° in this case) is the compass course required to make the necessary ferry angle. (Note: the units of length do not matter in this sketch: all that is necessary is that you are consistent from one line to the next when measuring.)

- With a standard boat speed (paddling speed) of 3 knots, the ferry angle will be 30 degrees. Making a straight-line course with an upstream ferry angle of 30 degrees, speed made good will be 2.6 knots. The crossing will take 46 minutes.

- If you increase your boat speed to 3.5 knots, the new ferry angle will be about 25 degrees and the resultant speed made good will be 3.2 knots. The crossing will take 38 minutes—*8 minutes faster* than with a boat speed of 3 knots.

- If you decrease your boat speed to 2.5 knots, the new ferry angle will be 37 degrees (approximately) and the resultant speed made good will be 2 knots. The crossing will take 60 minutes—*14 minutes longer* than with a boat speed of 3 knots.

- With a boat speed of 3 knots but with no ferry angle—simply letting the current push the kayak off course—the channel will be crossed in 40 minutes, but the kayak will have drifted 1 mile downstream. It will take an additional 40-minute paddle against the current to reach the intended destination. The full crossing will take 80 minutes—*34 minutes longer* than if you had used a ferry angle.

A modest increase in paddling speed from 3 to 3.5 knots gives good results, and maintaining a correct ferry angle puts that speed to good use. Time spent in the current and in the traffic of the channel is reduced. Paddling slower, or drifting with the current, adds considerable time to the crossing. In a busy shipping lane, the least amount of time spent in the middle of the channel is safest. In most cases, paddling quickly and efficiently will be the preferred way to save time and energy. Proper consideration for navigation, coupled with good paddling technique and a strong, healthy body, result in less work and greater overall safety.

If you paddle enough years, sooner or later you will get caught out, having to find your way home in the fog or at night. Prac-

Life Isn't Always Fair

Have you ever felt that a following current does not provide all the boost you might expect? Well, it is true.

If you're paddling at 3 knots, a 2-knot current 40 degrees off your stern increases your speed by 1.2 knots.

The same 2-knot current 40 degrees off your bow decreases your speed by 1.8 knots.

The same geometry works for speed made good in winds. Paddling into a headwind reduces your speed more than a similar tailwind increases your speed. It's not intuitive and it's not fair.

tice the more technical aspects of navigation when you don't need them, and they will be ready for you at that moment of need.

Communicating Your Position

In times of trouble when you require help, you will need to communicate your position. Different forms of communication are effective over significantly different distances. The priority is to use a tool appropriate to the circumstance. Following are some of the most useful methods of emergency communication. (See the section "Communication Gear" in chapter 4, "Safety and Rescue Gear," for more details on these and other methods of communication.)

VHF Radio

Marine VHF radios are in common use by pleasure boats and commercial vessels. Any vessels monitoring VHF channel 16 within the range of your radio broadcast (approximately 5 miles for the 5-watt transmitters often used by kayakers) can be contacted for information or assistance. VHF channel 16 is the International Distress Safety and Calling channel monitored by the US and Canadian coast guards, commercial vessels, many pleasure craft, and in some cases marinas, lighthouses, and other shore stations.

For seeking help in serious, possibly life-threatening distress, you can place a *Mayday* call. A Mayday call follows a specific sequence and has absolute priority over all other transmissions.

To make a Mayday call, turn to VHF channel 16 (156.8 MHz) and follow this sequence:

1. State the distress signal "Mayday," repeated three times.

2. Give the call sign or other identification of the station in distress, repeated up to three times.

3. Give the location of the distress situation. When possible, give the bearing and distance in nautical miles from a known geographic position.

4. State the nature of the distress and kind of assistance required.

5. State the number of persons involved.

6. Provide any other pertinent information.

7. End the message by saying "over."

A Mayday broadcast puts into action an official emergency response and must be taken with great seriousness. Help should be requested when it will do the most good. Waiting until the situation turns to tragedy can cost lives and put rescue personnel at greater risk.

For an urgent situation relating to safety that is not as critical as a Mayday emergency, you can place a *Pan-Pan* call on channel 16.

Horizontal arms or paddle: stop, remain in place, potential hazard.

Horizontal waving arms or paddle (may include whistle or other alarm noise): urgent stop, hazard imminent, look around, your safety is in jeopardy. Avoid the hazard.

Vertical arm or paddle: move ahead; come to me, toward me. I need your assistance.

Arm or paddle at an angle: move forward to the right/left as indicated.

Vertical arm or paddle waving (may include whistle or alarm sound): urgent, move ahead toward me, paddle faster toward me. I need your immediate help.

Visual signals can be used when out of voice range. These are the most common paddle signals.

This call follows the same sequence and content as a Mayday, except that your broadcast begins by stating the urgency signal "Pan-Pan" three times. A Pan-Pan call has priority over all other transmissions except a Mayday.

A third type of broadcast is called a *Sécurité* (*"say-cure-e-tay"*), which is a notice that affects safety to navigation. For example, a kayaker crossing a channel in low visibility might consider broadcasting a Sécurité message to notify local marine traffic of the kayak's position.

To make a Sécurité call, give the signal "Sécu-rité" three times followed by the call sign of your station. Then state the safety notice, give any other pertinent information, and end the call by saying "standing by on channel one-six."

Other Electronic Communication

Where there is adequate station coverage, cell phones are very useful for communicating position. The general procedures developed for radio communications work well in calling with a cell phone for assistance.

A satellite phone offers global communication and may be a viable alternative for kayak expeditions in areas not served by cell phones.

A personal locator beacon, beaming its one-way signal to satellites and to ground and air stations, can tell search and rescue organizations where you are. The Coast Guard and marine electronics suppliers can provide detailed information.

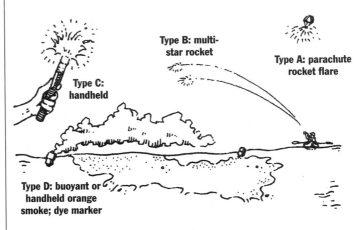

DAYLIGHT SIGNALS

Type B: multi-star rocket

Type A: parachute rocket flare

Type C: handheld

Type D: buoyant or handheld orange smoke; dye marker

Signal flares come in a variety of types and vary greatly in their use and effectiveness. Flares need to be replaced at regular intervals as specified by coast guard regulations. Coast guard regulations in different jurisdictions may require that specific types of flares be carried.

Visual Signals

In large waves or swell, it can be difficult for a paddler to communicate position or other information to fellow members of the kayak group or to other boats in the area. You can use a set of simple, well-understood hand and paddle signals for this purpose.

Gestures need to be large and have a clear meaning. A raised paddle can call a group together. A paddle held horizontally overhead usually means "Stop, do not proceed." An agitated motion up and down increases visibility of the horizontal paddle and stresses the meaning. In general, vigorous waving and agitated motions of any sort need to be interpreted as signs of concern, danger, or calls of distress.

Flares are also valuable visual signals for gaining attention and assistance. Among flares available to kayakers are handheld flares, parachute flares, and smoke flares, as discussed in an earlier chapter.

Tripping

7

In tripping, the concepts of safety management discussed earlier in this book are pressed into the service of a safe passage and personal adventure. A trip of only a day or two involves all the same elements as a trip of two months. Often the most significant difference in preparing for a longer trip is that one must carry less gear in order to make room for more food. On a one-night outing, we need little food and can therefore pack more gear. Our level of concern is usually greater for longer journeys, which may explain why more accidents occur on single-day outings than on overnight trips.

Any trip has three phases: planning, implementation, and reflection.

- *Planning* focuses on identifying potential problems, gathering information, and deciding on a course of action to address the potential problems. The principles of risk assessment (as discussed earlier) are brought into play at this stage.

- *Implementation* is of course the trip itself: the plan put into action. The principles of risk management guide our routines along the way.

- *Reflection* simply means reviewing the planning and the trip itself in order to improve our future actions and to recognize what is being done well. During a multiday trip, reflection, planning, and implementation recur often as we update decisions for the continued trip ahead.

The goal of the three phases of tripping is to maximize safety, minimize harm, and allow for a comfortable and enjoyable trip for everyone. Many of the steps and techniques in each phase can and should happen simultaneously, and some may have to be done more than once.

Though every trip has all three phases, the level of detail and formality of each phase can vary greatly. Plans for day trips in local waters can be less formal than plans for a week along an unfamiliar coast. Your level of experience will dictate how much time you need for planning.

Paddler's Logbook

Despite its name, the paddler's logbook is not simply a book with notes in it. A paddler's logbook is really a set of tools to help in planning, implementing, and reflecting on the trip. The logbook is not always a written document. Parts of the logbook can be written; a discussion may be sufficient for other parts.

Whether or not you choose to write down the details depends on the needs of the group and the demands of the trip. There is no need for a written menu on a day trip, but organizing and packing three weeks' worth of groceries into a kayak requires a detailed written list.

The paddler's logbook involves a variety of documents, lists, and information. They include:

- A trip contract—an agreement among members on critical aspects of the trip.
- A float plan, detailing the route and timetable for the trip.
- Weather information, both reports and forecasts.
- Navigational information, such as a dead-reckoning log.
- A daily journal, or diary.
- Checklists, including menu, equipment, and budget.

The paddler's logbook is used to plan better trips and make better decisions. A critical step in decision making is gathering information, and the logbook is a major aid in that task. Memory is inconsistent, and information is easily forgotten; when in doubt, write it out.

Trip Planning

There is no such thing as a "perfect" trip in which everything goes exactly as planned; you can't plan for every contingency. The real purpose of planning is to ensure that you are able to deal effectively with whatever problems come your way. Trip planning focuses on the first three stages of the decision-making process: identifying potential problems,

A simple waterproof notebook is a fundamental piece of navigational equipment.

gathering information, and deciding on a course of action to address these problems. Done well, trip planning will significantly enhance the safety of a trip.

Where to Go

Decide where you want to go. If you are unsure of a destination, gather information on several options and review the advantages and disadvantages of each before deciding. In-

Have an alternate plan. Sometimes the beach you planned to camp on will already be occupied.

formation you will need in making a decision includes:

- Ease of access.
- Difficulty of the trip, including distances and expected terrain, sea conditions, and weather.
- Experience of the group.
- Equipment available.
- Time available.
- Money available.

Area Information

With a destination in mind, begin to gather detailed information on the area. Information you will need includes:

You will spend more time in camp than sitting in your boat. Choose campsites wisely.

(GREG SHEA)

- Local hazards, such as localized winds, currents, surf, or reefs.

- Potential camping sites or other accommodations.

- Land access restrictions: native lands, ecological reserves, military sites, private land, park lands—and any necessary permits.

- Alternative access and egress points.

- Local resources, such as outfitters, fishing and sailing clubs, or water taxi services.

A lot of this information is available on charts and topographic maps. Local guidebooks and an Internet search will yield additional resources. Sea kayakers will also find a lot of useful information in *Coast Pilots* and other publications for the coastal commercial marine industry and the sailing community.

Who to Go With

Clearly define the demands of the trip, including likely sea conditions, skill needed, equipment needed, proposed route, and probable lengths of the daily paddles. Ask each member to detail their experience and training, and ask them if they feel that they are up to the demands of the trip. The smallest group you will travel with is a group of one, yourself. The solo paddler is responsible for all decisions and outcomes. Solo paddling has its own rewards and risks: be prepared. The advice of "three at sea" provides for a greater variety of alternatives when things go wrong.

In the early planning stages of a trip, it is important to conduct a risk assessment, identifying potential hazards and the compensating skills, equipment, and judgment necessary to manage the hazards safely. For example, a trip along an exposed coast will require surf skills, helmets, and the judgment to determine where and when to land and launch. Groups need navigators, cooks, rescue leaders, entertainers, natural-history interpreters, cultural interpreters, and others to have safe and enjoyable trips. Take the time to assess the group's assets and weaknesses of the group. A critical step is to choose a leadership structure. (See "Leadership" in chapter 1.) The group must determine an appropriate structure, designate responsibilities, address identified

The solo paddler should have an unstoppable roll, steady nerves, and excellent judgment.

(GREG SHEA)

As the planning evolves, periodically check with each trip member to review any new material and to make sure assigned tasks are being completed.

Pre-trip Meetings

To simplify the lines of communication, it is often useful to arrange for one or more pre-trip meetings with as many group members as possible. The initial meeting can be fairly loosely organized, allowing members the opportunity to express opinions and explore ideas. At the end of the meeting, a list of things to do can be drawn up and further meetings and communications can be planned.

If the trip goals and itinerary are already clearly defined, the first meeting can be used to state expectations, itinerary, and assign responsibilities so everyone has a clear un-

hazards, and reinforce weaknesses. Assets should be integrated into the trip for the enjoyment and safety of all, and weaknesses should be addressed through thoughtful planning. Consider adding members to address weaknesses or take the time to build the needed resources within the existing group to ensure a successful trip.

It is a good idea to collect basic information from each person for the paddler's logbook. This information will facilitate communication, and can be useful in an emergency. Information for each person should include:

- Name, address, and contact information.
- Emergency contact person.
- Medical information, including doctor, medical benefits provider, and health care number.
- Special medical considerations, including existing conditions, allergies, and any medication.
- Dietary needs, desires, and restrictions.
- Relevant training, including radio license, first-aid training, and CPR training.

Traveling in larger groups has both benefits and complications. The size of the group and the individual skills of the members play an important role in planning a safe and enjoyable trip.   (GREG SHEA)

derstanding of what is expected of them. It is useful to have a chart, guidebooks, and photographs on hand to help group members visualize the trip and to generate enthusiasm. Further meetings can be used as deadlines for specific tasks, including menu planning, logistics, and developing the itinerary.

It is important not to overburden group members with deadlines and endless meetings. Be realistic, and rely on e-mails and telephone calls to handle the little details.

Budget

All trips have associated costs. Start a draft budget early in the planning process and identify as many of the costs as possible. These may include food, transportation (cars, gas, water taxis, ferries, airplanes), permits, rental equipment (kayaks, VHF radios, satellite telephones, camping gear), guide services, and incidental expenses (telephone calls, charts and maps, vehicle parking).

Some group members have more time than others to help with trip preparation. Consider allocating costs according to the work that each person contributes toward the trip. Those who have less time to assist in preparation can perhaps pay a little more. If everyone is too busy to spend a lot of time on trip planning, consider hiring a guide or outfitter to organize the trip. Make sure everyone is aware of the likely costs of the trip and what they are expected to pay. Budgeting will minimize surprises and ill feelings.

Itinerary

As the trip approaches, a more detailed itinerary should be established. This does not mean that every day of the trip has to be mapped out with every campsite, distance, and rest stop plotted on

a chart or map. It does mean that everyone has to agree on the destination, length of the trip, and the general itinerary.

In addition, detailed notes on alternative takeouts, nearby medical services, and transportation should be included in the paddler's logbook. Much of this information will be used to complete a float plan. With this information in place, the group can focus on other pre-trip considerations.

Food

The old expression says that an army travels on its stomach. This is equally true for people traveling by sea kayak. Food and water are what drive the engine that powers the sea kayak. They are also important in the prevention of common risks such as hypothermia, sunburn, and sore muscles.

A common approach to food planning is to follow a detailed menu for each meal, including snacks and quantities. The challenge for many groups is in coming up with a varied, interesting, and nutritious menu. Some people turn to a camping cookbook; others rely on prepackaged, dehydrated meals available from grocery and camping stores; still others prepare and package their own meals

You will need a hearty, sustaining meal at the end of a day of kayaking. (GREG SHEA)

using favorite recipes from home. All three strategies work well; many kayakers use a combination.

Keep a copy of the menu in the paddler's logbook to expedite food preparation at meal times and minimize the work required on the next trip. The challenge of this style of food planning is that it locks the group into a set menu and doesn't necessarily allow for changes based on weather conditions or other needs.

A more flexible approach is sometimes preferred. One such strategy is called the pantry menu, which requires that the group pantry be well stocked with a variety of foodstuffs. Simply open up the pantry and organize a meal based on the group's preferences and needs for that meal. The challenge is getting the overall quantities right to ensure enough food for the entire trip.

Many experienced paddlers use a blended strategy, planning a variety of meals but leaving the final choices to the day, or combining the ingredients as preferred. There are also restaurants, pubs, and cafes along many stretches of coastline. Consider stopping off, warming up, and relaxing. Not only is it a nice break on a trip, but it also builds companionship and respect between kayakers and the many other users of coastal waters.

Equipment

As with menu planning, it is useful to develop a list of gear and keep it with the paddler's logbook, facilitating packing on future trips.

Food for Thought

Weather conditions were the best that our group had encountered all week as we planned our paddling along Scotland's Isle of Skye. The forecast for the next day was for westerly winds between about 12 to 20 knots. We decided to paddle northwest from Elgol for about 4 miles, up into Loch Coruisk, where we planned to stay a single night.

During the night, wind and rain came at us with a passion. The wind, accelerating down the Cuillin Mountains and directly into the sea, thrashed our tents. In the morning, there were no "maximum 20-knot winds." Instead we were hit with winds up to 40 knots.

The winds off the mountains were seriously affecting local conditions, while out at sea conditions didn't look as bad. Should we stay on the stormy shore or try to paddle through the winds and return to Elgol? Among the considerations that nagged at us as we tried to reach a decision was the simple fact that we had brought enough food only for a single overnight.

We reckoned we could battle the wind to the Isle of Soay, only about 2 miles away, and then run with the weather back into Elgol. We decided to go for it. What a battle it turned out to be. One of the paddlers simply couldn't make any headway against the wind, so we had to put him on a towline. The others were managing, inch by inch. The first 500 yards seemed to go on forever. We struggled on, and conditions began to ease as we got farther from the base of the mountains. When we finally reached Soay, we collapsed in exhaustion on to the beach. After rest and some lunch, we made an exhilarating run back over to Elgol.

On reflection: Carry more food than you're likely to need, so that critical safety decisions aren't based on such an issue.

—Mike McClure

Rendezvous by Moonlight

I had agreed to rendezvous with my fellow paddlers that evening somewhere along the east end of the strait. We hadn't decided on a specific meeting point because we wanted to keep our plans flexible. As agreed, at 4 P.M. I broadcast a call on my VHF radio. No response. I paddled out to a prominent headland in the strait and had an early dinner. Every half hour, I placed the same call. Still no response.

Finally, at 7 P.M., I got a reply. The others were coming up into the east end of the strait after exploring some islands and a freshwater lake. They were running late and wanted to know if I had established a campsite. I invited them over. As it got dark, I lit a small fire on the point to help them find me. Eventually I saw the glow of a flashlight. I called on the radio and told them where to land. By 9 P.M. we were all together, enjoying the clear night and recounting our adventures.

Although there were a couple of anxious moments, the communication protocol that we had established as a group was successful. We regularly use VHF radios to communicate, and we follow a set schedule when we separate. In this case, it brought us all together safely.

On reflection: Established communication protocols are an important part of traveling on the water.

—*Michael Pardy*

In general, equipment can be divided into two categories: personal gear and group equipment.

Personal gear includes clothing, camping equipment, toiletries, and amusements. These items can be left to the individual members to organize. If anyone is short an item or is uncertain about what is appropriate, other group members can offer advice or lend extra equipment. In order to conserve space, some members may decide to share tent space, while others may prefer a private retreat at the end of the day.

Shared gear usually includes the kitchen, tarps, first-aid kit, repair kit, communication equipment, and library resources. The sharing of these items conserves space and saves money.

Items that can be considered either personal or group equipment include charts and maps, compasses, GPS units and other navigation equipment, tide and current tables, kayaks, and kayaking accessories. Our pref-

erence is to include them in personal gear because it emphasizes each individual's responsibility for his or her own safety.

A group member who is not familiar with the use of this equipment would not be expected to supply it all personally. But be sure the lack of skill and knowledge is not a safety concern for the trip. This is an excellent opportunity for that individual to acquire new skills.

Communication Protocols

The group needs to choose communication equipment and determine how they will use it on the trip. The geographic range of the equipment must be appropriate to the location and purpose. Communication within the group will obviously rely heavily on face-to-face conversation, but on the water the group should strongly consider additional communication tools such as paddle and whistle signals. Outside communication can be established through the use of flares, radios, and other equipment. Each member of the group must be familiar with the advantages, disadvantages, and protocols governing each piece of communication equipment. (See the section "Communication Gear" in chapter 4, Safety and Rescue Gear.)

Transportation

It is necessary to arrange transportation for all the gear and people to and from the launch site. Depending on the location and the route, a variety of options are possible. Most trips are loops, starting and ending in the same place. Other options can open up a wider range of itineraries and destinations. Water taxis, ferries, shuttle vans, and airplanes can extend the range of options. Contact local outfitters and tourism offices for advice, because they usually have a handle on what transportation options are available. Some of them may be willing to run a shuttle for a group of kayakers for a nominal fee.

Paddlers may be coming from a variety of locations to meet in a central place. Make sure everyone is familiar with the rendezvous point and schedule. Have backup plans if someone is late or has transportation trouble. The use of cell phones or a central contact number can make all the difference.

Regardless of which transportation options the group uses, see that there is sufficient room for all the equipment and that vehicles are as safe as possible. Long drives, high speeds, heavy loads, crowded vehicles, and awkward loads on the roof of a car all impose a high risk potential. It is considered good manners to share the costs associated with transportation, including ferries, gas, and, if the trip is a long one, a pre-trip tune-up for a group member's car. Include these costs in the budget for the trip.

Float Plan

A kayaking group needs to prepare a float plan that lays out its travel plans, including destination and most likely routes, campsites, and dates and times. Carry one copy of the

Car Trouble

Eight of us were heading out to the coast to spend a week paddling. My wife, son, and I got a head start on the drive to the put-in, because travel with a 5-year-old can take time and we didn't want to hold up everyone else.

Our car broke down a couple of hours from home. The mechanic at the garage said it would take at least two days to get the parts and make the repairs. We called the other members in our group, who were traveling not far behind us. For once I was grateful for cell phones!

We met at the garage and crammed our stuff into the other cars, but there was no room for our double kayak. I called a kayak outfitter out on the coast to arrange a rental. The garage agreed to make the repairs and hold our car until we came back through. We then spent six glorious days in the sun, paddling and exploring.

On reflection: Contingency planning is essential, and in this case our informal contingency planning was a success. We carried a cell phone, so were able to get help from our group, and we knew how to contact an outfitter, so we weren't left up the coast without a kayak.

—Michael Pardy

float plan in each kayak and leave one with a responsible person back home—giving this person clear instructions on what to do in the event the group does not return on schedule. Information in the float plan will be used by emergency response personnel in the event a search or rescue is needed. (See sample form for providing float-plan information, in the appendix.)

Trip Contract

The trip contract is an agreement to be used in the spirit of working together toward common goals. This contract, or agreement, among trip members details the goals and expectations of the trip, individual responsibilities, and decision-making procedures. Spelling out these details minimizes the confusion and lapses of communication that so often plague multiday coastal trips. The trip contract is not intended to be a legal document. In the event of a dispute, the contract is there to be used as a reference to allow for a calmer, more structured discussion.

Be as clear as you can when establishing goals. Many conflicts and ill feelings on trips are the result of poorly articulated goals, which can also lead to accidents. Goals should be set for the physical and social characteristics of the trip. By this we mean such expectations as the distance traveled each day, the kinds of sea conditions and weather the group will paddle in, and the expectations of group members regarding leadership, camp chores, and other issues. The accompanying sample contract covers the basics that should be found on such a document.

The Trip

All the planning is put to the test on the trip itself. If the planning is thorough, the group will have anticipated and reduced a great deal of the risk, thus ensuring a safe and enjoyable trip. There are also several activities that need to be carried out during the trip in order for the group to maintain a high level of safety.

Beach Talk

Before heading out onto the water each morning, take a few moments to review the day's itinerary, including potential water and food stops. This daily check is called the beach talk. If everyone is involved in this process, there are fewer questions and disagreements about routes and stops. This review is an opportunity for each person to make plans for the day. If there are limited landing sites along the route, extra food and water can be placed close at hand and bathroom breaks anticipated. Potential hazards can be identified and alternative strategies developed. This should include an evaluation of the weather, sea state, and terrain of the proposed route.

Communication protocol should be reviewed. Some groups rely on voice communication. Paddle and light signals, and electronic communication as well, can also be used on the water as long as everyone is familiar with the signals. Signals allow group members to explore and travel with flexibility. In times of difficulty, the signals help to organize and carry out rescues.

Finally, consider how the group will travel on the water that day. If sea and weather conditions are good, each person can have a lot of latitude for exploring. In more demanding conditions, group members can agree to more clearly defined boundaries and leadership.

Travel Formations
Kayaker groups can choose from a number of travel formations. One in particular works well for groups of intermediate paddlers traveling on an open coast, because it allows for flexible organization while ensuring that everyone stays within voice and visual range. Simply designate one kayak as the *home* or

TRIP CONTRACT

Trip contracts, like the sample provided here, are critical for communicating common goals and expectations.

Goal	To relax and enjoy the natural and cultural beauty of Esperanza Inlet.
Dates	August 10th to 17th including travel days (8 days total).
Proposed Route	Launch at Little Espinoza Bridge, travel out to Rosa Island, around the outside and along the north side of Nuchatlitz Inlet to Belmont Beach and back.
Expected Sea Conditions	• Weather—Winds 15 to 25 knots; possible fog; rain and drizzle likely. • Seas—1 to 3 meters; 1 knot currents except at mouths of tidal lagoons up to 6 knots. • Terrain—Mixed, rocky shorelines, with moderately steep pebble/stone beaches, occasional sandy beach; frequent landing options in Nuchatlitz Provincial Park, limited landing in Esperanza Inlet and Nuchatlitz Inlet. Parts of the trip are exposed to Pacific Ocean. • This is an intermediate trip with lots of options if the weather is poor.

Members and Skill Level	Name	Kayak Skill Level	Camping Skill Level
	Dave	experienced	experienced
	Maryanne	intermediate	experienced
	Merrill	novice	intermediate
	Satchiko	beginner	intermediate
	Lisa	beginner	intermediate
	Rowan	novice	intermediate

Distance Each Day	8 to 12 miles or 3 to 4 hours, whichever comes first.
Environmental Guidelines	Restrict paddling to winds less than 18 knots, seas less than 1.4 meters, 1 meter surf, crossings less than 3 miles.
Kayaks	• Singles with at least one double to accommodate weaker paddlers. • All the kayaking equipment will be rented in Campbell River and transported by the group. Maryanne is responsible for renting the kayaks. The rental comes with paddle, PFD, skirt, pump, a few spare paddles, and paddle float.
Safety Equipment	• Dave/Maryanne will provide VHF radio, 1 type A flare, and 3 type B flares. They will also bring a towline. • Each member is responsible for their own self-rescue equipment including paddle floats, pumps, and immersion clothing. • Each member will bring 3 type B flares. • Each member will bring immersion clothing (wetsuit/fleece/paddling jacket combo or dry suit).

TRIP CONTRACT (continued)

Meals	• Breakfasts and lunches in family pairs. • Dinners shared.
Camping Equipment	• Each couple is responsible for their own camping equipment. • Kitchen equipment will be provided by Dave and Maryanne.
Transportation	• Dave/Maryanne and Rowan/Lisa have agreed to drive. They have appropriate roof racks on their cars.
Leadership and Decision Making	• Dave is the most experienced paddler, and will take responsibility for route, weather, navigation, and rescue; Dave will discuss his thinking with the entire group where time allows and in particular, he will defer to the needs of Rowan and Merrill, who have never kayaked before. • For non-kayaking related decisions, the group will make decisions through consensus.
Budget	• Rowan will keep the budget. • Rough estimate of the cost per person is $150. • All the costs associated with renting equipment, transportation, and permits will be shared equally by the group. Each person will provide Rowan with $100 by July 15th as a deposit. • Final tallies and any moneys owed are due at our post trip dinner, August 27th.
Pre-trip Meetings	• Informal through telephone and e-mail. • Group will meet on July 15th at the lake for a trip planning and skills review session including wet exits, rescues, and strokes.
Dropping Out	• After pre-trip session, a member can cancel his/her space, but forfeits his/her deposit.
Post-trip Meeting	• August 27th at Satchiko's—Pot luck and slides. Please RSVP.
Other Considerations	• Staying at each campsite at least 2 nights (conditions allowing). • Allowing group members time to explore on their own. • Bringing lots of guidebooks and local histories.

lead boat, or navigator, and everyone else must travel with that boat. The group forms a pod on the water, ensuring that everyone is close by in times of difficulty and allowing for easy communication.

For additional safety, individuals can buddy-up. This way, there are at least two sets of eyes watching every paddler. The home boat can be changed on a regular basis, giving everyone a chance to lead. Along more challenging coastlines, the kayak of a more experienced paddler can be designated as the home boat.

Updating the Paddler's Logbook

As the trip unfolds, set aside time each day to add information to that collection of checklists, journals, and other documents that is known as the paddler's logbook. The logbook with all its components serves as a record for the trip—a repository for the information, observations, and insights of the group.

Routine information including the daily weather forecasts, itineraries, water sources, campsites, and other points of interest should be recorded. In addition, personal experiences and reflections can be included. This information is particularly useful if the group faced either exceptional success or difficulty during the day. The information and comments will provide a basis for reflection and for planning future trips. These records are especially helpful whenever members of the group travel back to the same area.

On-trip Meetings

Over the course of the trip, set aside time for the group to meet occasionally to review its objectives, adjust the itinerary, or make other important decisions. These meetings are different from the quick daily beach talk that simply sets up the day's plan.

These occasional meetings can seem artificial and even appear intimidating to some people. They should be used with care and understanding, allowing each member an opportunity to speak without being criticized. Many problems facing groups stem from a lack of honest communication. The sessions are an avenue for maintaining clear lines of communication and dealing with problems and tensions as they arise, before they get worse. These meetings may not be necessary for groups in which there is already an open, ongoing dialogue between all members throughout the trip.

Trip Reflection

Take time after the trip to get the group together and reflect on the experience. Were the goals of the trip met? Were revisions necessary? What problems developed, and how were they handled? What were the successes

When Memory Fails

Three of us were 10 miles down a rough coast looking for a particular small creek with a beach. It was a good place to camp. Jake was in our group, and he had been there five years before; no one else knew this stretch of coast. It was obvious Jake was feeling some stress, because according to his memory we should have arrived at the creek already. We were all a little nervous. We had come inside the reef specifically to find this site, and it was a long and exposed paddle back out and around the reef to the next suitable beach.

Suddenly Jake yelled, "There it is!" The stream, not marked on the charts, was a great site, with beach camping on flat stones, lots of driftwood for fires, and fresh water. And we were the only people there. The beach was hidden by a series of tightly packed islands with narrow channels between. Later that night, after dinner and a swim, Jake pulled out his old logbook. In it, he had mentioned the site from his prior trip, but he hadn't made accurate notes on its location. He didn't make the same mistake twice.

On reflection: Memory can be shaky and inaccurate. A detailed paddler's logbook can add greatly to the enjoyment and safety of a trip.

—Michael Pardy

How Strong Was the Wind?

The five of us were admiring the slides from our latest trip. One picture reignited a debate. It shows us sitting under a tarp, with a choppy sea in the background. There was a light drizzle. The picture reminded us of the debate we were having under the tarp. The weather had been mediocre at best for the preceding three days and we were tired of being stuck under the tarp. We had come to paddle, but we hadn't done much so far.

The debate hinged on how strong the winds were. There were periodic whitecaps, and according to the Beaufort scale, the wind should be in the 10- to 12-knot range, easy enough for our intermediate abilities. The problem was, it felt stronger. To make matters worse, our weather radio had died on the first day of the trip. As a result, we continued to put off our launch.

As we sat in the comfort of our living room that evening, enjoying the slides, Anne settled the matter for us. She called the Weather Service and got the reports from those days. Sure enough, the wind had been blowing 18 to 22 knots. Our instincts were right.

On reflection: Our experience had helped us make a good decision. Reviewing this decision reinforced our judgment and added new bits of information to our toolbox for future decisions. (We also learned to bring more than one radio on a trip.)

—Michael Pardy

of the venture? What can we learn for use on our next outing? The paddler's logbook will be invaluable in this process as you look back at the trip just completed and ahead to those yet to come.

A post-trip meeting can also tidy up any loose ends, including sorting out the budget and returning equipment. The meeting should be fun for everyone, with a chance to look at each other's photos and to reminisce on the kayaking time together. After particularly challenging trips, it can be instructive to ask each group member to write up individual impressions of the trip. The differences in perception can be startling.

Decide on the lessons learned from the trip, and write them into the paddler's logbook as a starting point for the next adventure. These can be lessons for the group, and for just a single individual. Group lesson: There was not enough tea on the trip. Make a note in the logbook to bring more next time.

Stop occasionally over the course of the day to check your position and listen to the weather broadcast. Keeping a weather log in your paddler's logbook will help greatly in interpreting weather information as broadcast and as it unfolds on site. (GREG SHEA)

Individual lesson: One paddler realized that his 15-year-old sleeping bag just doesn't do the job anymore. Make a note in the logbook to remember to bring a replacement bag on the next trip.

Important on-trip decisions can be reviewed with the benefit of hindsight. Was it in fact a good idea to stay on the beach that day because of the threatening weather forecast, or should we have gone out on the water anyway? Decisions can be evaluated and additional information can be brought to the discussion. Reflecting on the kayaking experience is a step often shortchanged, but it is in the reflective process that we learn our most valuable lessons.

Self Rescue

8

Self rescue involves a variety of techniques designed to undo the short-term consequences of a capsize. If one member of a group is in need of a rescue, it is likely that others may also be busy taking care of themselves and may not be immediately available to help. The best use of self-rescue techniques is to get independently back to full function before your paddling buddy has a chance to help.

The goals of a self rescue are to:

- Get yourself back in the kayak.
- Get the water out of the kayak.
- Ensure your stability.

This chapter focuses narrowly on techniques for an individual paddler to use in carrying out a self rescue. Chapter 9 covers the topic of assisted rescue, and outlines techniques by which other paddlers can help a person get back safely into the kayak after a wet exit. Chapter 10 discusses the broader context of a rescue, covering all the planning and implementation of a rescue as it involves every member of the paddling group.

Paddling truly alone, without any support, brings risks and rewards that need to be thoughtfully considered. Supplementary res-

cue gear cannot replace the need for the skill and judgment necessary for solo coastal paddling, and simply staying near to shore does little to reduce the risks. Most serious incidents involving inexperienced solo paddlers happen near shore, where unanticipated conditions prevent the paddler from completing a self rescue. In apparently sheltered waters, offshore winds and tidal currents have been the cause of a number of serious incidents involving unprepared solo paddlers. These unfortunate icons of individuality usually end up using flares, arm waving, or other means to summon help.

A self rescue is much more than a single technique. It is a medley of judgments, techniques, skills, and confidence. Individual techniques learned and practiced on good days must be sufficient to work on a bad day. Decisions during a rescue should center on what to do, not how to do it.

Novices and beginners typically capsize a time or two in calm water near the beach or in the bay while learning how to control a kayak. They need reentry techniques that are easy to learn, and lots of practice with able partners. The first rescue technique to learn is the wet exit, followed by a walk to shore or a swim to the edge of the pool. But this is not enough offshore. So the novice then learns to

A roll is the quickest, simplest means of recovering from a capsize. It may not be the quickest to learn, but then learning usually occurs in controlled conditions and you can take your time.

(GREG SHEA)

Hanging onto your paddle when capsizing is easier than losing it and having to swim for it, but learning any technique that helps you stay in your kayak is worth the effort.

(GREG SHEA)

encountered. Rough-water practice is necessary. Competent instruction and experienced paddling buddies will keep beginners safe while they learn.

First encounters with rough water are best shared with a group of veteran paddlers, ready to lend a hand. A beginner's perception of risk may be a great deal higher than that of experienced partners. In this safe but challenging environment, the beginner has the opportunity to test and improve skills. Courses or club events that include tidal currents or surf will also teach techniques appropriate to storm-tossed rescues.

Rescue techniques described in this chapter are generally arranged from simple to complex. We first present the techniques that use fewest hands, fewest pieces of gear, and the fewest number of steps. Reliability is the paramount quality of a rescue technique; it has to work when you need it. Simple is better.

Efficient self-rescue techniques:

- Require the least effort.
- Are quick, simple, and above all else, reliable.
- Are necessary even when traveling in a group. Other group members may be busy with their own problems and unable to assist.

reenter the kayak in deep (but calm) water following a wet exit.

Meanwhile, the student's paddling skills improve rapidly, and he or she soon wants to venture away from the beach, and then out of the bay into the rougher conditions of the strait. Now even more training and practice in self rescue are required for the larger waves, stronger winds, and tidal currents that will be

Rolling

Rolling is by far the simplest and most effective rescue technique. Far too often, rolling is given credit as the best technique but is the last skill to be taught. The purpose of the technique is to turn a capsize into a roll of the kayak so that paddler and boat are returned upright.

Novice kayakers can begin to learn to roll on their first day. With the aid of a rigid paddle float, a diver's mask or nose plug, and the guidance of an experienced instructor, some novices will complete a roll or two; then they are hooked. They usually have a strong desire to continue, and more importantly they leave with an understanding that with time and practice, they can soon learn to roll their kayak dependably in calm water. It takes a good deal of practice in a variety of sea conditions before a paddler learns a reliable roll, but the earlier you start practicing, the sooner you will have command of this most valuable rescue technique.

Rolling requires consistent technique and timing, not personal strength or power from the paddle. Each kayak with its paddler and cargo rotates at a given speed. The paddler simply rolls in time with the natural rhythm of the kayak. A loaded kayak rolls more slowly than an empty kayak. If the anxious paddler gets ahead of the kayak's natural roll, the roll will not be successful.

A roll is a complete rescue technique. It starts with a capsize and ends with the paddler right side up in the kayak, which remains dry on the inside. Rolling a loaded kayak requires no additional strength or technique; the principal difference is that the timing is slower.

Many of the variety of roll techniques can be done with a regular paddle grip. If more leverage is required, an extended paddle grip can be used. (See "Sweep Roll" later in this chapter.)

The best way to learn the roll is in small steps, with many small successes along the way. Any amount of progress at learning to roll is a success. In learning the roll, you learn to handle the kayak tilted, on its side, and upside down. The process of learning to roll greatly improves your edge

control, brace turns, recovery braces, and overall confidence. In this way, the learning to roll improves your general paddling skill, increases your safety, and reduces the potential need for a complex assisted rescue.

There is a psychological factor involved in hanging upside down in a kayak, immersed in the sea. To learn to roll, you need to be confident sitting upside down. It may take barely five seconds to perform a roll, but any time spent upside down seems very much longer than it is.

Many articles and books offer good advice on rolling in waves, current, and wind, with the paddle in one hand, without a paddle, or with a sealskin float; it is all great fun. Rolling in rough seas after an unexpected capsize requires presence of mind that only comes with experience. Learning to roll proficiently on both sides is a worthwhile goal, but learning to roll on one side with one reliable technique will usually be enough to get the job done.

The Basics of Rolling

Most rolling techniques follow the same principles. Each paddler develops a personal interpretation best-suited to that individual's body and boat. Common names for some of

It is crucial to keep your head low throughout the recovery phase of a roll.

Magic

My first lesson in rolling took place in a cool, calm lake. Near shore in 3 feet of water, my instructor explained a few things, then told me to capsize and give it a try. He was close by to help if I had any difficulty.

How would this roll be possible? My paddle was 7 feet long and there was no way I could roll with it in only 3 feet of water. My instructor had to be wrong. Patiently he told me to just go ahead anyway, to stop thinking about it and just do it.

I capsized to the right, pushed my paddle out to the side, paused, and then felt his helping hands. With a tug on the paddle and a flick of my hip, I was upright. My first roll was complete. But I still did not understand how I could have rolled with a 7-foot paddle in 3 feet of water. My first assumption was confirmed: rolling is part magic.

On reflection: It was actually more ordinary than that. It turns out that I was only doing a half roll, and the paddle never really left the surface.

—Doug Alderson

Reach well up before starting your roll.

tice: gravity does most of the work, and you just need to be calm and confident. The last quarter of the roll is similar to a high brace. The key elements to develop are confidence and timing, through enough practice to train the body to accurately perform the same movements under stress.

Sweep Roll

A sweep roll works well for beginners and is particularly good for a paddler with a flexible lower back and a kayak with a low rear deck. Set up for the roll by leaning forward on one side of the kayak, and finish the roll leaning forward on the other side of the kayak. The forward-leaning posture keeps the shoulders in a safe and strong posture throughout the roll.

During practice, there is the opportunity to set up before you capsize. In reality the setup will often happen after the capsize. In any case, establishing this setup position is the starting point for the part of the roll that really counts.

these techniques are sweep roll, screw roll, brace roll, C to C roll, and Pawlata roll. Each one prescribes certain movements of the paddler, grip on the paddle, and motion of the paddle through the water. Paddlers debate the precise description of each and often proclaim that one is better than another. In fact, the fundamentals of these techniques are similar. The greatest success comes from good coaching that will help a beginner learn the one technique that is best for him or her.

The first half of a roll requires little prac-

To establish the setup position before capsizing, lean as far forward as possible with your head near your right knee. Push your hands as far overboard as possible, reaching to put your knuckles in the water. To get a good angle on the paddle blade for its sweep through the water, slightly rotate your wrists to push your knuckles forward.

Capsizing toward your hands and staying well tucked and low to the deck with your nose to your knee will help the kayak make a full ¾ rotation. It will take a second for the kayak to capsize and finish rotating. Realize that you have not moved.

Sweep Roll 1

Once capsized, your kayak has to roll over. Stay in the setup position and wait for your hands and paddle to clear the surface. Notice here that the paddler has taken a modified grip with the paddle off center.

2

The paddle sweeps across the surface out to a perpendicular position, and the kayak begins to rotate and be back underneath you.

3

With the head still low in the water and the shoulders coming to the surface, the paddler uses both body and paddle blade to complete the roll.

4

You should finish the roll sitting upright. Even at this final stage, bring your head up last. The kayak has rotated, placing the paddler on the left.

Practice holding your breath and making three attempts to roll before you decide to exit your kayak. This is an aspect of rolling that is often overlooked.

Sweep your paddle out to a position perpendicular to the kayak. The back hand remains almost still, and the forward hand swings the paddle. The paddle blade should sweep an arc on or near the surface. A slight up-angle on the paddle blade will help the paddle blade sweep near the surface and provide some welcome lift and rotation to the kayak. During this sweep the kayak is beginning to rotate—keep the momentum up in a graceful continuous motion. During the sweep, your body comes naturally out of the forward tuck with your head out over the center of the cockpit. You don't have to think about that—it will happen as you sweep the paddle. Keep your right forearm close to perpendicular to the paddle shaft as in a good high-brace.

As the paddle nears the perpendicular position, do two things at once: commence a high brace (pulling down gently on the paddle), and bring your head low along the wa-

Extending the working length of the paddle by adjusting the grip during the setup will provide additional leverage. The longer effective paddle length will make the sweep slower, so the timing will vary from a standard roll. With practice, many paddlers prefer to keep a consistent grip, firmly holding onto their paddle at all times.

ter to your back deck. Take care to keep your shoulders in a safe posture, with the forearm perpendicular to the paddle shaft.

C-to-C Roll

The leaning back posture of the sweep roll can be a challenge for some paddlers. Kayaks with a high seat back or high back deck do not allow for leaning back. A C-to-C roll is essentially the same as a sweep roll but finishes in a forward leaning posture. A C-to-C differs from a sweep roll in that the paddler starts and finishes in a forward-leaning position. The C-to-C roll uses a high brace to the front.

Rolling a Loaded Sea Kayak

A loaded sea kayak can have enough inherent stability that it may not want to roll a complete revolution. A properly loaded sea kayak will have a significant amount of the weight placed low along the line of the keel. This weight increases the stability of the kayak. To complete a full roll, this weight will have to be lifted out of the water. The buoyancy of air trapped in a dry suit or dry top can also inhibit a full 360-degree roll.

A half roll is sometimes preferred over a full roll. A half roll occurs when the paddler capsizes and rolls back up on the same side. Rolling techniques can be done either as a full roll or a half roll.

Mental Training

To make your roll work effectively under challenging conditions, you need to train both body and mind. The untrained mind reacts poorly under stress. With the anxiety of a sudden capsize, any thoughts of rolling can be overwhelmed by the instinctive urge to get out of your kayak. You need to learn how to

Capsizing to the right, the paddler has assumed the setup position to roll back up on the same side. (GREG SHEA)

The paddle has moved from the setup position and swept out to the side of the kayak as in the sweep roll. (GREG SHEA)

With a sweep of the paddle and a hip-flick the paddler has rolled in a forward leaning posture referred to as a C-to-C roll. (GREG SHEA)

create a positive mental image that makes it possible to execute a roll when you really need to.

Self-talk is a recognized mental training technique that helps in learning skills, correcting errors, increasing focus, and building confidence. Self-talk is something you can practice any time. Make sure that your talk focuses on success. Keep your conversation on a strong successful roll.

Practice positive imagery. Imagine yourself in the conditions that make you feel anxious and stressful—then continue the image through to a relaxed and successful outcome. Unexpectedly capsized in a steep wave, you see that all around you, the water is swirling and turbulent. Move into the setup position and feel the motion of the crest of the wave as it passes over the upturned keel of your kayak; then the water becomes still. Checking for a good forward lean and proper paddle orientation, reach up, sweep out, flick, and you have rolled back up on top of the water and are gliding over the next wave.

Replay this mental videotape often, until it pushes out the image of an anxiety-driven wet exit. Create an image of a successful roll that has you upright and on your way almost immediately. Take as many opportunities as possible to practice this positive imagery. Think it through while waiting in the line at the grocery store or at home before falling asleep, as well as on paddling days.

At the same time, press on with your physical training. Practice unexpected capsizes. For that, you need to paddle on moving water. The safest place to practice on moving water is in small tidal races or in spilling (not dumping) surf. There, in the company of other skilled paddlers or a qualified instructor, you can experience unanticipated capsizes. While you are at it, you will likely get a chance to practice assisted rescues and various towing techniques. You may need a helmet and a plastic boat that will stand up to bumping on rocks. With mental preparation,

Bombs Aweigh

The day's plan was to practice rolls in the surf. New to the group, I was introduced as an experienced paddler: "Don't worry about him, he has a bombproof roll."

This lofty introduction had a measure of truth to it. I had practiced long and hard in the pool and in sheltered coves. I could roll consistently, with apparent expertise. I launched from the beach, feeling confident and comfortable.

Not long afterward, I found myself hanging onto the stern toggle of my kayak as it washed up on shore. As I gathered up my paddle and kayak, I pondered what had gone wrong.

I paddled back out to watch the others. Playing in the waves, they were capsizing and effortlessly rolling up. They seemed to have a relaxed and controlled response to capsizing in turbulent water. While their first attempts were not always successful, they appeared to accept the situation with grace. Suspended at the surface of the water, they would relax, then complete the second half of their rolls. It was clear that I was still a beginner with a great deal to learn.

On reflection: Rolling in the real world is not just a matter of knowing how to roll, but also having the ability to apply that technique in conditions that catch you off guard.
—Doug Alderson

you can respond to the unexpected and use positive images to guide you to persist until you succeed.

There will come a time when circumstances will conspire to make things particularly difficult. The next wave may be a rogue that flips you like a hotcake on a griddle, and you are suddenly and unexpectedly upside down. Because you have practiced positive imagery, a vision of a strong, successful roll occupies your mind. You are relaxed and confident, thinking "I can do this." You go through the motions mentally, then physically. But this time, the roll doesn't work and the kayak remains upside down.

Your head clears the surface as your paddle blade dives for the bottom. With a positive mental state and with a clear image of what you must do physically, you prepare for your second attempt. At this point, you have several alternatives: reset and repeat, change sides, or finish by sculling up.

Reset and repeat: Go with your strength and repeat your best technique, since you have trained mentally and physically for this one sequence and its successful outcome. Swing your body back under the kayak, reestablish the setup position that you started with, and keep a calm head. Roll up on the same side on which you made your first attempt.

Change sides: Being able to roll both left and right can have advantages. After a failed first attempt, it may be easier to set up and roll in the other direction. The momentum of swinging your body back under the kayak can help you complete your second roll. The failure of the first attempt may be due to the contrary effects of current, strong wind, or breaking waves. In these circumstances, rolling up on the other side may be more effective. However, determining which side is best to roll up on while in this difficult situation requires a particularly clear head. Only good mental training will free you to have the presence of mind to consider which side to use.

Scull up: Failed rolls are often at least 50 percent successful. The paddler often reaches the surface, but in an unstable position that leads to a repeat capsize. Rather than submerging to set up for another full roll, the paddler has the alternative of sculling for support or executing a high brace. As a follow-up to a partially successful roll, this technique has the advantage of offering the opportunity for a breath of air, although taking a breath while still unstable takes good timing. A positive mind-set can help keep you from inhaling the moment your face breaks the surface, when you might inhale a stray splash of water. A cool head may permit you to get a controlled breath when it is safe to breathe.

Sculling is essentially sweeping the paddle back and forth continuously to provide support. Here a paddler has paused at the surface. Exploring the region between upright and inverted helps gain confidence and skill.

Persistence in difficult conditions is more about mental training than practical skill. Focus on the one successful roll necessary to get the job done. In safe and rough conditions, you can practice rolling left and right, and even practice feigning an unsuccessful first effort, then set up for a second effort. You can also practice capsizing and coming up on the same side in a half roll. It is good practice to capsize in different postures or with the paddle in one hand, making you find the correct

Taken by Surprise

My friend John and I had punched out through the shore break to paddle in a swell that was running about six feet. Conditions weren't good for surfing: the waves were long, fast, and dumping. I picked a small wave to ride in on. I had my heart set on getting at least one good ride, so I tried to rudder-stroke out of a broach. I held the stroke too long, and when the wave broke, I couldn't brace into the wave fast enough. Over I went.

Being upside down in the breaker was not at all like capsizing in a whitecapping wind wave. Kayaking in high winds, all of the action is above the surface: spray from the bow lashes my face, the roar of the wind rumbles in my ears. Capsizing brings with it a measure of calm. It's quiet and still underwater.

But out in the shore break, the capsize took me into a maelstrom of noise and turbulence. I was caught off guard. If I considered rolling, the thought of it went out of my mind so fast that it didn't even register. I had lost my bearings. I bailed out, making a quick wet exit.

On reflection: I felt embarrassed; surprised too. All that practice rolling, and I did a wet exit. I knew I could hold my breath, I knew I could get into the setup position, I knew I could roll—but I bailed out. I had all of the tools, but I lacked the patience and the composure to put them to use.

—Chris Cunningham

setup position when upside down, blind and disoriented. Try a partial roll and then sculling for support, and don't forget to try rolling a fully loaded boat. If you have made three attempts and you are not yet right side up, there is still a long list of things you can do after your wet exit.

The Wet Exit

A variety of circumstances can cause a paddler to exit a kayak. Making a wet exit from an overturned kayak will get your head back above water, but it is only the beginning of a longer rescue process. A self rescue that begins with a wet exit has three parts:

- Wet exit—the paddler gets out of the kayak.
- Reentry—the paddler gets back in the kayak.
- Pump-out—the flooded cockpit is emptied.

It is common to practice wet exits in the comfort and control of a heated pool. Safety and rescue classes are conducted in sheltered lakes and bays, during summer. In the familiar and comfortable surroundings of warm, calm freshwater, the novice kayaker learns to capsize, pause, remove the sprayskirt, and calmly exit the cockpit, all the while holding onto both paddle and kayak.

In a short time, the kayaker will be capsizing, hanging upside down watching the fish go by, and carrying out a wet exit with playful acceptance. Confidence is an important part of skill. Early lessons in flatwater include standard reentry techniques that work in these calm conditions.

As a student's paddling skills get better, the ability to handle wet exits and reentry also needs to improve, with training and practice in rougher sea conditions. The consequences of exiting a kayak in a rough sea are unforgiving, and the ensuing rescue can be complex and difficult.

A touring sea kayaker needs to practice dealing with the surprise and stress of an unexpected capsize.

Take the following steps to complete a wet exit after you have capsized in your kayak:

1. Hang on to your paddle with one hand or with an armpit.
2. Release the sprayskirt by pulling the release loop in one motion, outward and then upward.
3. Clear the rear of the sprayskirt from the back of the cockpit coaming.
4. With hands on the coaming near your hips, lift your bottom fully out of the seat and toward the back deck.
5. Exit while holding onto the paddle and the kayak.

As sea conditions become more vigorous, hanging onto the paddle and the kayak becomes increasingly difficult, and at the same time increasingly important. If you can hold onto only one thing, hold onto the kayak. Not only is there probably a spare paddle on the back deck, there may also be a radio, flares, and a host of other important gear in the kayak.

Swimmers separated from their kayaks make for complex rescues. The first step in such a rescue is to bring the swimmer and the wayward kayak together—a big challenge. Wind can blow an unoccupied kayak away faster than any swimmer can move. In an instant, one breaking wave can push a kayak beyond reach.

Solo Reentry

Once a paddler has completed a successful wet exit, the next challenge lies in getting back into the kayak—and quickly. The most successful solo reentry is one in which the paddler is able to get back into the kayak so quickly that nearby assistance has not yet had

Gone with the Wind

It was a blustery day, just right for practicing wet exits and solo reentries. I had installed new rigging on the back deck of my kayak, designed to hold a paddle securely for a paddle float reentry. I wanted to test it in rough conditions.

I put in at a boat launch ramp that ran down to the water between rocky outcrops. Three-foot waves battered the adjacent shore, and winds were blowing at 18 knots. With my partner supervising in case of mishap, I first did a couple of rolls before submitting to swimming in water that was at 50°F (10°C).

Fifty yards from shore, I purposely capsized and made a wet exit. My neoprene skull cap, dry top, and wet suit kept me warm enough. I inflated my paddle float and installed it onto the paddle blade. Meanwhile, the onshore wind had pushed me onto a rocky point at the entrance to the boat launch. With the paddle in one hand, I pushed the kayak to get it away from the rocks.

I pushed the kayak only 3 feet, but I was never able to reach it again. One moment I was in control, holding onto the kayak, and the next moment it was gone. The wind took it away, well beyond my ability to retrieve it. It quickly traveled 30 feet across the entrance to the boat launch and bounced ashore on low rocks, leaving bits of gel coat in the intertidal zone.

On reflection: Letting go of your kayak is never a good idea, even if you are right next to shore.

—Tony Bridge

---

time to arrive. Although good advice tells us to paddle with one or more paddling partners, a dependence on others to come to your rescue is fundamentally unsafe. Each paddler is independently responsible for personal safety. Traveling in groups adds to safety, but the group does not replace the need for personal skill and judgment.

During cold-water immersion, it is imperative that the paddler's torso be out of the water as soon as possible. Reentering a flooded cockpit has the paddler's torso out of the water, but in an unstable kayak with a high potential for a second capsize. If another kayaker does arrive on the scene, this second person can help support the rescued kayak and aid with the rest of the rescue.

You don't get a second chance to make a first attempt. During your first attempt at getting back into your kayak, you will have the most energy and the least stress. Each unsuccessful attempt at a rescue draws from you a significant amount of physical and psychological strength. The ability to use self-rescue skills decreases as anxiety and fatigue quickly increase. If it takes a little longer to get it done right the first time, the extra time has been well spent.

Reenter and Roll

There are occasions when even the most proficient paddlers, who seem to have the ability to roll up in almost any circumstance, find themselves making a wet exit and then swimming alongside the kayak. If you are one of these people with excellent skills at rolling, reentering the overturned kayak and executing a roll may be the quickest and simplest way to recover from a capsize and wet exit.

After your wet exit, you are holding onto your paddle and your kayak. With luck, you will be both on the upwind side of the kayak and on the side of your best roll—but of course it will not always work out that way.

For a reentry on the right-hand side of the overturned kayak followed by a right-handed roll, hold onto the kayak and the paddle with your left hand. (You can also hold the paddle under your armpit; a paddle leash can be insurance against losing it.) Lie on your back and slide your feet into the cockpit—left foot on the left side of the cockpit and right foot on the right side of the cockpit. Sounds sensible, but the kayak is upside down, so you will have to cross your legs, left ankle crossed over the top of the right. While keeping your head above water, rotate your body slightly away from the kayak; aim your bum at the cockpit seat. Slide in as far in as you can. Relax and take a couple breaths.

You now need to get your bum into the seat and your feet on the footrests. With your right hand, reach back and across your bum and grab the far side of the cockpit coaming—as if to scratch your left hip in a very peculiar way. Take a breath, relax, and pull yourself fully into the kayak. Your head is underwater and your bum is in the seat. Take the time to get seated with feet, knees, and thighs braced in place. With a little practice, this can be done in about 2 seconds.

You are now back in your kayak, paddle in hands and ready to roll up. The cockpit is flooded, causing the kayak to roll much more slowly than normal. Set up for the very best roll you can. Slide your left hand along the paddle shaft to the paddle blade, keeping your hand there, and check the orientation of the blades; the extended paddle grip will increase the chance of a successful roll. An extended paddle will also take longer to sweep out and will be more in time with the slowly moving flooded kayak.

Once in your setup position, sweep slowly, and then at the right time give a strong hip flick. As always, keep your head low. If the roll is imperfect, be ready to give a supportive sculling stroke to finish off.

The greatest difficulty with the reenter

Duff's Scramble

I was attending a sea kayak skills symposium on Orcas Island, in Washington state, eager to see Chris Duff's presentation on self-rescue techniques. Chris had paddled solo from New York to Florida to the Mississippi to Canada and back to New York; he had paddled around England, Scotland, and Wales, then around Ireland; he had paddled around the south island of New Zealand. I was certain he would have something interesting to show us, and I was not disappointed. He even demonstrated a technique that is usually considered simple and unsophisticated—just scrambling back into the boat.

Swimming perpendicular to his kayak, feet near the surface, he said, "Grab the front of the cockpit rim in one hand and the rear of the cockpit rim in the other hand, then just get in." Literally before my jaw could drop, he had pulled himself up and, with a half twist, was sitting in the cockpit with his legs hanging over the side. "Now you just have to slip your feet inside," he said.

He repeated the move several times, each time scrambling instantly back into the kayak with just as much dexterity on his part and just as much amazement on mine.

On reflection: Sometimes we can overlook the simple; but simple is not easy for everyone.

—*Doug Alderson*

Holding onto the paddle, the paddler is laying out flat on the surface and grasping the cockpit rim. From here, the kayaker pulls up onto the back deck and swings a leg over.

(GREG SHEA)

Keeping his weight low, the kayaker moves well forward onto the cockpit, ready to drop his buttocks directly down into the seat.

(GREG SHEA)

Sculling his paddle on the water for support and balance, the kayaker swings his legs into the cockpit. The next tasks are replacing the spray skirt and pumping the water out of the cockpit.

(GREG SHEA)

and roll is having the composure to take your time. You are out of your kayak because something exciting has happened, and it is difficult to slow yourself down. The total time you will have your head underwater is about 5 seconds, but your adrenaline-charged body is in a time warp; 5 seconds may seem a very long time.

Scramble

Simply scrambling back into the kayak is an option. Some paddlers are particularly adept at this technique, while for others it remains entirely elusive. If the kayak is overturned, grasp the cockpit rim and flip the kayak over. Then move to the stern and, facing the bow, straddle the kayak. Shuffle forward along the back deck like a cowboy riding a horse—a back deck clear of gear is an advantage here. Scull your paddle on the water for support and balance.

Paddle Float Techniques

Several solo reentry techniques take advantage of the very helpful attachment of a rigid foam or inflatable float to one blade of a paddle. An inflatable float provides more buoyancy than its rigid counterpart but must be inflated by mouth before it can be used.

Paddle Float Reenter and Roll

Use of a paddle with a float attached to one blade, instead of just the paddle alone, can greatly increase the success rate of any reenter and roll technique. The foam float is quick to install on the paddle blade and will sweep through the water without undue drag; the inflatable float takes more time to inflate and attach, but the increased buoyancy can be beneficial.

Throughout the reenter and roll, keep the paddle perpendicular to the kayak. The additional flotation will keep the paddle on the surface and add some support for a reliable roll.

With a paddle float securely attached to the paddle blade the kayaker is putting his feet on the footrests and his buttocks into the seat.

Firmly seated in the kayak, this paddler is leaning back and using an extended paddle grip to begin the roll.

The paddler has successfully come upright. Leaving the paddle float on the paddle adds support while putting on the spray skirt and pumping the water out of the cockpit.

Paddle Float Outrigger

Use of a paddle float as an outrigger provides stability on one side of the kayak as the swimming paddler climbs back into the cockpit. In this technique, one blade of the paddle is secured flat onto the deck of the kayak, usually by rigging or bungee cords installed for that purpose. The blade with the float is in the water, and the result is additional flotation and an outrigger effect.

The paddle float outrigger works especially well in calm conditions. In difficult sea conditions, it is difficult to manipulate rescue devices such as a paddle float while maintaining a hold on the kayak and the paddle.

If you need additional support for balance, use a paddle float on the end of your paddle.   (GREG SHEA)

Without specialized deck rigging to hold the paddle blade on the back deck, it can be held by hand.   (GREG SHEA)

This kayak is outfitted with sturdy bungee on the back deck. The paddle blade is slipped beneath the bungee to hold it at right angles to the kayak. For further aid, a sling of rope is looped around the coaming. The bottom of the sling should hang at a depth convenient to step into.

The paddle-float outrigger adds stability, and the sling assists the paddler in climbing onto the deck.

Keeping some weight on the outrigger ensures that the kayak won't capsize in the opposite direction.

Back in the kayak, the paddler leaves the outrigger in place until the skirt is attached and the cockpit is pumped out.

Paddle Float Outrigger and Sling

A sling is a loop of line used to create a stirrup, or step, for the swimmer to step into as an aid to getting out of the water and into the kayak. A sling can be made from 12′ of floating 3/8″ diameter line tied into a loop with a water knot. A sling, secured around the cockpit coaming, can be used in conjunction with a paddle float outrigger. Adding a sling will take longer, but it may be a necessary support for a tired or weak swimmer.

Getting the Water Out

When the cockpit is flooded, you need to get the water out. Good kayak design that minimizes the volume of the cockpit and a good pumping system will put you safely back on your way. Unless you are close to shore in calm conditions, leaving the water in is not an option, because it makes for a very unstable kayak.

A variety of pumps are available, offering

A foot pump provides hands-free pumping when you might need your paddle the most.

several solutions to the fundamental safety concern of a flooded cockpit. (See the section "Gear for Removing Water" in chapter 4, "Safety and Rescue Gear," for details on pumping systems and techniques of packing to help minimize flooding.)

A *foot pump* mounted on the front bulk-head permits a solo paddler to empty out a cockpit with the sprayskirt in place and while paddling. A mounted *electric pump* is fast and easy to use, but maintenance is a serious concern. The ability of the electric pump to move lots of water quickly makes it suitable for a double kayak. A *portable hand pump* is inexpensive and easy to carry along, but both hands are needed to operate it. In rough conditions, a paddle float outrigger may be necessary to add enough kayak stability to allow a single paddler to have both hands free to run the pump.

To help limit the amount of water that can enter areas other than the cockpit, empty or partially loaded compartments should be filled with air bags. An added advantage of having air bags in a partially loaded compartment is that they will hold loose items in place.

Assisted Rescue

9

A variety of assisted-rescue techniques are available to undo the short-term consequences of a capsize. As with self rescue, assisted-rescue techniques are judged on two criteria: simplicity and reliability.

The goals of an assisted rescue are to:

- Get the paddler back in the kayak.
- Get the water out of the kayak (before or after the paddler is back in the boat).
- Ensure the stability of the rescued person's kayak (often accomplished by towing).

Bow Rescue

The simplest assisted-rescue technique is the bow rescue (sometimes also called the Eskimo rescue). Its advantages are that the paddler remains seated in the capsized boat and water is prevented from entering.

In this technique the affected paddler must decide to remain submerged and to draw attention to the capsize by banging on the overturned hull. A nearby paddling partner must quickly offer a helping hand, paddle shaft, or kayak bow, providing the capsized paddler something to grab on to in order to pull him- or herself upright.

This technique leaves the capsized paddler in a vulnerable position. A successful recovery requires tenacity on the part of the victim to hold his or her breath while upside down waiting for assistance, and speed and precision on the part of the rescuer.

Learning a bow rescue is part of the progression of learning to roll. Like a roll, a bow rescue is a complete rescue, in that the kayaker remains seated and returns upright with no water in the cockpit. Because it requires a second paddler, this rescue technique is usually slower and more difficult than a roll. If you are interested in using this method, practice it with your paddling partners so they know how it works and are aware you will be expecting their help after a capsize.

The most difficult part of waiting for a bow rescue is holding your breath and remaining confident that your partner will quickly arrive. Some paddlers have an enormous commitment to staying in their kayak and will hold their breath for extraordinary lengths of time. You can extend your hang time by swimming with your kayak, twisting up to get an all-important breath of air and checking to see if anyone is coming to your aid.

The angled-approach bow rescue. Approaching the overturned kayak at an angle is preferred. The rescuer's bow can make contact and slide down to meet the victim's hands.   (GREG SHEA)

Assisted Reentry

The goal of an assisted reentry is to get the capsized kayaker back into the kayak. Reentries are often described in fine detail, showing exactly how the kayak should be oriented and specifying a sequence of steps to follow. When a rescue needs to be quick, however, the orientation of the kayak and a prescriptive set of steps become less important. With prac-

A bow rescue with side presentation. When the kayaks are parallel, the rescuer places the victim's hand onto a paddle shaft. It is best to place the victim's hand onto something stable and let the victim take control of rolling up.

(GREG SHEA)

Strong paddling techniques on the part of the rescuer are all-important. To get quickly to the rescue, a kayak must be turned, accelerated forward to approach the overturned kayak at the correct angle, and slowed down just before contact.   (GREG SHEA)

tice, an assisted rescue can be effective with the kayak in any orientation and with a wide variety of methods for the swimmer to reenter the cockpit.

Communication is a key component of any assisted technique, and communication is vastly improved by prior practice, making both parties familiar with shared technique and equipment. It is a matter of judgment on whether to return the paddler into a flooded cockpit or to first tip out the water. A fully loaded touring kayak in rough seas, with a small cockpit volume and a foot pump, would lead to a decision to reenter the flooded cockpit and then pump the water out. A lightly loaded kayak in calm, warm seas, with a large

Assisted side-by-side reentry—holding onto the kayak. A firm grip on the deck lines is necessary to keep the kayak stable. Leaning on the kayak, using your body, adds considerable support to the raft. If deck lines are not available, the rescuer will need to lean over, give the kayak a good hug, and hang on. (GREG SHEA)

cockpit, would suggest tipping out the water prior to reentry.

As a rescuer, knowing your abilities and the limitations of your equipment is only half the story; you also should know the capabilities of the victim and of that person's equipment.

Side by Side

In the quick and reliable technique of side-by-side assisted reentry, a rescuer paddles to the kayak of the person in the water and pulls alongside. The rescuer grasps the other kayak

Hand in Hand

A low swell was rolling in, and the surf was 3 to 4 feet high. I was the last to leave the beach. Twice as I began to secure my sprayskirt, the boat was knocked sideways by incoming waves and the cockpit took water. With two paddling partners waiting for me outside the surf, I simply pushed the half-flooded kayak out into deeper water, jumped in, and paddled out through the surf with the sprayskirt unattached.

Lloyd came over to lend a hand. We tucked the paddles under the deck bungees on Lloyd's kayak and began to pump out my cockpit. Between the two of us, there were too many hands and not quite enough communication;

during the pumping, I capsized, with no paddle.

We were close to the line of surf and I really did not want to wet-exit, swim, and run the risk of being swept back to the beach to start all over again. I stayed in the overturned kayak, reached up, and slapped on the overturned hull. I felt a helping hand in mine, and with head down and a quick flick of the hips, I was upright, spluttering, and we resumed the pump-out.

On reflection: The bow rescue can really work when you need it—as long as you can stay cool while submerged, and can count on a good partner to race to your aid.

—Tom Hukari

The side sit. Don't overlook a very simple technique like this. As when exiting the edge of a swimming pool, some paddlers will kick, twist, and land seat first in the cockpit.   (GREG SHEA)

The "my-deck" approach. This orientation has advantages when the swimmer has difficulty climbing onto a high-volume kayak and when a smaller rescuer is trying to support a kayak for a larger swimmer. The rescuer's boat sits lower in the water, so the swimmer can submerge the bow, climbing on and using it as a step onto his own kayak.   (GREG SHEA)

and keeps it stable while the paddler in the water climbs back aboard.

In most cases, the kayaks can be in any orientation while the paddler is getting back into the boat. Adaptability is an important aspect of any technique. Unless the paddler has a specific physical need to reenter the kayak in a particular way, orientation should have little effect on the reliability or speed of an assisted side-by-side reentry.

Face Up

The face-up technique, sometimes called British style, is an adaptation of side-by-side assisted reentry. The rescuer keeps both boats stable while the paddler in the water floats feet up and face up between the kayaks, head toward the front, and grasps both kayaks. The trick then is to throw one leg into the cockpit of your kayak and follow by pulling yourself up and into the boat.

Rescue Sling

Rescues often involve swimmers who are weak from cold and fatigue and unable to get into a kayak without some assistance. Sea conditions or an injury might also cause an otherwise capable swimmer to be unable to perform a self rescue or even reenter a kayak

The British-style or face-up technique. Reentering the cockpit from a position between the two kayaks can be done in a feet-first, face-up orientation. This can be quick and easy if you are limber enough to keep your head well back. One advantage of this style is that the paddler drops into the cockpit facing forward.   (GREG SHEA)

that is being firmly held by a rescuer. A rescue sling, looped around the cockpit coaming, provides a step up for the swimmer.

The sling is typically made of a piece of line or webbing, usually 12 to 15 feet long. It can be standard gear or improvised from a towline.

All-in Reentry

If conditions are rough enough to capsize one kayaker, it is likely that others will also cap-size. In this situation, the capsized individuals must help one another get everyone stabilized and back in the kayaks with the water out.

Some people may be able to self-rescue by rolling, then go to the aid of others. Alternatively, a paddler in the water can hold onto another person's kayak, stabilizing it while that person gets back in. The rescued person can then go to work as a rescuer, using assisted-rescue techniques. One such approach is shown in the accompanying sequence of photos.

In one approach to mutual rescue, both swimmers get on top of the overturned kayaks. With the kayaks overturned, breaking waves will not fully flood the cockpits. (GREG SHEA)

One kayak is turned upright and the swimmer reenters. It may be best to partially pump out one kayak before rescuing the second swimmer. (GREG SHEA)

The second swimmer then reenters his kayak. (GREG SHEA)

Both kayaks are pumped out now. The raft should stay together, providing support for each paddler until both are ready to commence paddling. (GREG SHEA)

Scoop 1

A disabled paddler can be returned to a cockpit with little or no self-help. First the swimmer's feet are floated into the kayak, which is held on edge. The lower edge of the cockpit should be down in the water to allow the victim to float in. This is hard for the rescuer to see; fully flood the cockpit before the scoop begins.   (GREG SHEA)

2

Continue to hang onto the victim and provide support; if he is unconscious or seriously injured, the victim may flop onto the rescuer.   (GREG SHEA)

3

Once the swimmer's legs have been stuffed and pushed into the cockpit, the kayak is pushed down and the victim is held low on the back deck. Attempts to lift the victim are usually unsuccessful; it is much easier to push down on the edge of the kayak and roll the kayak beneath the victim. Holding the victim's PFD shoulder strap with an upturned fist and pushing down on the kayak with the elbow can be effective. Tell the victim to stretch out and lay well back.   (GREG SHEA)

Scoop

In some circumstances it may be necessary to physically scoop a capsized paddler back into the kayak—in effect, scooping up the paddler with the cockpit of his or her own kayak. It is a technique that requires some coordination and strength on the part of the rescuer. This technique is commonly used to help a kayaker with a dislocated shoulder or other serious injury. The photographs show how this can be done.

Hand of God

In some unusual circumstances, a kayaker may become trapped upside down in a kayak, perhaps unconscious. In this situation, the rescuer paddles alongside the overturned boat, then reaches across its bottom to the far side and reaches down to grasp the trapped paddler by the PFD shoulder strap. Raise the victim to the surface and proceed as with the second half of the scoop rescue.

Getting the Water Out

Another goal of assisted rescue is to get the water out of the capsized kayak. This can be done at the beginning, middle, or end of a rescue depending on the demands of a particular situation and the preferences of the rescuer and the person being rescued.

Assisted Bow Tip-out

The fastest technique to remove the considerable volume of water in a flooded cockpit is an assisted bow tip-out. If the kayak has a stern bulkhead just behind the seat, a bow tip-out is very quick.

With the kayaks at right angles, you as rescuer should bring the bow of the capsized kayak onto your kayak's deck. To assist in lifting the bow, the swimmer can push the stern down. It may also be necessary to slightly rotate the kayak.

The cockpit will hold enough air to create a suction force that is difficult to release in a straight lift. Holding the bow up and the stern down will quickly empty the cockpit of almost all water.

To avoid hurting yourself as you roll the kayak right side up, be sure to roll it away from your face. The swimmer, pushing down on the stern, must be careful to keep fingers clear of a rudder and its associated steel cables.

With the cockpit now mostly clear of water, you can bring your kayak alongside the other kayak, and the swimmer can reenter using one of the various reentry techniques already discussed.

If time and sea conditions permit, a bow tip-out and assisted reentry will get the swimmer back into a nearly dry cockpit without the need for substantial pumping. With heavy kayaks and doubles, this rescue can be physically challenging. Practice in calm conditions with loaded boats before relying on it in rough conditions.

In some circumstances it may not be possible to tip the water out with a bow tip-out.

The hand of God rescue is similar to the scoop. Reaching well over the overturned kayak, grasp the victim's PFD shoulder strap or any available handhold.

(GREG SHEA)

The last step of the hand of God rescue involves raising the victim to the surface and pushing down on the upper edge of the kayak, bringing the victim and kayak to an upright position—just as in the scoop rescue.

(GREG SHEA)

A more stable but time-consuming technique is to drag the flooded kayak upside down across your own cockpit in an X, and teeter-totter the kayak back and forth, eventually getting the water out. The X is very stable and is also suitable for on-water repairs. For boats without bulkheads or large cockpits, this can be a useful technique.

Quite often the water in the cockpit can be emptied out prior to the swimmer getting back in.

Pumping

Another option for water removal, of course, is to pump the water out. The kayak may have an installed foot pump, and the rescued person can begin using it as soon as he or she is back in the cockpit. A hand pump can also be used, and sometimes it is helpful to use more than one pump at a time to get the water out faster.

In some circumstances, hand and foot pumps will not get the water out fast enough because water sloshes back into the kayak, a problem with kayaks that have insufficient buoyancy. Double kayaks in particular can have this problem, and often rely instead on a faster electric pump.

Flooded Compartments

Watertight bow and stern compartments are more of a hope than a promise. Hatches come loose, neoprene covers are forgotten, deck seams leak, keels wear through and leak, skeg cables leak, and there is the occasional hull puncture. A great deal of thought goes into clearing the water from a flooded cockpit, but a flooded compartment is just as serious. In the case of a hatch leak, a jury-rigged repair

may be temporarily sufficient. When the hull is damaged, pumping may not be an option.

With a partially loaded sea kayak, prevention is the best option. Fill up any empty space in the compartments with air bags, which will prevent the compartment from completely filling up with water.

With fully loaded sea kayaks, the challenge is greater. You may be able to pump some water out with a hand or electric pump. If some of the gear in the hatch is packed in dry bags, this will prevent the compartment from filling completely. The compartment may have to be partially unpacked before the water can be removed.

One of the advantages of a day hatch compartment is that it is so small that flooding it does not seriously compromise the stability of the kayak. At least for the short-term you can leave it flooded and deal with the problem later.

Towing

The final goal of an assisted rescue is to stabilize the formerly capsized kayak. Stability means to be in control of your kayak—that is, in control of the angle, motion, and tilt of the boat. Any technique that provides balance, maintains direction, and generates motion is a stabilizing technique. The most common assisted-rescue techniques for stabilizing a kayak are towing and rafting up.

Towing is an indispensable safety and rescue technique. Towing can improve safety in a variety of situations and be an instrumental part of a rescue. In a wind or a current, towing can keep a slower paddler with the group. Towing a distressed paddler to shore or to calmer water can keep a situation under control, preventing the need for a rescue. In a difficult rescue, towing can keep kayaks in place or move them away from hazards.

Towlines

Towlines are best when used as a specialized piece of gear, dedicated to use in towing. Towline systems attach to the paddler's body or to the kayak. (See the section "Towlines" in chapter 4, "Safety and Rescue Gear," for more information on towlines.)

Towlines require several basic features. Every towline should:

- Float.
- Absorb shock.
- Have a method of quick, reliable, one-hand release.
- Include an attachment clip that is easy to use and reliable.

Towlines can be any length, but generally vary from 5 to 50 feet. Long towlines are used for towing over long distances and when moving a victim away from a hazard. Short lines, sometimes called pig tails or cow tails, are used for quick tows over short distances. One towline can provide a range of lengths, as with a 30-foot line that can be daisy-chained down to a 10-foot line. Another option is to use a cow tail onto which you add a longer line as needed.

Practice with your towline in a variety of

conditions. Using towlines in rough water can be deceptively complex. Always carry a knife in a secure and accessible spot on your PFD to cut the rope if it ever becomes necessary. Beware of becoming entangled in a towline.

Bags, belt, and the towline itself can get tangled in a rudder or in gear stored on the back deck. Take care to release these types of systems at arm's length away from the kayak.

Contact Rafted Tow

A *contact tow*, quick and simple to set up, is limited to towing over short distances. In this technique, the towing kayak rafts up with the other kayak. The paddler in the other kayak, perhaps sick or exhausted, grasps or leans on the rescue kayak to maintain the rafting configuration. The rescuer then paddles in a normal fashion or with an offset grip on the paddle, moving both kayaks forward.

When the goal is to begin towing the distressed paddler as quickly as possible, it is important to make contact without fussing to turn the kayaks around one way or the other. When time permits, however, a face-to-face orientation is preferred, allowing easy communication.

Keeping the kayaks together can be difficult. Practice different variations in a variety of conditions and choose the ones that work best for you. The use of rudders or skegs can help keep the kayaks on track.

Attaching a cow tail or other short length of towline makes the contact tow considerably more effective. With a line attached, the rescuer can concentrate on moving the raft forward. Maneuverability is improved, and in rough conditions the tow is easier to control.

When only two paddlers are on the water and one paddler is sick or injured, a contact tow may be the only option. In this situation, an in-line tow would leave no one to stay next to the paddler in trouble to help stabilize that person's kayak.

If the paddling group includes a double

kayak, a tired or ill paddler in a single kayak can exchange places with someone in the double.

In-line Tow

The in-line tow is useful to assist an otherwise able paddler in keeping up speed or maintaining a desired course in a wind or current. With a properly prepared towline, an in-line tow is quick and easy to attach.

Towing downwind with following waves, the towline needs to be longer than the distance between waves so that the trailing kayak does not get pushed forward into the towing kayak. The paddlers must try to keep in touch, though communication may be difficult. Both persons can paddle in order to make good forward progress. From this basic model, many variations are possible to suit a variety of needs.

In-line Rafted Tow

A paddler in distress often will be unable to continue paddling or to safely maintain the stability of the kayak. This paddler is likely to capsize, creating an even more difficult rescue. The paddler may require medical attention or face-to-face emotional support that can only be provided by another kayaker who is rafted with the paddler. This technique provides for these rafted kayaks to be towed.

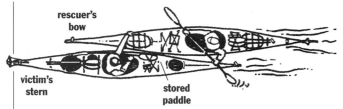

Contact tow. Quite simply, the two kayaks come into contact without the use of any lines or devices; the rescuer paddles the raft forward. The rescuer might choose to take an offset grip on the paddle to extend his or her reach over the victim's kayak.

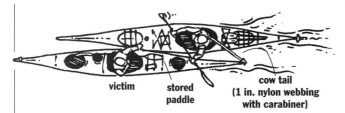

Cow-tail contact push tow, or toggle tow. Using a cow tail, as shown, the rescuer propels the raft forward. Forward motion draws the kayaks together and the raft is quite stable and maneuverable. The victim's rudder or skeg should be retracted, and the rescuer's rudder should be deployed.

In-line tow. An able-bodied paddler may need help making forward progress or keeping a straight course in a strong wind. Rudders and skegs should be used as needed. Communication between paddlers can be difficult.

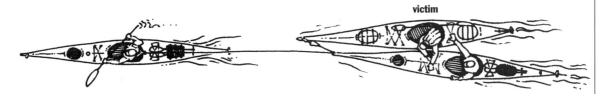

In-line rafted tow. A tired or disabled paddler may need the support of a partner. The towline is run under the perimeter lines on the helper's deck and then to the victim's boat. In this way, the helper can move forward to disengage the towline if necessary.

In-line/push tow combination. This is a particularly effective arrangement for two rescuers. Both rescuers can paddle forward. The victim is supported and can be reassured by face-to-face contact.

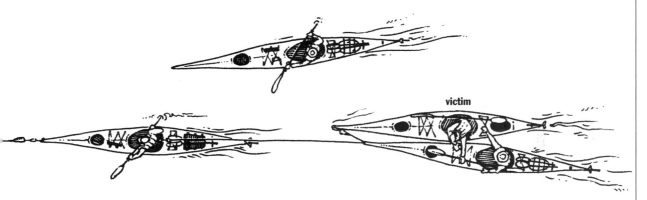

In-line rafted tow with multiple towboats. Additional kayaks in the tow will ease the load and increase forward progress. Communication is difficult, and a leader outside of the tow can pass along instructions and information.

To attach the towline, pass it beneath the perimeter lines of the support kayak and then clip into the perimeter line or end toggle of the victim's kayak. This arrangement keeps the two kayaks together. If the towline needs to be let go, the support person can paddle forward and release the towline from the victim's bow. Deploying skegs or rudders will help if the raft is hard to keep together or steering in the wind is difficult.

Adding additional tow kayaks in series to the in-line tow increases the efficiency and spreads out the effort among several paddlers. A second kayak clips into the bow of the first tow kayak. There is concern for the tow kayak that is between the lead kayak and the raft, because this kayak is now hooked up front and back with rope. Good teamwork and communication are important. A kayaker not involved in the towing

A Kayaker Disappears

At Race Rocks lighthouse, near Victoria, British Columbia, the wind was recorded at 55 knots. Nearby, four kayakers were trying to paddle just a few hundred yards more, to the entrance of a bay that would provide a change in course, some shelter from the wind, and a safe landing site.

David and Ted were side by side in front, with Rene and Brian just 30 feet behind. The howling wind and the waves breaking against the rocky shore 200 feet to the right made voice communication between the two pairs of kayakers impossible. David kept looking over his shoulder to keep track of the second pair.

As he looked one time, Rene gave an OK signal. The next time he looked, he could see Rene still paddling hard, but Brian was nowhere in sight. In the steep waves, it would be difficult to find an overturned kayak.

Ted paddled farther offshore to get a better line of sight down the gap between the shore and a downwind island. David turned and ran downwind while Rene scouted the nearby shore. Now all three searchers were out of range of any communication, and each paddler was alone.

At that point, David saw Brian standing on a beach in a tiny sheltered cove cut into the rocky shore. He had feared being blown onto the shore where waves were breaking dangerously against jagged rocks, so he had decided on his own to turn and run downwind, and he found this place to land.

David's concern now turned to the safety of Ted and Rene, who were still to windward looking for Brian. Staying outside the cove, David managed to raise their attention. Soon all four were together in the haven of the cove. They had ended up in an out-of-the-way place, and it took until evening to get everyone home safe.

On reflection: This is a situation where use of a towline might have been sufficient to assist Brian in making the short distance to the bay and to safety in a known location. A tow might have kept the group moving forward together and prevented a long and stressful day.

—Doug Alderson

can be very helpful in coordinating the rescue.

V-tow

Two towing kayaks can each be attached directly to the towed kayak, forming a V pattern. Communication between the tow kayaks is better than with an in-line tow, but this tow is not as simple or effective. The towlines will be at an angle to the direction of movement, causing more drag through the water. When crossing eddy lines or paddling in crosswinds,

it is difficult to maintain the separation of the towing kayaks.

Towing in Place

There are times when a tow is used to keep a raft of two or more kayaks in one place. Rescuers may be helping an injured paddler, repairing a damaged kayak, or assisting a paddler who is reentering a kayak.

This type of tow can keep a raft from drifting into danger. The pull of the tow can be against the wind, for example, keeping the

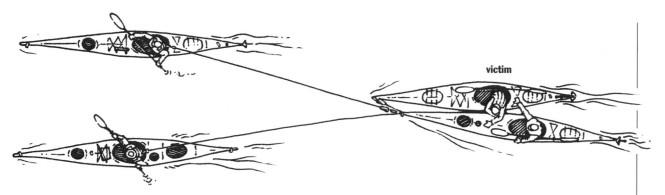

V-tow. Two towboats can be attached directly to the raft. This configuration tends to be awkward in rough seas and current. The proper separation of the towboats is important. Too much separation drags the towlines through the water, causing unnecessary resistance; too little separation and the paddlers begin to collide. An in-line tow is usually preferred.

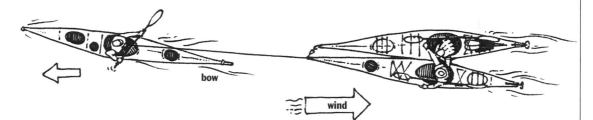

Towing in place. There are times when a tow can be used to stop kayaks from drifting with the wind or current. In some cases, to assist in communication, the towing kayak can go in reverse.

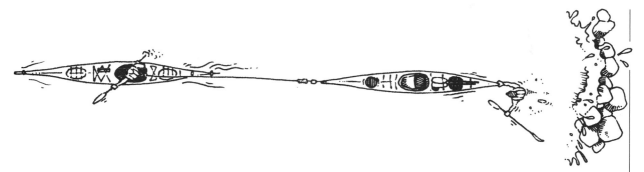

Extrication from a hazard. At times, a kayaker may need to be towed away from an imminent hazard. Before the swimmer reenters his or her kayak, one or more rescuers can tow the kayak and the swimmer to a safer location.

raft pointed upwind into the waves. In this situation, it helps if the towing kayaker can paddle in reverse, and thus face the raft. Towing in reverse is more awkward than towing while moving forward, but there is an advantage in being able to see the raft and observe the situation closely.

Towing from a Hazard

A tow can pull a kayak away from a hazard. This method could be used, for example, in a situation where a paddler has made a wet exit from a kayak near rocks and is in a place too dangerous for a standard rescue. In this case, you might be able to tow the kayak and the swimmer, holding onto the stern toggle, to a safer place, where the rescue can then be completed.

A similar tow works when rescues are conducted in strong current. Capsizes often occur where moving water meets still water. As the kayak crosses the eddy line, sudden forces can upset the paddler. A rescuer can place a towline onto the stricken kayak and tow across the current back toward the eddy. With the swimmer still holding onto the kayak, a second rescuer can move in to help with a reentry.

Towing a Swimmer

On a breezy day, a capsize followed by a wet exit sometimes results in the paddler losing touch with the kayak. On a rocky shore with breaking waves, it might even be safer for the swimmer to avoid contact with the kayak.

In these cases, the swimmer and the kayak must be rescued separately. In a group rescue, one paddler can catch the wayward kayak and tow it back. Another rescuer can tow the swimmer out of harm's way prior to reentering the kayak.

Simply having a swimmer lie face down on the rear deck of a rescuer's kayak is an excellent early step in such a rescue. This gets the swimmer's torso out of the water, especially important if the rescue is taking place in cold water.

A kayak with a swimmer flopped over the rear deck is certainly easier to control than one with the swimmer hanging off the bow. However, if the swimmer needs only to be transported a few yards, the bow will do. The rescuer can paddle forward or backward.

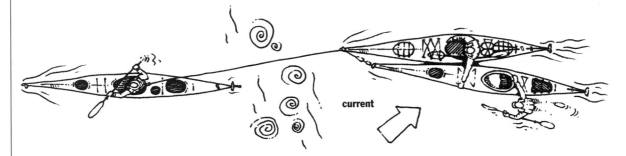

Towing to safety before reentry. During a rescue in a current or near hazards a towing kayak in combination with an assisted reentry can keep the raft safe while the reentry is completed.

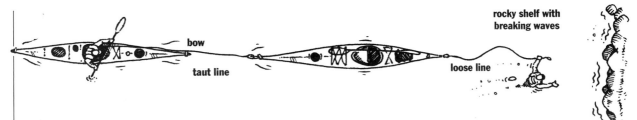

Towlines can be used in a wide variety of difficult situations. If it becomes necessary to land on a rocky shore, a paddler can exit his or her kayak with a towline in hand. A partner at the other end of the towline can provide enough control to keep the abandoned kayak from surging onto the rocks. Once the swimmer has arrived on shore the first kayak can be retrieved. The second paddler can then approach the shore with someone on shore to help with the landing.

On Deck

It was the end of a long weekend and we had to land in larger surf than we would have wished. One oversize, plunging breaker hit Tony full force. Unsuccessful at rolling up, he made a wet exit.

Any rescue attempt to get him back into his boat would be too dangerous in the surf. He was tired and cold, and getting him into shore was the first priority. Valiantly he hung on to his kayak and paddle, and it took a lot of persuasion before he followed my demands to let go of everything and swim onto the back deck of my kayak. One of the other paddlers would fetch his boat and paddle.

With Tony on the back deck, we headed in.

On the way, another large set of breakers came through. As the kayak began to roll over, I shouted "Off!" He understood completely and slid off my deck. I rolled up, shouted "On!" and we were again heading in. But we both knew that waves come in sets. "Off!" I shouted again, then the roll, then "On!" Three times we played our game before both of us, now nearly exhausted, made it safely to shore.

On reflection: It is important to keep energy in reserve to cope with the unexpected. A stressful rescue is very tiring.

—Michael Pardy

Keeping Together during a Rescue

In a rescue situation within a kayaking group, it is common for some of the paddlers to be involved in the rescue while others must stand by to await the outcome. In a large group, it generally will not be helpful to have everyone directly involved in the rescue. The waiting paddlers have to stay together during a difficult time. There are several techniques for accomplishing this.

The Raft

The idea is simple. Line all the kayaks up cockpit-to-cockpit, lay the paddles across the cockpits, and use arms and hands to hold the paddles down. The resulting raft is surprisingly stable. It is a social configuration that can provide physical and emotional support to paddlers in a stressful situation. Most importantly, it keeps them together. The raft

Simply hanging onto the bow may be sufficient to return a swimmer to safety. (GREG SHEA)

A swimmer on the back deck can be transported a good distance in quite rough water. (GREG SHEA)

Swimmer to the Rescue

It was winter and we were out kayak surfing. It was very windy and cold, the surf was irregular, and the bigger sets were breaking hard well out. I had a close encounter of the swimming kind with a steep plunging wave, and my kayak and I made it back to shore at about the same time.

I was standing above the beach trying to warm up while watching the others make their way in. One pair of paddlers had paused in the soup zone about 150 feet offshore. The kayaks were sitting sideways to the incoming waves. I turned and said to a friend, "They had better get out of there."

The words had hardly left my mouth when I looked back and saw one paddler in the water. The capsized paddler was on the seaward side of the kayak, hanging on. A long minute elapsed and there was no action by the swimmer or the other paddler.

I walked down to the water's edge and tried to get the paddler's attention. Waves were engulfing the overturned kayak. It was high tide, and the larger waves were now lifting driftwood logs into the water. Standing waist deep in the water, I still could not get anyone's attention. Chest deep, I made one more shout without a reply before beginning to swim out.

At the kayak, the swimmer reported a dislocated shoulder. There was no way she would be getting back into the kayak. Gripping both kayak and paddle, she wouldn't let go of anything. Although close to shore, we were not making any progress in. The longshore current was drawing us along the beach to what must be an outgoing rip current.

With waves breaking over our heads, the other kayaks were not much help, and anybody to seaward was a distinct hazard. In spite of my repeated shouts, a throw line from a kayak was not available. With each wave I swam hard, trying to push kayak and paddler along, but it was very slow progress. A good set of waves finally pushed us closer in, where the soup pushed us the last 50 feet. Several people on shore rushed to help, and the ambulance was called.

On reflection: I left the beach thinking that I would swim the victim in on her back; it didn't work out that way. Communication with other potential rescuers was very difficult. A towline would have made the rescue quicker and easier.

—*Doug Alderson*

also makes an excellent platform from which to perform any number of tasks, including kayak repair and administering first aid.

The raft has some inherent weaknesses. No one is steering or paddling, so the raft is at the mercy of the waves, wind, and current. A raft will also drift faster than one or two kayaks together. The raft can become separated from the other kayaks because it will drift faster.

Paddling in Place

Another strategy that works well is to have the group paddle in place. In practice, this means keeping the boats headed upwind and into the waves. This strategy has the advantage of keeping everyone together, but under his or her own power. If the situation changes, it is easy to reorganize and pull out extra resources that might be required to complete a rescue. This formation can be difficult for new paddlers, leaving some people feeling unsupported during a difficult situation on the water.

The Buddy System

Faced with a demanding environment, it is useful to organize paddling buddies. This system ensures that an extra set of eyes, ears, and hands is looking after each paddler. It also helps reassure new or uncertain paddlers, because a stronger paddler can be paired with a weaker one.

This system also improves the numbers game. A group of eight paddlers can be thought of as eight autonomous units or as four units of two paddlers each. This improves communication and reinforces existing supports within the group. Leaders have less to worry about. This system works well in conjunction with paddling in place. Once the group is secure, attention can be focused on the unfolding rescue.

The raft works well with new paddlers or in situations where a stable platform is needed, as in a kayak repair, or sending a radio message.   (GREG SHEA)

Damage to the Kayak

Lots of little and not so little things can happen to gear while on the water. Serious problems such as a damaged rudder cable, a broken paddle, or a leaking kayak are not uncommon. These problems are sometimes

Paddling with a partner provides companionship and an extra set of hands in the event of a problem.   (GREG SHEA)

experienced during a rescue, or can in themselves result in the need for a rescue. They require attention, often involving teamwork among paddlers.

Broken Rudder Cable

Many paddlers rely on a rudder to steer their kayak, and if the cable breaks, they are at a serious disadvantage. Also, in many kayaks the loss of the cable means that the cockpit pedals, which are used as footrests, are now loose, and the paddler is no longer held as firmly into the kayak.

In these cases, the rudder cable must be repaired. Find out where the break occurred. If it is within the cable housing on the inside of the kayak, there is not much that can be done, except to paddle to shore and replace the cable.

If the break occurred at either end of the cable, it is possible to temporarily tie off the cable so that the rudder and pedals can still be used. Most cables are made of an aircraft-grade braided stainless steel cable, which is very stiff and slippery. The only knot we have found that will hold is a friction knot, but it shortens the rudder cable considerably, which in turn offsets the pedals. You can shorten or lengthen the pedal on one side to correct this.

Rudder cables are prone to breaking, so an extra length of cable, pliers, and a screwdriver need to accompany each trip. Practice replacing the cables at home, and regularly check them for wear. Cables rarely break in calm conditions. Consider how to do this repair while on the water. The easiest method is to raft up and get someone to tie off the cable. If it is broken in the cockpit, the paddler can fix it while being supported.

We encourage paddlers to learn to maneuver their kayaks without the aid of a rudder, even if the boat has one. There are situations and techniques where a rudder is appropriate, but in general it is important not to rely on the rudder too much.

Leaking Kayak

Most kayaks leak at one time or another. In most cases, the stability of the kayak and the safety of the kayaker are not compromised because the intake of water is minimal. Repairs can wait until shore or the end of the trip.

However, there can be more serious problems. Situations where a kayak develops a leak serious enough to require an on-water repair are few, but it doesn't take much imagination to set up a scenario that has a kayak along an exposed coastline hitting a partially submerged rock. Paddlers have been in situations where a small stone lodged under the seat slowly wears a hole through the hull, or a deck seam comes apart.

The kayaker with the leaky boat needs to raft up with another paddler and look for the hole. If it is found, it can usually be quickly patched with a two-part epoxy putty stick or plumber's Denso Tape (duct tape does not adhere to a wet surface).

If the location of the hole is uncertain or out of reach, the two paddlers have a useful technique at their disposal. The paddler in the leaky kayak can climb onto the deck of the assisting kayak and face the paddler as they both straddle the kayak and hang their feet into the water on either side. From this position, the disabled kayak can be pulled up and across the assisting kayak. The resulting crossed, or X, configuration is very stable, allowing the paddlers to look for the hole and to patch it.

Lost Hatch Cover

Whether a hatch cover is lost on shore or on the water, the answer is the same: cover the hatch with something waterproof and secure it in place. The easiest solution is a heavy-duty plastic bag secured with a bungee cord. In a pinch, paddlers have used dry bags, raincoats, and even an inflatable paddle float. A square of yellow or orange plastic and a short length of rope or bungee fit easily into a cockpit back or the pocket of a PFD.

Broken Foot Brace

Foot braces (footrests, or pedals) commonly break for two reasons: the mounting screws come loose, or the mechanism that holds the pedal in place fails.

Most foot braces are mounted through the hull of the kayak with large screws. If the screws loosen, two problems result: water gets in, and the brace is no longer secure in the kayak. The best thing is to replace the screws, either on shore or while rafted up with another kayak. If replacement screws are not available and the loose screws will not tighten, cover the hole or holes with Denso Tape or a bit of Ding Stick.

If the mechanism that holds a pedal in place fails, try resetting the pedal. If this doesn't work, try jamming a bit of tape, wood, or anything else behind the mechanism to secure the pedal. If nothing works, you'll have to paddle without it.

Jammed Skeg

A retractable skeg often becomes jammed in the skeg box by rocks and other debris as a boat is launched. Forcing the skeg down often ends up kinking the cable. The best solution is to support yourself on a second kayak while a third paddler works to free the skeg from its housing.

If the skeg is really stuck, a knife or other long, thin, stiff object can be used to remove the debris. Many paddlers use a hockey skate lace tightener or a hemostat (a type of medical pliers) to free the skeg. You can also drill a small hole in the bottom of the skeg, attach a bit of fishing line or twine through the hole, and pull on it to release the skeg.

Broken Paddle

There is not much to be done about a broken paddle except to carry a spare on the deck. Reaching the spare paddle can be difficult in rough conditions. Practice getting it out and deployed quickly.

Some paddlers recommend carrying the spare paddle on the front deck, where it is easily accessible and out of the way of equipment like towlines and paddle floats. More common in North America, however, is to carry the spare on the back deck. In either location, consider the layout of the deck and equipment carefully and practice retrieving important equipment quickly and reliably.

Another useful skill is to practice paddling short distances with a single blade, like a canoe paddle. If a paddle breaks it may be easier to just hold onto one end and paddle with the good blade, or retrieve only one half of the spare set. This is especially true in rough conditions or near hazards, where it is important to keep paddling to ensure stability. Some paddlers carry only one half of a spare paddle.

Guidelines for Effective Rescue

10

A rescue is the last line of defense in managing safety, and encompasses all the decisions, actions, and techniques necessary to return a kayaker to full function after an accident. The four lines of defense in safety are:

1. Planning.
2. Physical and mental skills.
3. Self rescue and assisted rescue.
4. Outside rescue.

Planning anticipates potential problems and designs strategies to avoid, accept, and reduce harm. Physical and mental training prepares us for accident prevention and response. Rescues are what you do when something goes wrong.

In the natural world, where risk factors constantly change and are especially difficult to predict, some hazards are obvious and others are hidden. The trip plan may be for a comfortable journey, but miles from outside help, the group must also be able to cope with trouble. While it is pleasant to paddle in conditions well within our skill level, it is inevitable that we will venture out into environments that challenge our abilities.

There is a tendency in our anticipation of hazards to focus on open-water risks. In fact, most accidents occur within 100 meters of the sea's edge. Launching, landing, and forays near shore are more likely to result in an accident than offshore paddling, but heightened awareness near shore will minimize such risks.

Most sea kayak accidents are minor. Good planning and early intervention will ameliorate or even stop severe accidents. A successful rescue is as much a result of good judgment as good technique. We must quickly choose how to be effective in our interventions, tailoring our responses to suit the circumstances. By definition, the victim is the first one on the scene, and may have the resources for a self rescue. In all cases, the person in trouble must make every effort to be active and helpful in the rescue.

Rescues are often complex and full of surprises, and no one technique works in all situations. The variables are too many. Over our years of paddling, we have encountered an almost endless number of complications during rescue, including kayaks that drifted away, jammed rudders, broken rudder cables, punctured hulls, leaky skeg control cables, broken deck hardware, deflated paddle floats, faulty pumps, defective flares, broken paddles, and lost hatch covers, along with kayakers suffering from seasickness, dislocated shoulders, leg cramps, panic, or hypothermia.

Preparation for dealing with a rescue begins long before the trip itself. Before leaving on a trip:

- Practice rescue techniques, learning who does what and how. Be familiar with each other's gear.

- Discuss probable scenarios and leadership roles.

- Balance the need for self-sufficiency with reliance on the group for rescue.

- Have the right rescue gear. Keep it in good working condition and replace worn or suspect gear. Remember that your rescue may depend on other people's gear.

- Identify access and egress points along the route. Identify the location of emergency response services including Coast Guard, hospitals, ambulances, helicopters, and water taxis, and communication protocols to reach those services.

Throughout the trip, anticipate problems and devise risk management strategies. Place yourself in a position to observe, to be observed, and to be nearby when the unexpected occurs. Most incidents (in which potential for harm exists) and accidents (in which harm has already occurred) are the culmination of a chain of events. Safety management will allow for early detection and intervention, so that the chain can be broken and the harm minimized.

A key characteristic of a successful rescue is effective leadership, which ensures a timely and reliable response to an incident or accident. Unfortunately, leadership is often lacking as group members attempt to deal with the stress of a rescue. Leadership during a rescue is as much about psychology as about physical ability. Leading a rescue requires clear and focused thinking and an ability to remain in control of the situation. It is often best for the leader to stay at a place that is best for communication and control. When there are other hands available to carry out the rescue, the leader's responsibility is to observe, assess, and direct the operation.

Sea conditions may not allow for an assisted rescue. Even when traveling in a group you may have to rely on your own resources.

(GREG SHEA)

Groups must identify leaders in advance. There is no time during a rescue for this debate. Agree on a rescue leader. Because the rescue leader could also be a victim, or be unavailable, have a backup leadership strategy. Rescues are seldom simple, you will often have to improvise.

Rescue Decisions

Rescues do not follow from normal daily events; rescues follow incidents or accidents. Rescues impose time constraints, high levels of stress, and serious potential consequences on rescuers—challenges that are barriers to good decision making. Decisions must be made quickly and acted upon in a timely manner because of the increased potential for harm.

The steps in the decision-making model introduced in chapter 1 can be applied to a rescue: Identify the problem, gather information, make a choice, take action, reflect on the outcome.

Identify the Problem

When a rescue situation arises, the group needs to mobilize an effective and timely response. This process begins by identifying the problem, and at the same time specifying a desired outcome. Next comes the gathering of information. These steps are often overlooked in times of crisis as would-be rescuers rush to help.

Practice Makes Perfect

Here's the training scenario I was given: We are paddling along an exposed coastline with limited landing options. I am leading the group in and around some rocks, exploring the intertidal zone. Suddenly one of the kayakers capsizes about 150 feet behind me. The boat is still—a telltale sign of an unconscious kayaker.

I take it from there. I back-paddle to the capsized boat, reach over, and pull the kayaker to the surface. The paddler flops into my arms. He is unconscious, but he is breathing strongly and steadily.

There is little I can do on the water. I call the others over and organize a rafted tow to a boulder beach about 100 yards away. There is no place to easily land a kayak, so I give my kayak to another paddler to tend while I get into the water and swim toward shore, towing the unconscious paddler in his kayak.

On shore another kayaker and I carry the paddler onto a flat spot higher up on the beach.

I make a Mayday radio call, asking for urgent assistance. I continue to monitor the unconscious paddler and also direct the others in establishing a temporary camp.

My scenario was over, and the "unconscious paddler" miraculously recovered. The debriefing began. I was asked what my priorities were during the rescue. I said my priorities were first to ensure the safety of the group, then to get the paddler to shore so we could administer first aid, and then to arrange for evacuation of the victim.

On reflection: It was not an easy scenario, and it challenged my decision-making ability. All my training and practice over the past few years paid off: despite the stress, I was able to process a lot of information in a short period of time to complete a successful rescue.

—*Michael Pardy*

Out of My Mind

The morning broke with a forecast for increasingly poor weather; ocean reports offshore were for swell of 12 to 15 feet. Within our sight, the sea conditions looked much smaller and manageable. In the half light before dawn, the three of us quietly broke camp and readied our boats.

Just before leaving the beach, we confirmed with each other that venturing out on the next leg of our paddling trip was an acceptable thing to do. Many miles of difficult paddling lay ahead, along miles of steep cliffs that offered no chance of going ashore. All was ready, and we departed the shelter of our little beach. Seas were 4 to 6 feet, with a headwind at 20 knots or more and gusts to over 30. At times we were going backward.

About 90 minutes after leaving the beach, Dave called over to me: "Where is your PFD?"

My PFD was gone! I have never paddled without the safety and flotation of a PFD jacket. It didn't seem possible that it could have blown off. It took several seconds for me to realize that I had never put it on. I must have left it on the beach.

On reflection: We were so intently focused on the weather that a fundamental safety preparation was forgotten. It's difficult, but essential, to keep the basics in mind at all times. A buddy check before leaving the beach is always a good idea. Look over your buddy to see if he or she and his or her kayak are ready to go: hatches locked down, gear secured on deck, PFD on and zippered, and if he or she has a sunny disposition ready for the challenges of a day out paddling. If you check them, he or she can check you.

—Tom Hukari

Gather Information

Take time to assess the scene. Determine the likely causes of the accident. Identify hazards (such as rocks, current, or surf) and likely resources (such as other paddlers, convenient beaches, or other boats). Prepared with this information, rescuers will be better able to mobilize a response that does not put anyone else at risk.

This assessment includes initial planning to meet the three critical priorities of any rescue: secure all members of the group, extricate the distressed paddler, and rehabilitate the paddler. Based on the information gathered during this part of the rescue process, rescuers can devise appropriate strategies to address each of these priorities and can define and weigh the options for action.

Make a Choice

Choose the most appropriate option for action. Keep it simple and reliable. Simple, reliable rescue techniques ensure a quick response and minimize the potential for harm. This also reduces the stress faced by rescuers and other group members.

Complex rescue situations may require some combination of techniques, but the goal is the same: a simple, reliable response. For this reason, it is important that would-be rescuers have a variety of tools in their rescue-technique toolbox.

Simple rescue techniques require little or no extra equipment and have few steps; reliable rescue techniques have a high chance for success in rescue conditions. These two needs must be balanced when choosing a strategy.

For example, contact tows are a simple rescue technique but are difficult to maintain over long distances; as a result, they are not as reliable as an in-line tow over long distances. In a rescue where towing over a long distance is necessary, the slightly more complex (more gear, more steps) in-line tow is more reliable (less fatiguing), and is probably the best option.

Would-be rescuers often freeze at this stage of the decision-making process because they are unable to process and organize the quantities of information bombarding them. They simply cannot decide on a course of action. The best remedy in this case is to do something, anything. Make a decision. If the decision turns out not to be the most appropriate, at least it will provide valuable new information that can help rescuers make new and better decisions.

Take Action

Once the most appropriate option has been identified, act on it. As the rescue unfolds, continue to assess the situation, assuring that things are getting better and not worse.

Things to Do during a Rescue

- Assess the situation before rushing in to help.
- Plan for the safety of the entire group before calling for outside help.
- After the incident, stay with the victim, who is unlikely to be able to look after himself or herself.
- Keep buddies together. Do not let anyone travel alone unless it is absolutely necessary.

Ensure that your safety and the safety of other group members is maintained.

If the actions do not solve the identified problem, go back around the decision-making cycle: gather more information and attempt other rescue techniques. Trial and error can be costly both physically and psychologically, however, prolonging the rescue, increasing stress, and continuing the exposure to harm. The best actions are based on the best information.

If there is no obvious answer to the problem, you will have to improvise. Many of the rescue techniques used by paddlers today are the result of improvisation during rescues. There is no single right answer for any rescue. Even the best plans can go awry as equipment fails, people behave unpredictably, or the vagaries of weather, sea, and terrain bring new challenges. Be flexible, stay focused on the goal, and keep trying.

Even after the immediate crisis is resolved, the rescue is not over. The original cause of the accident may still be present. Another large set of waves may return, or the victim may remain seasick and nauseous. The incident may have introduced new hazards: fear, hypothermia, a flooded kayak. A premature sense of renewed safety is a significant hazard in itself. The victim of a rescue is often tired, cold, and highly stressed. The best way to assure a full recovery is to go ashore, and in severe cases evacuate the victim.

Reflect on the Outcome

The reflective phase can begin even during the rescue; if there is time, record important information in the paddler's log. The sooner the recording process begins, the better the information will be during reflection. Information should include:

- Weather.
- Sea state.
- Terrain.

- Location.
- Witnesses (names and contact information).
- Brief description of the event.
- Ongoing condition of the victim.
- Actions taken and reasons.

Once the rescue is over, review the log and add any additional information. Evaluate your decisions and actions with the benefit of hindsight. Identify problems, try to find their source, and draw lessons for future rescues.

Rescue Priorities

During a rescue, the leader and rescuers must act on a set of three priorities:

1. *Secure all members of the group.* See that kayakers who are not in distress are kept safe while the rescue proceeds.
2. *Extricate the distressed paddler.* Remove the disabled paddler from harm, or remove the harm from the paddler.
3. *Rehabilitate the paddler.* Provide additional aid until the rescued person is able to resume the trip or is evacuated.

Secure the Group

The first priority of a rescue is to secure the overall situation and keep the leader, rescuers, and unaffected group members safe. The rescue cannot begin until the safety of the remaining group members is looked after.

The rescue leader must decide how best to ensure the safety of the group. Managing the group is relatively straightforward on land: members will not drift off due to wind, waves, and currents. Nevertheless, take the time to ensure everyone's safety. Each person wants to feel useful, so ask members to heat water, prepare food, set up camp, secure gear, and carry out other support tasks; this is a great way to keep everyone active and involved.

Several techniques can be used to manage a group on the water, keeping them together and out of danger. The techniques include rafting up, paddling in place, and the buddy system (see the section "Keeping Together during a Rescue" in chapter 9, "Assisted Rescue"). Once the group is secured, the leader will be able to draw paddlers into the rescue as required. With a well-trained group this can happen spontaneously, and the leader need only observe and confirm that others are aware of what has occurred and are responding appropriately.

Extricate the Paddler

The second priority of a rescue is to ensure the safety of the paddler in distress. This involves choosing which rescue technique or combination of techniques will be the simplest and most reliable to get the paddler back in the kayak, remove the water, and regain stability. The paddler requiring rescue should be an active participant, working quickly and efficiently to ensure his or her own safety.

In the best case, the paddler self-rescues. A roll is the simplest and quickest self rescue after a capsize. If the roll is unsuccessful, the paddler can still self-rescue with a wet exit and one of the various methods of solo reentry (see chapter 8, "Self Rescue"). Other kayakers can assist in a self rescue that is under way, increasing its reliability and speeding the return of the affected paddler to full function.

If unable to complete a quick self rescue, the paddler will require assistance. Rescuers can choose from a variety of assisted-rescue techniques that clear the kayak of water and get the swimmer quickly back into the cockpit (see chapter 9, "Assisted Rescue"). As difficult sea conditions, an injured paddler, or other factors increase the complexity of the rescue, the time the victim spends in the water increases and the likelihood of an effective rescue decreases. In choosing a rescue

The Inattentive Paddler: Disaster in the Making

With instructions to paddle together as a pair, Ian and Geoff, two intermediate paddlers in our kayak rescue class, were to ferry 500 yards across a 2-knot current. Waves were 1 foot and the wind was 10 knots. One-third of the way across, Geoff was 50 yards ahead. Unknown to him, Ian was instructed to stop paddling and simply wait until his partner came back to check on him.

About 10 minutes later, Geoff arrived on the far side of the channel.

"Where is your buddy?" I asked.

Shocked and dismayed, he looked into the distance, barely able to see the drifting kayak.

Having drifted for 10 minutes, Ian was a quarter-mile away, downstream. Paddling quickly, Geoff rushed off to help. It took another 5 minutes to reach Ian. If Ian had capsized and needed rescue, he could have been in the water for 15 minutes before Geoff arrived.

On reflection: When conditions rise to challenge your abilities, it is difficult to pay attention to the needs of others. When the going gets rough, it is particularly important to keep an eye on your paddle buddy.

—Doug Alderson

technique, the needs for speed and reliability must be balanced.

Rescues that present multiple challenges require a variety of rescue techniques. An effective rescue leader will deploy a range of resources, including equipment carried by the group and the various skills of its members.

Rescue techniques seldom work as practiced because unanticipated twists invariably enter the scene. Be persistent and flexible. As new challenges arise, solve them and move on to the next challenge. Narratives of rescues consistently highlight an important point: the rescue seldom proceeds as planned. Variations and other techniques will have to be tried before the rescue is over.

In preparation for dealing with a future emergency, it often helps to paddle in groups of three, providing the opportunity for a wide variety of rescue strategies—as long as the three kayakers keep within close range of each other. As conditions deteriorate to the point where someone might capsize, members of the group should move closer together, ready to lend assistance. As simple and reasonable as this sounds, it can be quite difficult to keep a group together. A kayaker's awareness of others is reduced when he or she is anxiously paying attention to personal safety. Strong and confident general paddling skills enable a kayaker to free the mind for the concerns of the group.

Rehabilitate the Paddler

The third priority of a rescue is to provide additional aid to secure the rescued paddler until that person is able to resume the trip or is evacuated. This may take 10 minutes or it may take 10 hours. It can involve first aid and treatment for hypothermia and shock, figuring out how and where to go ashore, setting up a camp, and deciding whether to evacuate the victim.

Hypothermia and Shock

The most serious and common threats to a paddler after being rescued from immediate danger are hypothermia and shock. Treatment should begin soon after the paddler is back in the kayak. Treatment includes reassuring the person, protecting him or her from the elements, and adding additional insulation, especially to areas of high heat loss (head, neck, torso, and groin).

The simplest strategy is to remove as much wet clothing as possible, add dry insulating clothing, and cover the head and neck. If the person is able to swallow, you can offer warm water from a thermos. If treatment is not possible on the water, get to shore quickly. (See the section "Hypothermia" in chapter 2, "Health and Fitness.")

Getting Ashore

Once the immediate situation on the water has been addressed, the leadership must decide whether the rescued paddler and the group can continue with the planned itinerary. In most circumstances this means getting to shore and reassessing the conditions that led to the rescue.

Along exposed coastlines, it may take several hours before a suitable beach or landing site is reached. During that time, exercise extreme caution and monitor the condition of the rescued paddler and other group members. The time lag between extricating and rehabilitating the victim can be put to good use developing strategies for bringing the paddler back to full function, including a possible call for outside assistance.

If the victim is unable to continue paddling alone, it may be necessary to set up a tow, using one of the various towing techniques (see the section "Towing" in chapter 9, "Assisted Rescue"). Towing can require a lot of energy and quickly exhaust rescuers. En route to shore, the rescue leader must anticipate such secondary challenges and come up with solutions.

Once ashore, the rescue leader should oversee establishment of a camp, provision of food and water for the group, and addi-

Between a Rock and a Hard Place

Six of us were paddling in and around the rocks and sea caves of Port Renfrew off the west coast of Vancouver Island. There was a low southwest swell, little wind, and no currents. The conditions were ideal for practicing our paddling skills. Near the rocks, the low swell translated into a 3- to 5-foot rise and fall. One spot offered a real challenge: a 30-foot flake of rock had split off the cliff, creating a 10-foot-wide channel. Rocks on either end meant that a dogleg approach and good timing were important.

Most of us made it through, but one paddler missed the timing and ended up against the cliff on the dogleg. The rise and fall of the swell caught his kayak, and up and over he went.

I surfed through the slot to help as the others went along the outside of the rock. I clipped a towline into the capsized kayak and got the swimmer onto my back deck as I paddled out against the swell. Partway out I asked a second kayaker to come and get the swimmer, making it easier for me to tow the empty kayak away from the rocks. I directed a third kayaker to empty the water out of the capsized kayak and to steady the boat for the swimmer to get back in.

The whole incident was over in 5 minutes. Damage was minor. Nevertheless, we headed back to the beach for an early lunch and a mental pause before facing more challenges.

On reflection: Good teamwork and lots of hands can turn a fairly complex rescue into a straightforward operation.

—*Michael Pardy*

tional aid for the rescued paddler. The camp may be temporary, but it will provide physical and psychological support for the group, relieving some of the stress of the rescue. It also gives everyone something to do, keeping them active and warm and out of harm.

The important decision now is whether to continue the trip as planned. Determine whether the rescued paddler is able to continue the trip—and whether this person is willing to continue. Or is an evacuation necessary? If so, will it require a night landing by helicopter, or will a detour to the nearest marina suffice? Once ashore, some of the stress and time constraints of the rescue are lessened and the pressure to make a quick decision is reduced. Take the time to stop, think, observe, and plan. Use the paddler's logbook to record information to aid in the decision-making cycle.

Evacuation

One of the most serious decisions a group will ever make is whether to evacuate one of its members. Evacuation must be considered if a member of the group is experiencing any of the following:

- A serious condition of injury or illness that is deteriorating.
- Persistent vomiting or diarrhea.
- An inability to tolerate fluids.
- Severe pain.
- Inability to paddle at a reasonable pace due to a medical condition.
- Severe ongoing bleeding from a wound, or in vomit or stool.
- Worsening infections.
- Chest pain not directly associated with muscles or bones of the chest.
- Psychological disorder that impairs the safety of the person or group.
- Effects of near-drowning.
- Large or serious wounds and burns includ-

ing compound fractures (bones protruding through the skin, deformed fractures, fractures that impair circulation, dislocations of major joints, impaled objects, suspected spinal injury).

- Effects of any accident involving a large mechanism of injury (such as falls of more than 7 meters, or about 23 feet, or being hit by a kayak in the surf zone).

There are three levels of evacuation:

- *Urgent:* Injuries and illnesses that pose an imminent threat to life (such as heart attack, stroke, severe internal bleeding, rapidly deteriorating level of consciousness).
- *Semi-urgent:* Injuries and illnesses that require medical attention, but can be secured and have no anticipated complications (such as broken bones and dislocations).
- *Non-urgent:* Injuries and illnesses that do not require additional medical attention but prevent the paddler from continuing the trip (such as sprains, soft-tissue injuries including blisters and minor burns on the hand, and some illnesses).

The level of seriousness of the injury or illness will determine the type of evacuation. Most evacuations are rated as semi-urgent or non-urgent and can be carefully planned and organized. If the affected paddler is ambulatory, he or she should be escorted by at least two other competent paddlers to the nearest access point or medical facility. If the paddler is not ambulatory, the group needs to help the person prepare for travel and then provide transportation to the nearest facility.

Outside Help

Many groups are not sufficiently equipped or trained to carry out an urgent or semi-urgent evacuation on their own. Instead they must rely on outside assistance. The kind and quality of outside assistance depends on the communication equipment available to the group, location of the trip, and training and experience of the emergency response personnel. Evacuation may be by water, land, or air.

The decision to bring in outside help is an admission that the group is not capable of managing its own safety. This is a difficult admission, and not one made lightly. After this point, the group is no longer in complete control. In the eyes of the outside rescuers, the group has become a victim.

A competent paddling group will carry contact numbers with them for emergency response agencies, including phone numbers and radio frequencies. In calling for help, the needs of the outsider rescuers have to be considered. Emergency personnel assume a measure of risk in coming to your aid. They will have additional rescue techniques and strategies at their disposal. Listen to them and respect their leadership.

Evacuation by water is the most likely option for most sea kayakers. The primary concern with a water-based rescue is whether or not the evacuation further compromises the safety of the victim. For example, can this paddler wear a PFD? In a capsize, can the person wet-exit and swim? Members of the group

can transport the person themselves or rely on outside resources such as water taxis, the Coast Guard, or maritime vessels in the area. In all cases, be clear on the trade-offs between the benefits of getting the victim out to additional aid and the risks involved in transporting that person to the aid. Sometimes other evacuation options may be preferred.

Evacuation by land can by mobilized in many cases. This option will usually be used only with a person who can walk. Carrying a person, even over moderate distances and with a stretcher, is extremely difficult and imposes a high level of risk. It may be possible to send two or more members of the group out over land for additional resources, leaving the affected paddler in the temporary care of other members.

Evacuation by air may be the only option in remote locations and in urgent situations. Planes and helicopters can arrive quickly, but they may be hampered by high winds, poor sea conditions, dwindling daylight, or limited landing sites. Do your homework before a trip and talk to airplane and helicopter operators about their needs in the event of an evacuation. Air evacuation should be considered a last resort.

Appendix

Mental Shorthand for Decision Making

Over the course of a kayaking trip, the group will have to make many decisions. Most of these decisions are routine and easily acted upon, covering things like campsite selection and food choices. At times the group will have to make important decisions regarding such issues as route choice and rescues. These crux decisions must be made with the best information and in a timely manner to help ensure safety.

Risk is not evenly spread out through the trip. Instead, risk tends to be concentrated at these cruxes. For example, the decision to leave the beach each morning is a crux because that decision sets in motion a unique series of events and eliminates others. Crossing a shipping lane is also a crux because of the higher risk involved.

Decisions during a trip follow the basic steps in decision making detailed in chapter 1: identify the problem, gather information, make a choice, take action, and reflect on the outcome. Many paddlers rely on a mental shorthand to help in making decisions on the water. There are a variety of these

shorthands, each involving a mental exercise, and no single one is completely satisfactory. Add them to your toolbox of skills, and combine them as needed to help collect and sift through information and reach decisions that minimize the potential for an accident. Whenever you use one of these exercises, it is helpful to record the process and its results in the paddler's logbook for later reflection.

This section describes several of these mental shorthands or models and discusses how they could be applied in a hypothetical case study involving a sea kayaker named Katia. First we'll describe Katia's situation, then we can consider how various decision-making exercises might apply.

Case Study: Katia's Story

Katia is an intermediate sea kayaker, with several multiday trips logged and lots of day paddling. She can execute a roll on one side that is more or less reliable on the ocean. She is paddling with two friends of similar experience and skill, and they plan to paddle for three days before meeting some other friends and continuing on with them for another week. Katia has paddled in this area once before. Each of the three wears immersion clothing and a PFD every day on the water.

Their second night out, they camp in a bay 12 miles from their scheduled meeting point with the other group. The next day they must paddle around a headland for 2 miles. There are no landing sites along the headland. The chart indicates currents of up to 2 knots and tide rips along the face of the headland. Once around the headland, the terrain is mixed, with rocky outcrops, cliffs, and the occasional stone beach. There are some other campsites along the proposed route.

When they get up in the morning, the wind has picked up to 15 knots, according to the weather radio, and clouds are moving overhead. The forecast is for deteriorating weather late in the day. The wind is moving against the flooding current along the headland, and they can see choppy waves and the occasional whitecap at the nearest point of the headland.

Each of the three kayakers has paddled in similar conditions with the local kayaking club, but always under the supervision of a more experienced paddler. Katia tries her VHF radio and then her cell phone, trying to contact the other group. She is unable to get through, possibly because signals are blocked by the land surrounding their sheltered bay.

If they delay their launch,

they will miss the rendezvous with their friends.

Red Light/Green Light

This is the simplest model for making decisions. It asks a simple question: should I paddle or not (red light or green light)? The answer is easy in two situations: if the conditions are within the abilities of all members of the group (green light); and if the conditions are outside the abilities of all group members (red light). The decision becomes more complex when there is some uncertainty about conditions. Paddlers must collect as much information as possible, use their judgment, and make a decision.

This sounds straightforward, and it can be. The secret is in gathering the right information. Traditionally, information used in this model is collected for three categories: sea state, weather, and terrain. We include a fourth category: the paddling group itself.

After gathering information in each of the four categories, we can give a red light or green light designation to each. In the case of Katia and her friends, we might get a result like this:

- Sea state: Wind against current, choppy waves, and an occasional whitecap. Green light.

- Weather: Strong winds, clouds moving overhead, deteriorating weather. Red light.

- Terrain: Headland with no landing options; some camping beyond the headland, but generally limited landing options. Red light.

- Paddling group: Intermediate experience; each member with comparable skill and knowledge; some experience with

roll; all wear PFDs and immersion gear. Green light.

Experience tells us that these conditions will be challenging for the group, but potentially within their ability. The complexity of the information will make this decision a difficult one for the group. The red light/green light model has provided some useful information and may help them make a good decision by encouraging them to ask questions and to recognize that there may be some deficits in their skills, knowledge, and experience.

If the situation for Katia and her friends was even more challenging, the decision on whether to paddle might be easier. For example, if there was a 4-foot dumping surf on the destination beach, or if Katia was ill, it would be easier to decide to stay in camp.

The challenge with this simple model is that it does not accurately capture some of the nuances of the situation. We can add some texture to the stark contrast of the model by adding a third option, a yellow caution light. Assign one of three choices to each category: green light for go, red light for no-go, and yellow light for maybe.

A red light in any one of the four categories is usually interpreted as a no-go situation, a veto. Obviously, four green lights means a go. Uncertainty comes when you have one, two, three, or four yellow lights. Usually one yellow and three green is interpreted as a go, and three or four yellow as a no-go. When we have two yellow and two green lights, judgment comes especially into play. Our rule of thumb: When in doubt, be conservative.

A clear answer may not emerge, but the goal is to narrow

the uncertainty. Using this model, Katia and her fellow paddlers might come up with this outline:

- Sea state: Current, winds, whitecaps. Green.

- Weather: Deteriorating. Yellow to red.

- Terrain: Limited landing options. Yellow.

- Paddling Group: Moderate skills, proper equipment. Yellow.

According to our standards, Katia and her friends should not follow their original plan to meet the other group. They must consider alternative plans and evaluate them as well. Perhaps they can leave later, or hike up the hill behind the headland to try the radio and cell phone again. Maybe this is a good day for relaxing in camp.

The Numbers Game

The numbers game asks the decision maker to rank the severity and accumulation of risk factors in seven categories. The risk is assessed in each category on a scale of 1 to 5, with 5 indicating the highest risk. The decision maker is encouraged to write down the assessments; you can use the checklist accompanying this discussion.

This process permits a more personal expression of level of acceptable risk than with the red light/green light model. It allows the decision maker more judgment in the final decision. Using Katia's situation, results of the numbers game might look like this:

- Self-reliance: Group traveling together; is self reliant. Risk 3.

- Knowledge: Good kayaking knowledge. Risk 2.

- Judgment: Moderate to good judgment. Risk 3.

KAYAKING RISK FACTORS CHECKLIST
This checklist of kayaking risk factors helps define acceptable risk.

> > INCREASING RISK > >

SUPERVISED						SOLO OPEN WATER
SHELTERED WATER	1	2	3	4	5	CROSSING
WELL TRAINED		KNOWLEDGE				**FIRST TIME**
EXPERIENCED	1	2	3	4	5	KAYAKER
AWARE		JUDGMENT				**UNAWARE**
PRUDENT	1	2	3	4	5	RECKLESS
SURF LANDINGS		SKILL				**WET EXIT AND REENTER**
RELIABLE ROLL	1	2	3	4	5	FREQUENT SWIMMER
CALM WIND		WEATHER				**STIFF BREEZE**
STABLE	1	2	3	4	5	DECLINING
CALM SEA		SEA STATE				**STEEP WAVES**
NO CURRENT	1	2	3	4	5	SWIFT CURRENT
20°C WATER		TEMPERATURE				**SEA ICE PRESENT**
WELL DRESSED	1	2	3	4	5	POORLY PREPARED

Top row headers: SUPERVISED — **SELF RELIANCE** — SOLO OPEN WATER

- Skill: Strong kayaking skills. Risk 3.
- Weather: Deteriorating. Risk 3 to 4.
- Sea state: Rough. Risk 3 to 4.
- Temperature: Water temperature cold, but group well dressed. Risk 2.

One approach to using this model is simply to add up the total score. In this case, the total is 19. While the score in and of itself does not indicate excessive risk it does provide a guide, allowing decision makers to consider their options. Katia could lower the score, and the overall risk, by altering one or more of the factors. The weather and the sea state pose significant risk in this situation. The weather cannot be changed and in this scenario, there are no alternative routes. Katia and the group will have to wait for better conditions or accept the total risk.

The structure of the red light/green light model and the numbers game can be constricting, especially in complex situations. Some other models are more open-ended, allowing for a more nuanced assessment.

Lemon-aid
The lemon-aid model asks the decision maker to collect lemons (dangers). For each danger, the decision maker must decide if the danger will be accepted, avoided, or reduced. Lemons representing the dangers that will be avoided are discarded. The other lemons are figuratively squeezed into a glass to create lemon juice.

Lemons representing dangers that will be accepted are squeezed straight into the glass. Lemons representing dangers that will be reduced are also added, but along with some sugar, making the juice sweeter. As new dangers are faced, they are likewise turned into lemons and added to the mix, creating an ongoing change in the balance between sweet and sour.

Members of a group must decide on the appropriate balance that best suits their taste.

The lemon-aid model highlights the important point that dangers faced by kayakers are cumulative, and that safety management is an ongoing process of gathering information and making decisions. Unless the group makes a decision about dangers as they arise, they must accept the higher level of risk.

For Katia, there is a sour glass of lemon-aid indeed. Deteriorating weather, current against wind, limited landing options, and lack of radio communication all add unsweetened lemons to the glass. To sweeten the drink, her group has immersion gear and some experience and skill in these conditions.

They can avoid the dangers altogether by staying on the beach. They can improve radio communication by climbing up onto the hill behind camp. If they decide to leave the beach, there are limited route options. Once around the headland, they could establish another camp if the weather and sea conditions continue to deteriorate. All in all it is a sour drink, but it does give Katia and her friends a basis for reaching a decision on how much risk they want to assume.

What If . . .

Another popular open-ended model is the "What If . . . " exercise. It asks the decision maker to assess the potential consequences of a decision. The decision maker will also consider harm-reduction strategies to minimize the severity of consequences, and avoidance strategies to bypass dangers.

Katia and the two paddlers with her must ask themselves what will happen if they leave the beach. There is a possibility they will not be able to handle the conditions. If this is the case, do they have sufficient reserves of skill and knowledge to deal with this worsening situation? Are there alternative plans, such as waiting until evening or until tomorrow? What are the consequences of these decisions? When does the tide change, and will this result in an improved sea state around the headland? Many judgments come into play in this model.

Katia and her friends will be feeling some pressure to meet the other group as planned, which will make the decision all the more complicated. Much of the consequence of their decision depends upon the contingency plans they have made with the group they are meeting. Will these other kayakers expect Katia to paddle in these conditions? What will they do if she does not show up? A proper communication protocol for both groups, and improved radio and cell reception, would answer these questions.

Regardless of the decision-making strategies used, Katia and her friends must in the end use their own judgment to decide if they have the skill and knowledge to handle the sea conditions, weather, and terrain. These mental exercises are aids in applying judgment, but are no substitute for it.

Environment and Paddling Levels

The table below shows the basic relationship between a paddler's skills and the sea conditions at hand. Many aspects not shown on the table also contribute to the relative safety of a situation, such as the number of paddlers in the group, their health, the time of day, and local geography. Making the necessary judgments to match the skill level of the paddler with the environmental conditions is an important part of deciding to head out to sea. When the paddlers' level of skill meets or exceeds the maximum predicted environmental level the situation could be judged as safe.

	NOVICE	BEGINNER	INTERMEDIATE	ADVANCED
BASIC SKILLS	First season of paddling. Two days of instruction. Practices forward paddling and turning.	Second season of paddling. Additional week of instruction. Practices, edge control, bracing, rudder srokes, draw strokes.	Additional week of instruction. Practices rough water rescues, capsize recovery, rolling. Takes overnight trips, paddles a loaded kayak.	Practices in surf or whitewater. Practices rough water rescues. Rolling in waves and current.
KNOWLEDGE AND EXPERIENCE	None	Understands that there is much to learn and wary of overextending themselves. Experienced day trips in several locations.	Understands marine weather reports and forecasts, uses compass and chart, tide and current tables to predict sea conditions.	Extensive broad knowledge and the ability to combine information to make complex decisions in new situations.
SELF RESCUE	Wet-exit and paddle float reentry.	Wet-exit and paddle float reentry.	Rolling successful 50% of the time. Reenter and roll with a paddle float.	Rolling successful near 100% of the time. Reenter and roll.
JUDGMENT	Unable to judge conditions for themselves.	Can judge existing conditions for themselves. Checks marine weather forecast.	Uses current tables, weather forecast, and charts to judge conditions for themselves.	Able to judge conditions for themselves and others in the group.
LEADERSHIP	Should paddle with person of greater ability.	Day trips with other beginners.	Leads short trips in conditions appropriate for the group.	Leads multi-day trips in conditions appropriate for the group.
ENVIRONMENT* **WIND kn**	< 10	< 15	< 20	> 20
WAVES ft.	< 0.5	< 1	< 3	> 3
SWELL ft.	< 1	< 2	< 3	> 3
CURRENT kn	< 0.5	< 1.5	< 3	> 3
LANDINGS *At each level there are combinations of environmental conditions that would make conditions unsafe.	Easy, sheltered enclosed water.	Easy, sheltered open water, within a large bay.	Frequent landing opportunities, open coast, may require maneuvering around rocks or small breaking waves. Travels out and around prominent headlands between large bays.	Infrequent landing opportunities, open coastal, surf, difficult maneuvering around rocks with breaking waves. Travels along open crossings and inaccessible shoreline.

Float Plan

A float plan can be a formal document such as this form or an anecdotal, or verbal note. The complexity of the float plan is dependant on the length and complexity of the trip. Each paddler should carry a copy of the float plan in their kayak, in case of accident or other misadventure. If found in open water, a kayak that has drifted off the beach will start a coast guard search for possible victims. A float plan onboard will simplify an otherwise long and costly process and you are likely to get your kayak back.

Trip Name: _____

Date(s): _____

Leaders: _____

Vehicles: _____

Name of Driver: _____

Latest Return Date: _____ Time: _____

Number of People: _____

Number of Singles: _____ Number of Doubles: _____

Color and Style of Boats: _____
_____

BASIC TRIP PLAN

Launch Time: _____ Return Time: _____

Put-in: _____

Route _____
_____
_____

Take-out: _____

Alternative Route/Contingency Plans: campsites, route, put-in/take-out _____
_____
_____
_____

Number and color of tents: _____
_____

Number and color of tarps: _____
_____

Type of communication equipment (VHF, EPIRB, Weatherone, cell phone and number): _____
_____
_____

Type and number of flares: _____

In Emergency, please contact: _____

Lines and Knots

A good line should be strong, supple, rot-resistant, and hold a knot well. In general, lines used for kayaking should not stretch or absorb much water, and lines for towing should float. Two features of line that must be considered are the material it is made of and the construction of the line. In most cases, you get what you pay for; the better lines are more expensive. The best lines are made of synthetic fibers.

Material

Polyester has excellent characteristics and is a good all-round choice. Polyester is strong, and resistant to degradation from sunlight. It stretches very little and absorbs little water. The most widely known trade name for polyester is Dacron.

Nylon is strong and highly elastic and able to absorb shock loads. Nylon deteriorates more rapidly than polyester when subjected to direct sunlight, and it stretches when it absorbs water.

Polypropylene fibers make strong, lightweight rope. It does not ab-

sorb water. Polypropylene is subject to deterioration when exposed to direct sunlight. It is often used for floating line.

Polyethylene is similar to polypropylene, but is heavier and not as strong. It deteriorates quickly in direct sunlight.

Kevlar is a very strong fiber and does not stretch. To counteract the deteriorating effects of sunlight, Kevlar rope meant for out-of-doors use has a protective outer jacket made of polyester. Kevlar ropes are expensive.

Spectra is the strongest of fibers, made of a polyethylene with an ultra-high molecular weight. Spectra meant for out-of-doors use has a protective outer jacket of polyester. Spectra floating lines are high strength and high quality; they are also expensive.

Construction

Twisted strand is the most common construction for lines made of natural fibers; many synthetic ropes are also available in twisted strand construction. Easy to splice, it has many applications but is generally not preferred for kayak safety applications.

Single-layer braided (single-braid)

lines are usually floating lines of lesser quality, often made of polypropylene.

Double-layer braided (double-braid or yacht braid) line is strong, soft, and less prone to kinks and tangles than twisted strand. It feels good in the hand and holds knots well.

Kernmantle construction consists of a braided sheath around an unbraided fibrous core. A combination of materials can be used to make a strong, durable rope. The construction and the fibers used can make the line stiff and less easy to tie and hold a knot.

Webbing is woven from nylon or polyester and is found in a wide variety of applications. It is soft, strong, and can be sewn. It is used for straps on deck, on PFDs, and on packs. It can be made as a hollow weave and is a good material for cow tails and rescue stirrups.

Authors' Choice

For deck lines and general use: double-braided quarter-inch polyester.

For towlines: kernmantle or double-braided polypropylene floating line.

Knots for Safety Lines

Water Knot

The water knot is used to tie two ends of a line together. The method for tying it follows the same tracing principle as above. It works well for tying the ends of nylon webbing together.

Figure Eight

The figure eight is an easy to remember stopper knot useful in many applications.

Figure-Eight Loop

Figure-eight loop bight of line.

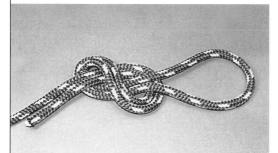

A figure eight tied with a bight of line is a quick way to form a loop on the end of a line. The figure-eight loop is sometimes preferred over a bowline because it holds well in all types of line, including stiff rescue lines that may not hold other knots well.

Figure-Eight Loop—Tracer

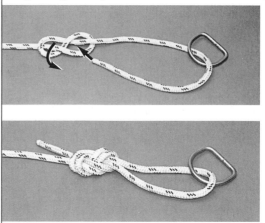

The figure eight used as a tracer knot forms a secure loop in the end of a line when passed through an eye. First, tie a figure-eight knot in the midportion of the line and then pass the working end back, following the original figure eight.

Figure Eight to Join Two Lines

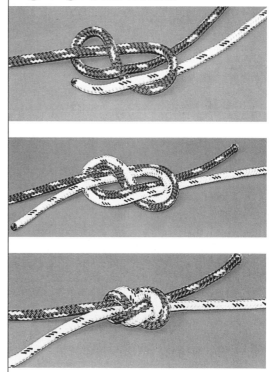

The same figure-eight tracer knot can also be used join two lengths of line together. The knot is very secure but may be bulky.

Larks Head

loop tied or spliced

The larks head knot is useful for attaching the end-loop of a long towline to a carabiner. When attached with a larks head knot the towline is less likely to move about the carabiner and trip open the gate. Fold the end-loop over upon itself (top photo) forming a double-loop. Pass both eyes of the double loop over the carabiner (bottom photo).

Spiral Hitching

Spiral hitching is more secure than simple whipping. It is useful for securing the end of a line after a knot is tied as in the anchor bend. Proper low-stretch polyester marine whipping twine must be used to keep the hitching tight.

Anchor Bend

The anchor bend is an excellent knot for securing the end of a line to a fixed object such as carabiner or D-ring on a towline. Because the hitch passes through the round-turn on the knot it holds well but is difficult to untie. Pass the line through the eye and "bend" it around one more time.

Pass the working end of the line beneath the standing part and tie a secure hitch by passing the working end through the bend.

Finish the knot by lashing the working end of the line to the standing part. After the knot has been water soaked and had tension on it during a tow, it can be difficult to untie.

Binding an End Loop

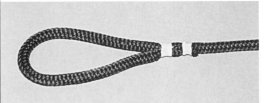

Spiral hitching is useful in binding the end of deck lines together or forming a loop. If an inch or two of the core of yacht braid is removed and then the line is bound into place, the result is smooth and strong.

Quick-release Sheet Bend

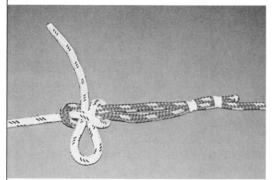

The quick-release sheet bend is used when an improvised quick-release is necessary. Pass the end of a line through a loop and around the standing part finishing the knot by folding a bight of line and passing it beneath the working part.

Friction Knot

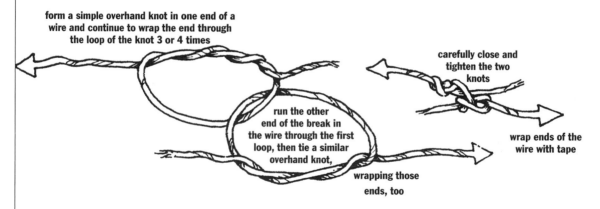

form a simple overhand knot in one end of a wire and continue to wrap the end through the loop of the knot 3 or 4 times

run the other end of the break in the wire through the first loop, then tie a similar overhand knot,

wrapping those ends, too

carefully close and tighten the two knots

wrap ends of the wire with tape

A friction knot will create a sturdy field repair if rudder cables break. A friction knot is simply a common overhand knot wrapped three or four times. Two interlocking friction knots will tie a broken cable together. Wrapping the finished knots with tape will keep the sharp wire ends under cover.

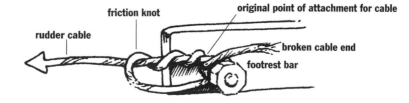

rudder cable

friction knot

original point of attachment for cable

broken cable end

footrest bar

If the cable breaks near its end, at the footrest or at the rudder, a friction knot can be tied around a bolt, through a hole, or at any other available location to affect a temporary field repair.

Knots for Around the Campsite

Bowline

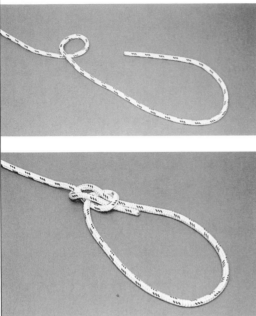

The bowline is the mariner's steadfast favorite. It is quick to tie and easy to untie. Some types of line do not hold a bowline very well and an end loop formed by a figure-eight knot is more secure for safety and rescue applications. To tie a bowline, form a loop in the line, then bring the bitter end up through the loop, around the line, and back down into the loop.

Clove Hitch

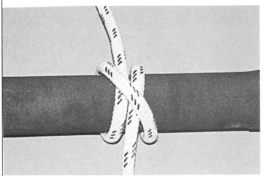

The clove hitch is a general-purpose knot for securing a line to a fixed object. Wrap the line once around the object and then pass the line over upon itself. A second wrap of line around the object is finished by running it beneath the second wrap and then finished by pulling the knot snug to create the friction necessary to hold it in place.

Rolling Hitch

A rolling hitch works well for tarps and tents. As fabrics stretch, the hitch can easily be pushed up the line to tighten guylines. A rolling hitch will take a strain when the line is pulled but the knot will move easily when grasped by hand. To tie a rolling hitch, wrap the working part twice around the standing part.

Pass the working part over the two wraps just formed and continue with another wrap in the same direction. Finish by running the end under the last wrap and making the knot snug.

If grasped in the hand, the rolling hitch will slide up or down the standing part of the line but will remain secure in place when subjected to tension on the line while in use. A rolling hitch works well for tarps and tents. As fabrics stretch, the hitch can easily be pushed up the line to tighten guylines.

Trucker's Hitch

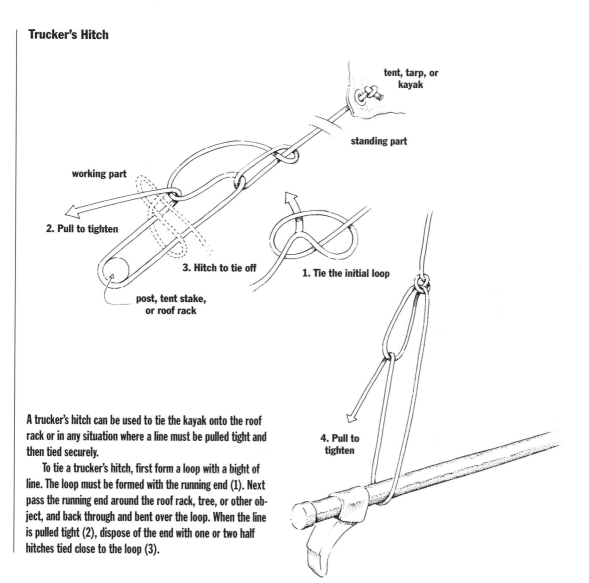

tent, tarp, or kayak

standing part

working part

2. Pull to tighten

3. Hitch to tie off

1. Tie the initial loop

post, tent stake, or roof rack

4. Pull to tighten

A trucker's hitch can be used to tie the kayak onto the roof rack or in any situation where a line must be pulled tight and then tied securely.

To tie a trucker's hitch, first form a loop with a bight of line. The loop must be formed with the running end (1). Next pass the running end around the roof rack, tree, or other object, and back through and bent over the loop. When the line is pulled tight (2), dispose of the end with one or two half hitches tied close to the loop (3).

Kits for Kayaking

Any roster of kayak supplies will include a first-aid kit and a repair kit. Following are lists of important items for both of these kits. A bivouac kit is valuable for safety on a day trip in the event of an unexpected overnighter; items for that kit are also listed.

First-Aid Kit

It is useful to organize your first-aid kit into a series of smaller pouches. This is a general list appropriate for a recreational paddler with basic first-aid training. If you are planning a trip to a remote location, you should obtain additional first-aid training appropriate to a wilderness setting. The quantity of each item will depend on the length of the trip. Consult your physician regarding prescription drugs.

Ouch Kit

Lots of adhesive bandages (such as Band-Aids)

1-inch cloth tape

Tincture of benzoin (helps tape adhere to damp and dirty skin)

1 pair scissors

100% aloe vera gel (provides a moisture barrier for small wounds and burns)

Safety pins

Tweezers

Traumatic Injury Kit

Large triangular bandages

Pressure dressing

Sterile gauze dressing

2-inch crepe wrap

Medicine Kit

Pain maskers (aspirin, ibuprofen, acetaminophen)

Antinausea medication

Antidiarrhea medication

Antihistamine

Personal medications

Repair Kit

A flexible and well-stocked repair kit will permit repairs in the field. Most repairs are minor and can be left until the end of the trip. A serious safety threat is posed by structural damage to the kayak, broken rudders and skegs, leaks in immersion gear, and broken stoves, and the repair kit needs to reflect these priorities. The equipment each kayaker carries and the length and remoteness of the trip will dictate the exact contents, but every repair kit should contain the following items.

- Pliers and screwdrivers to match nuts and bolts on the kayak
- Extra nuts and bolts to match the variety on the kayak
- Extra rudder or skeg cable
- Cord
- Urethane adhesive
- Needle and thread
- Neoprene and nylon patches
- Waterproof tape (duct tape, plumber's tape, roofing tape)
- Materials to repair tent pole (spare tent pole sleeve)
- Spare parts for stove

Additional items can include

- Clothing/fabric repair kit
- Spare gaskets for dry tops and suits
- Spare zippers

Bivouac Kit

A bivouac kit contains minimum gear for an emergency overnight bivouac, and can also provide temporary shelter for an accident victim. The kit must be small and durable enough to easily survive the rigors of repeated outings, and be convenient to carry on every day trip. The kit is in addition to normal day-trip supplies that include a change of clothes, lunch or snacks, and water.

- 10- by 10-foot sheet of plastic, as a tarp (6-mil plastic from a building supply store)
- Mylar space blanket
- 15 feet of duct tape (wrapped around a piece of foam)
- Folding knife
- 50 feet of eighth-inch line
- Compass
- Fire starter (ignition source and fuel)
- Survival bag (plastic bivy bag)
- Viscous towel
- Chemical light sticks
- Signal mirror
- Whistle
- Metal cup to collect and boil water

Resealable plastic bags taped together with clear packing tape make a convenient multichamber transparent first-aid kit. The kit needs to be stored in a waterproof dry bag.

Beaufort Scale

The often-cited Beaufort Scale provides a means to approximate wind speed by observing fully developed waves over open water. The sea kayaker must consider additional local factors of current, swell, and geography to evaluate wind speed and sea state.

Beaufort Number	Wind	Speed (kn)	Indications at Sea	Avg. Wave Height (ft.)	Min. Duration (hr.)	Min. Fetch (miles)
0	Calm	< 1	Sea mirror smooth	0	—	—
1	Light air	1–3	Sea rippled	0.05	0.3	5
2	Light breeze	4–6	Small wavelets, crests do not break	0.2	0.5	8
3	Gentle breeze	7–10	Small waves with some white caps	0.6–0.9	1.7–2.5	10
4	Moderate breeze	11–16	Wave are longer; fairly frequent white caps	1.4–2.9	3.8–6.6	18–40
5	Fresh breeze	17–21	Waves well formed; white caps everywhere. Probably some spray.	3.8–5.0	8.3–10	55–75
6	Strong breeze	22–27	White foam heaps up, begins to be blown in streaks	6.4–9.6	12–17	100–180
7	Strong wind	28–33	Waves heap up; wind starts to blow the foam in streaks	11–16	20–27	230–340
8	Fresh gale	34–40	Crests break into spindrift, foam is blown in well marked streaks	19–28	30–42	420–710
9	Strong gale	41–47	High waves, dense streaks, visibility affected	31–40	47–57	830–1,110
10	Whole gale	48–55	Very high waves with overhanging crests. Sea surface takes on a generally white appearance.	44–59	63–81	1,250–1,800

Glossary

Accident An experience with a harmful outcome (personal injury or property damage). Also see *event* and *incident*.

Actual risk The true potential for injury or loss. Also see *perceived risk*.

Aid to navigation Any of various devices, as a buoy, external to a vessel and intended to assist in determining position and safe course or to warn of dangers.

Air mass A large section of the atmosphere that has uniform temperature and moisture.

Apogee The point in the moon's orbit that is farthest from the earth. The tidal forces of the moon are reduced. Also see *perigee*.

Assisted rescue A rescue with the aid of at least one person in addition to the victim.

Back eddy An area of current flowing in a direction generally reversed to the predominant flow.

Backstop An obstruction to straight-line navigation that will stop forward progress. Used in piloting as a means of establishing a known position.

Bearing The compass direction to an object. Also see *course* and *heading*.

Boil Area of turbulent water where the current is vertical and resembles boiling water.

Boomer A large breaking wave that occurs only occasionally over a shallow rock.

Bow tip-out The technique of draining water from a flooded cockpit by lifting the bow and tipping the water out. Usually done by a paddler sitting in a kayak, before assisting a swimmer to return to the cockpit.

Cardinal buoy A buoy in the standardized Uniform Cardinal System that indicates the approximate true bearing of safe water from the danger it marks.

Chart A nautical chart. Shows water depth, shoreline, topographic features, aids to navigation, and other information important to navigation.

Course The intended compass direction of travel to a destination. Also see *bearing* and *heading*.

Cow tail A short towline semipermanently attached to a quick-release belt on or about the PFD. Usually 4 to 6 feet long. Also see *PFD*.

Cross bearing Two or more bearings or ranges that intersect. Cross bearings are used to determine a position. Also see *bearing* and *range*.

Cross seas Two wave patterns intersecting at an angle, creating a combined sea state with irregular waves.

Day beacon Unlighted beacon that indicates channels or mark hazards to navigation, especially in shallow bays, harbors, and inland waterways. A geometrically shaped visual indicator is normally attached to indicate the type of beacon.

Dead reckoning The process of determining a position from previously known positions and recent measurements of time, direction, and speed.

Dumping wave See *plunging wave*.

Ebb current The current that results in the outgoing tide; usually flows in the predominant seaward direction. Also see *flood current*.

Ebb tide The outgoing tide and the resulting decrease in water depth. Also see *flood tide*.

Event An experience with a harmless outcome, without consequence. Also see *accident* and *incident*.

Ferry angle The angular difference between the course and the heading necessary to keep a desired course when traveling at an angle to a current.

Fetch The unobstructed straight-line distance that the wind has blown over.

Float plan An outline of the navigational and logistical details of a kayaking trip.

Flood current The current that results in the incoming tide; usually flows in the predominant direction from the sea. Also see *ebb current*.

Flood tide The incoming tide and the resulting increase in water depth. Also see *ebb tide*.

Front The leading edge of an air mass.

Handrail A natural feature, such as a coastline, that aids in navigating during low visibility.

Heading The compass directions that the boat is pointing. Also see *bearing* and *course*.

Impact zone The near-shore where waves break as a result of interaction with the coast or the sea bottom.

Incident An experience that results in minimal harm (a "near miss"). Also see *accident* and *event*.

Knot A measurement of speed: 1 nautical mile per hour. Also see *nautical mile*.

Lateral buoy An aid to navigation that indicates the lateral limits of a navigable channel.

Line of position A natural or navigational range used to determine position.

Longshore current A current parallel to the beach, inside the surf zone. A longshore current is formed by waves breaking at an angle to the beach.

Map Generally refers to a topographic map that shows land features.

Nautical mile A distance of 6,080 feet (1.15 statute miles, or 1.87 kilometers). Based closely on an equivalence of 1 degree of latitude. Also see *knot*.

Navigation The art and science of knowing where you are and determining a safe route to your intended destination.

Overfall A breaking wave caused by current running over shallow water depth and suddenly dropping into deeper water.

Perceived risk The perception of risk where none exists, or a perception of high risk when actual risk is lower. Also see *actual risk*.

Perigee The point in the moon's orbit that is closest to the earth. The tidal forces of the moon are at their greatest. Also see *apogee*.

Period The time difference between the passage of two waves.

PFD Personal flotation device.

Piloting The art of navigating in confined waters, with frequent reference to geographic features and aids to navigation.

Plunging wave A wave with a breaking crest that falls vertically in a sudden and violent manner. Often associated with surf waves breaking on a steep beach. Also referred to as a dumping wave. Also see *spilling waves*.

Range A straight line formed by the visual alignment of two objects or the extension of a large object. A range can be a natural range (formed by use of natural or man-made objects) or a navigational range (formed by means of aids to navigation placed to form a range).

Rescue The act of intervening in an unsafe situation and altering it to become a situation of safety.

Rescue sling A loop of line or webbing used to aid a swimmer in reentering the kayak. The sling, also called a stirrup, can be secured to a paddle shaft or around the cockpit coaming.

Rip current A current that runs out from a beach, caused by the rush of water returning from the beach after a wave has broken on shore.

Risk Potential for injury or loss.

Risk assessment Identification and description of human and environmental dangers.

Rough seas Conditions of wind and waves that can bring paddlers near to the limit of their ability to maintain safe control and movement.

Running lights Lights on a vessel that indicate its type, direction of motion, and any special activities, such as towing.

Safety management A three-step cycle that includes risk assessment, risk management, and reflection.

Safety The full range of planning, preparation, and implementation of a plan of action to assure that a situation remains safe.

Sea state The overall sea surface conditions that result from the combined effects of wind waves, swell, and current.

Self rescue A rescue conducted by the victim, without aid of another person.

Speed made good The resultant speed of the kayak over the ocean bottom after taking into consideration all factors of current and drift in the wind.

Spilling wave Surf wave on a beach with a very flat slope that breaks by spilling the crest forward in a gradual release of energy. Also called a surging wave. Also see *plunging wave*.

Standing wave A wave, caused by water flowing over irregular bottom features or interacting with other currents, that keeps a stationary position in relation to the seafloor.

Stirrup See *sling*.

Stroke rate The number of paddle strokes per minute, usually counted on one side only.

Surging wave See *spilling wave*.

Swash Splashing, frothy water usually associated with the nearshore area of a beach where larger waves, already broken, produce turbulent whitewater.

Swell Long wavelength waves that form due to the transfer energy of smaller wind waves.

Tide rip Turbulent surface water caused by the movement of water through a restricted passage or interaction of currents.

Tip-out See *bow tip-out*.

Upwelling Upward, vertical movement of water that produces irregular currents and patterns on the sea surface.

Wind wave Newly formed waves created by wind.

Resources

Canadian Information Services

Canadian Hydrographic Service

www.charts.gc.ca/chs/
The Canadian Hydrographic Service (CHS) publishes marine charts, coastal pilots, and other resources useful to the sea kayaker. Their products are available through local retailers.

Natural Resources Canada

www.nrcan-rncan.gc.ca/inter/index.html
Natural Resources Canada publishes topographic maps and has some other useful information for sea kayakers. Topographic maps are available through a network of local retailers.

Nautical Data International Inc. (NDI)

www.digitalocean.ca/
NDI is the official supplier of electronic charts for Canadian Waters. NDI electronic charts are sold directly by NDI and are also available through a network of local retailers.

Environment Canada

www.weatheroffice.com
Environment Canada publishes and broadcasts marine weather forecasts for the entire country. Text versions of the VHF Marine Weather broadcasts are available online. In addition, synopic charts, satellite images, and Wave Action Models (WAMs) are available online through Environment Canada.

Canadian Coast Guard

www.ccg-gcc.gc.ca
The Canadian Coast Guard provides a variety of important services to sea kayakers and other maritime users. Copies of the small-boating safety regulations and other publications are listed on the site. A free sea kayak–specific publication will be available in the summer of 2003.

United States of America Information Services

Office of Coast Survey

http://chartmaker.ncd.noaa.gov/
The Office of Coast Survey publishes marine charts, electronic charts, coastal pilots, and other resources useful to the sea kayaker. These resources are also available through a wide network of local retailers.

Center for Operational Oceanographic Products and Services

http://co-ops.nos.noaa.gov/co-ops.html
CO-OPS has on-line tide and current tables for the US. Printed tables are no longer available through the government. Instead, various businesses use government data to publish tide and current tables.

National Weather Service

www.nws.noaa.gov/
The National Weather Service (NWS) publishes text broadcasts for the entire USA. In addition, synopic charts, satellite images, Wave Action Models, and other resources are available on-line through the NWS.

United States Geological Survey

http://mapping.usgs.gov/
The Geological Survey publishes topographic maps and electronic maps useful to sea kayakers. These products are also sold through a wide network of local retailers.

U.S. Coast Guard

www.uscg.mil
The U.S. Coast Guard provides a variety of important services to sea kayakers and other maritime users.

Other Resources

Electronic Tide and Current Tables

There are a number of shareware tide and current predictors available on-line. The coverage is excellent for some areas and weak for others. Check the data carefully before using it. You may have to supplement the information with tables and electronic data from government agencies.

- JTides is an excellent shareware tide and current predictor available on-line through www.arachnoid.com/Jtides/index.html

- WXtide32 is another excellent shareware tide and current predictor. It is available through any number of sites. Simply type the name of the program into your favorite search engine.

Magazines

Sea Kayaker

www.seakayakermag.com
The original sea kayaking magazine. Lots of articles on trips, techniques, and gear reviews, plus an international resources section.

Adventurekayak

www.adventurekayakmag.com
A Canadian sea kayaking magazine. Great material from across the country, with a wide variety of articles. Partner to *Rapid* magazine (www.rapidmagazineinc.com), a great whitewater resource.

WaveLength Paddling Magazine

www.wavelengthmagazine.com

Lots of on-line material, links, and a discussion group. A great resource, especially for those looking to paddle in the Pacific Northwest.

Atlantic Coastal Kayaker

www.ackayak.com

Lots of material and links. A great resource, especially for those looking to paddle in northeastern North America.

Sea Kayaking Organizations and Clubs

American Canoe Association

www.acanet.org/acanet.htm

U.S.-based network of organizations offering training and certification to recreational kayakers and instructors in canoeing, whitewater kayaking, and sea kayaking.

Canadian Recreational Canoeing Association

www.paddlingcanada.com

A Canada-wide network of organizations offering training and certification for recreational paddlers and instructors. Sea kayak curriculum as well as canoeing and whitewater kayaking. Publishes *Kanawa* magazine.

Sea Kayak Guides Alliance of B.C. (British Columbia)

www.skgabc.com

A British Columbia–based association of sea kayak professionals, outfitters, and retailers. Offers training and certification for guides and others wanting to develop leadership skills.

Association of Canadian Sea Kayak Guides

www.islandnet.com/~skguides/

A British Columbia–based association of guides. Offers training and certification for those interested in becoming guides.

Association of Eastern Canadian Sea Kayak Outfitters

www.aecsko.on.ca

Professional association of sea kayak outfitters. Offers training and certification for guides and others wanting to develop leadership skills.

British Canoe Union North America

www.bcuna.com/

A U.S.-based version of the BCU. Courses and certification for recreational paddlers and instructors.

British Canoe Union

www.bcu.org.uk

Instruction for recreational paddlers and instructors based in England. There is also an Irish Canoe Union (www.irishcanoeunion.com).

Other Links We Like

Princeton University Outdoor Action Program

www.princeton.edu/~oa/resources/outother.html

A great collection of resources for outdoor leaders.

Outdoor Network

www.outdoornetwork.com

A site for outdoor professionals. Lots of material on risk, safety, and leadership of interest to recreational paddlers and leaders as well. Electronic articles from the Outdoor Network newsletter.

National Outdoor Leadership School

www.nols.edu

Courses, publications, and more for skills development and leadership training.

Leave No Trace

www.lnt.org

A nonprofit organization dedicated to promoting low-impact

outdoor recreation. Material on low-impact camping is available for sale on the site.

The New South Wales Sea Kayak Club (Australia)

www.nswseakayaker.asn.au

Lots of great fun and interesting articles from down under.

Jersey Canoe Club

www.jcc.org.je

Great site from the U.K. with good links and most of the on-line material from the now defunct *Sea Paddler Magazine*.

WaterTribe

www.watertribe.com

A great on-line magazine from Florida with lots of links, articles, and other materials for kayakers and other small boaters. Lots of material on adventure/challenge racing including nutrition, training, and equipment. Some free downloads for kayakers as well.

CoastalBC.com

www.coastalbc.com

Lots of stuff about coastal BC, and more general materials including great links.

California Kayak Friends

www.ckf.org

Lots of great links, some articles, and other materials for sea kayakers.

Books

General Sea Kayaking

Alderson, Doug. *Sea Kayaker's Savvy Paddler: More than 500 Tips for Better Paddling*. Camden ME: Ragged Mountain Press, 2001.

Foster, Nigel. *Nigel Foster's Surf Kayaking*. Old Saybrook CT: Globe Pequot, 1998.

Gignac, Wayne, and John Rudolph. *The Complete Canoe Trip Planner*. Ancaster ON: Magnetic

North Wilderness Adventures, 1998.

Hanson, Jonathan. *Complete Sea Kayak Touring*. Camden ME: Ragged Mountain Press, 1998.

Hutchison, Derek C. *The Complete Book of Sea Kayaking*, 4th ed. Old Saybrook CT: Globe Pequot, 1995.

Johnson, Shelley. *The Complete Sea Kayaker's Handbook*. Camden ME: Ragged Mountain Press, 2002.

Rowe, Ray ed. *Canoeing Handbook*, 2nd ed. Nottingham UK: British Canoe Union, 1995.

Seidman, David. *The Essential Sea Kayaker: The Complete Guide for the Open-Water Paddler*, 2nd ed. Camden ME: Ragged Mountain Press, 2001.

Navigation

Burch, David. *Fundamentals of Kayak Navigation*, 3rd. ed. Guilford CT: Globe Pequot, 1999.

Eyges, Leonard. *The Practical Pilot: Coastal Navigation by Eye, Intuition, and Common Sense*. Camden ME: International Marine, 1989.

Moyer, Lee. *Sea Kayak Navigation Simplified*. Mukilteo WA: Alpen Books, 2001.

Wing, Charlie. *Boating Magazine's One Minute Guide to the Nautical Rules of the Road*. Camden ME: International Marine, 1998.

Leadership and Group Management

Baird, Brian. *Are We Having Fun Yet? Enjoying the Outdoors with Partners, Families, and Groups*. Seattle: Mountaineers, 1995.

Graham, John. *Outdoor Leadership: Technique, Common Sense and Self-Confidence*. Seattle: Mountaineers, 1997.

Priest, Simon, and Michael A. Gass. *Effective Leadership in Adventure Programming*. Champaign IL: Human Kinetics, 1997.

Weather and Oceanography

Lange, Owen S. *The Wind Came All Ways: A Quest to Understand the Winds, Waves, and Weather in the Georgia Basin*. N.p.: Environment Canada, 1998.

Moore, J. Robert, comp. *Oceanography: Readings from Scientific American*. San Francisco: W. H. Freeman, 1971.

Renner, Jeff. *Northwest Marine Weather*. Seattle: Mountaineers, 1993.

Thomson, Richard E. *Oceanography of the British Columbia Coast*. Ottawa: Department of Fisheries and Oceans, 1981.

West Coast Marine Weather Hazards Manual: A Guide to Local Forecasts and Conditions, 3rd ed. Ottawa: Environment Canada, 1999.

Safety and Rescue

Ajango, Deb, ed. *Lessons Learned: A Guide to Accident Prevention and Crisis Response*. Anchorage: University of Alaska, Alaska Outdoor and Experiential Education, 2000.

Backer, Howard D., National Safety Council, and Wilderness Medical Society, eds. *Wilderness First Aid: Emergency Care for Remote Locations*. Boston: Jones & Bartlett, 2002.

Broze, Matt, and George Gronseth. *Sea Kayaker's Deep Trouble: True Stories and Their Lessons from Sea Kayaker Magazine*. Ed. Christopher Cunningham. Camden ME: Ragged Mountain Press, 1997.

Isaac, Jeffrey. *The Outward Bound Wilderness First-Aid Handbook*, rev. ed. New York: Lyons Press, 1998.

Leemon, Drew, ed. *Adventure Program Risk Management Report*, vol. 3. Boulder: Association for Experiential Education, 2002.

Lull, John. *Sea Kayaking Safety and Rescue*. Berkeley: Wilderness Press, 2001.

Schumann, Roger, and Jan Shriner. *Sea Kayak Rescue: The Definitive Guide to Modern Reentry and Recovery Techniques*. Guilford CT: Globe Pequot, 2001.

Index